BEYOND
DIVISION

ALSO BY BILHA CHESNER FISH

Invincible Women: Conversations with 21 Inspiring and Successful American Immigrants

**The Resilient Lives
of Thirty Diverse
Israeli Women Leaders**

BEYOND
DIVISION

BILHA CHESNER FISH, MD
Author of *Invincible Women*

WICKED SON

A WICKED SON BOOK
An Imprint of Post Hill Press
ISBN: 979-8-88845-666-8
ISBN (eBook): 979-8-88845-667-5

Beyond Division:
The Resilient Lives of Thirty Diverse Israeli Women Leaders
© 2025 by Bilha Chesner Fish, MD
All Rights Reserved

Cover Design by Jim Villaflores
Cover Art by Bilha Chesner Fish
All photographs courtesy of the author and the women interviewed.

Post Hill Press
New York • Nashville
wickedsonbooks.com
posthillpress.com

Published in the United States of America
1 2 3 4 5 6 7 8 9 10

This book is dedicated to the women soldiers who have de-fended Israel since its birth and through ongoing conflicts, the women who gave their lives to my homeland, and the women who show bravery every day by striving to make life better for all of us.

TABLE OF CONTENTS

AUTHOR'S NOTE

THE SPARK FOR THIS BOOK came three years before the horror of October 7, 2023, and the bloodshed that has continued to soak the soil of Israel, Gaza, the West Bank, and Lebanon. It was 2020. I was living in New York City and the COVID-19 pandemic was all we thought about. It menaced our daily lives and exposed humanity's ultimate fragility. As a native Israeli, I was proud to read how Israeli innovation in science and medicine helped the world tame this Middle Ages-type curse. I thought about women I had already met, whose stories exhibited their strength and love for this amazing country, how they rose above inequity and embraced unity to work in their own ways to help Israel not only survive but flourish. As I had enjoyed the experience of interviewing accomplished women immigrants in America for my previous book, *Invincible Women*, and had decided to focus my next work on women in my homeland, as soon as travel was permitted, I went to Israel.

I conducted most of the interviews for this book in person and by zoom in 2022 and into fall of the following year, even though in early 2023 a different type of outbreak was erupting in Israel. Demonstrations over judicial reform caused philosophical rifts between the half of the population who believed that the reforms threatened democracy and those who supported the government's shift to the right. At times, I just couldn't bring myself to work on the book. Social hatred and infighting prevented people in the center of Tel Aviv from praying together during Yom Kippur. I wondered whether the title I had chosen *Beyond Division*—even the book itself—was still appropriate.

Then came October 7th and the world changed.

Hamas massacred thousands of Israelis and took hundreds of hostages. Courageous Zionists like Varda Goldstein, whom I spoke with in December 2023, lost members of her family and will never be whole again. Again, I could not imagine how the title could be relevant in the wake of unimaginable cruelty on that Black Saturday. Israelis, reservist soldiers, and innocent Gazans died on the battlefield. The war against Hamas is predicted to be the most devastating conflict since 1948. Its impact will outlive generations.

As the nightmare persists, however—as people mourn their loved ones, seek the safe return of the remaining hostages, and pray for peace—an unprecedented unity emerged in Israel. Women, especially, have shown the initiative and heroism I have long associated with my homeland. Paramedic Amit Mann rushed to help a doctor and nurse treat the wounded before she herself was murdered in Kibbutz Be'eri. Her beautiful voice lives on in a video and recording that an Israeli band created of her singing *Nothing Will Hurt Me*.

An all-female military tank unit battled the initial onslaught of terrorists from Gaza. Dozens of female soldiers were among those killed by Hamas on October 7 and more were subsequently killed in the line of duty near Gaza, on the northern border, and in the West Bank.

Thanks to Alice Miller, the Israeli pilot who successfully sued the Israeli military for her right to enlist in the Air Force Flight Academy, women are now combat pilots and navigators. In late October 2024, four female navigators flew in F-15 and F-16 fighter jets that targeted facilities linked to Iran's missile sites, a historic mission in direct response to a missile barrage from Iran.

I am grateful that I was able to include Varda Goldstein's survival story before my publishing deadline. But there are so many more stories I wish I could tell—about Israeli women, of many faiths, colors, genders, and ages who joined in battle with their male counterparts to defend Israel and invest themselves in a country that is truly "beyond division."

—Bilha Chesner Fish, October 2024

FOREWORD

PROFESSOR URIEL REICHMAN

PRE–SIX-DAY WAR ISRAEL IS THE foundation for Dr. Bilha Fish's memories and comparisons.

Raised in Haifa, the author now revisits Israel after the fifty years of professional accomplishments in the United States that followed her medical education in Bologna, Italy. Dr. Bilha Fish's journey interviewing different women, each of whom have a meaningful message to share, paints a unique picture of the mosaic that makes up Israeli society. The book tells of impressive women, creativity, and leadership, alongside the disappointments and pain that arise from cultural differences, conflicting worldviews, and inequality. The reality that emerges is multipolar and sometimes rife with anger. The Israel of 2024 is, indeed, a different place from the one Bilha left.

Between the lines of the interviews, one can also find the author's personal impressions, expressed with restraint and humility. The Haifa and Israel of 1966 are not those of today. The familiar landscapes of the country have been transformed, and other voices have impacted its original values, though the earlier ones still endure.

Bilha's new book is particularly significant today. The Israel of 2024 is experiencing a crisis in its regime and its principles. The division into tribes, pointed out by former Israeli President Reuven Rivlin, has developed into a rift between what appears to be two camps on the verge of conflict.

The question is how deep the dispute is, and whether it will be possible to overcome the division and hatred. The book's documentation of our societal reality from the perspective of women leaders may help in understanding the causes of the current polarization, but, more importantly, can also help us identify sources of unity and hope.

The voices of women leadership heard in Dr. Fish's interviews, though expressed from different angles, are the voices of humanity: the doctor who works through the night to save the life of an Arab baby; the president of a university who makes sure to provide opportunities for Bedouin students; the creator of an organization that secretly provides Israeli humanitarian aid, often risking their lives to do so in disaster areas around the world, including in hostile countries; an Arab social entrepreneur who persists, despite disappointments, in leading dialogues aimed at establishing discourse and understanding between Arabs and Jews in Israel; a world-renowned Israeli artist whose life's ambition is to promote reconciliation with the Palestinians that will lead to a two-state reality; a settler who accepts the principle of the Palestinian Authority and seeks solutions for residency, and even citizenship, for the inhabitants of Area C; a Druze leader who gave up a ministerial position because promises to amend the exclusion of the Druze from the Nation-State Law were broken; and a minister of Ethiopian origin who has suffered discrimination and fights for the integration of members of her community into Israeli society. The stories of the women mentioned here, and the others that appear in the book, amid all the criticism and controversy, demonstrate an aspiration for humanity, togetherness, and unity, for an Israel that is a home for all.

These stories illustrate that the profound crisis Israel finds itself in today is the consequence of the failure of a coalition system that allows a minority to enforce its extremist views, and not the result of a deep and irreconcilable rift in the nation. Dr. Bilha Fish's book is therefore not only one of promise and hope, but one that highlights the growing need for women in leadership.

———◦•◦———

Professor Uriel Reichman is an Israeli legal scholar and former politician. In 1994, he established the Interdisciplinary Center Herzliya, later renamed Reichman University, where he was president for twenty-seven years and is currently chair of its board of directors.

INTRODUCTION/MY STORY

BILHA CHESNER FISH, MD

"Create the kind of self that you will be happy to live with all your life. Make the most of yourself by fanning the tiny, inner sparks of possibility into flames of achievement."
—*Golda Meir*

GENTLE GUSTS TOY WITH THE sycamore branches near my desk as I review that day's patient files. The breeze carries bits of a familiar Jewish melody, the gift of a saxophonist who is a fixture on the steps of New York City's Metropolitan Museum of Art across the street.

I am reminded of a time fifty-five years earlier when I sat at my desk in Bologna, Italy. It was June 1967, and I was listening to classical music and studying for my first-year medical school exams. A news bulletin interrupted my concentration: Egyptian troops were mobilizing along the Sinai border with Israel. Forces from Jordan, Lebanon, Syria, and Iraq were stationed at key entry points. Egyptian President Abdel Nasser threatened to annihilate Israel in what would become the Six-Day War.

I fled to the airport in Rome, anxious to get home, to check on my parents in Haifa, to pitch in at the hospital and relieve Israeli Defense Forces (IDF) soldiers for active duty. Instead, along with several other Israeli students, I spent three agonizing days waiting for a flight.

I sat on cold floors and uncomfortable benches and thought about my father's life as a young Zionist. He and my mother arrived in Palestine in 1934, safe from the Nazis but separated from my mother's parents, who died in Auschwitz. Later, when my father was a member of the paramilitary Haganah, he and his team helped hundreds of refugees come ashore in violation of the British White Paper that restricted Jewish immigration.

I remember the evening when I finally knocked on my parents' door. I fell into their elderly arms as tears of happiness streamed down their faces. They were relieved that the impending disaster had been averted and they were overcome with pride in me. Their pledge to help establish an Israeli state in 1948 had inspired my own determination to protect our young country from the many enemies who believed it should not exist.

Over the next few days, we learned that Israel took control of the Golan Heights, Gaza, the Sinai Peninsula, and the West Bank. Jerusalem was reunited, a victory that reconnected the western half of the city with Jordanian-controlled East Jerusalem and its holy Jewish sites: the Old City and the Western Wall.

In our minds, reclaiming Jerusalem more two thousand years after the destruction of the First and Second Temples (in 587 BCE and 70 CE), and the forced diaspora of Jews, demonstrated on a world stage that we had rightfully secured our home and our birthright. The cost of that sweet victory in 1967, however, was high. Students I knew did not survive.

LIFE AWAY FROM HOME

I returned to Italy thinking my studies there would propel me to a career as a physician back in Israel but, instead, as Robert Frost had written, I took "the road less traveled and that has made all the difference."

In New York, I would open a radiology practice, establish a women's health center, and raise two beautiful and intelligent daughters. My journey might sound easy, but I struggled with "immigrant syndrome," a conflict between my head and heart. I concentrated on my education, my career, and my family. I was grateful to my adopted country. And yet, Israel was never far from my thoughts. There was always a hole in my heart, an emptiness, a feeling that I belonged somewhere else, that I should be somewhere else.

As these feelings grew, I sought to contextualize my life story within the timeline of significant events in Israel. In 1973, when I had a pediatrics internship at North Shore University Hospital on Long Island, IDF soldiers fought in the Yom Kippur War. During the first Israel-Lebanon war in 1982, I was working as a radiologist. Throughout the first intifada—the sustained protests and riots in the occupied territories from 1987 to 1993—I had already founded and was president of Manhasset Diagnostic Imaging. And while Israel responded to the second intifada (2000–05), the second Lebanon-Israel war (2006), and the Gaza War (2008–09), I had founded and was running Pathways Women's Health, a center that provided a holistic and educational approach to cancer treatment, and The Unbeaten Path, a series of health seminars for adolescents.

I came to the uncomfortable conclusion that Israel and I had long been on divergent paths. Writing this book would be one way to reconnect.

RESEARCH AND WRITING

My motivations were several. Personally, now that my parents are deceased, I sought to strengthen my ties to my motherland and create new memories to share with my children and grandchildren. I wanted to enrich the limited exposure I had with immigrants and minority communities during my typically short family visits. I wanted to better understand how multiculturalism is a blessing and a challenge to a country's evolution.

When I wrote *Invincible Women* in 2020, I interviewed twenty-one female US immigrants who came from countries including China, Egypt, India, Brazil, and Bangladesh. I learned about their expertise in fields as diverse as biomedical engineering, astrophysics, education, and fashion design. A new book would allow me to continue my research by focusing on the ways women contribute to Israeli society.

So why am I writing again about women? First, it makes sense. I am a woman and an immigrant, and I knew that I would have an immediate bond with women living in my homeland. And second, women inherently face intersectional barriers. I was anxious to learn how they meet the challenges of gender and religious bias, patriarchal systems, racism, profound gaps in economic equity, and constant physical threats.

My goal was to meet women who comprise the beautiful mosaic of voices that is Israel. I wanted to learn about their ethnic communities, their integration with Israeli culture, and their achievements so I could shed light on what life in Israel is like today.

I also believed that writing this book would be helpful. The rise in anti-Semitism and the popularity of the Boycott, Divestment, Sanctions movement have eroded international opinion regarding Israel. I saw the need for an objective image of Israel to counter the media's one-sided and hostile coverage.

I spoke with Israeli women who broke glass ceilings, who are pioneers in technology and medicine, who are artists, executives, and philanthropists. They represent religious and secular Jews, sabras (those Jews born in Israel), Christians, the Druze, Ethiopians, and Arabs. I met women scarred by the Holocaust and influenced by the miracle of Israeli statehood in 1948. Women of differently philosophies who share the pain of terror and warfare and who now are living under a parliamentary system reeling from five elections in less than four years. (After my initial interviews, I spoke with a family forever changed by the October 7, 2023, massacre and war with Hamas.)

MY JOURNEY HOME

I flew out of Kennedy Airport in early February 2022 and spent the next couple of weeks in the company of a wonderful friend and guide. I encountered landscapes that reminded me of the biblical stories I'd learned as a child. I moved from north to south and explored the country's natural beauty and iconic locations, from the mountains in Galilee, Nazareth, and the Golan Heights, through the lush Israel Valley with its vineyards and vacation spots, to the Negev desert's crescent-horned ibex and marvelous craters known as *makhteshim.*

I visited my old army camp at the top of Mount Carmel near the Stella Maris Monastery. It was sunset and my heart was beating fast in response to romantic memories of my youth. My eyes followed the beauty of the golden dome of the Baha'i temple down to Haifa's crowded port. When the sparkling evening lights emerged, I tried to locate the house where I grew up. I held back my tears. I imagined my father dressed in his white coat coming down for dinner after a long day in his dental clinic. I could almost see my mother returning from the market carrying watermelon to spoil me, her youngest daughter.

In the north I met Bothaina Halabi, a Druze artist whose vivid paintings of the Holocaust build bridges between cultures and provide beautiful tools for sharing historical lessons. Gadeer Kamal-Mreeh, also Druze and a former member of Knesset, explained her motivations for bringing equality to all people in Israel. Kira Radinsky is a Ukrainian-born entrepreneur, data scientist, and researcher who uses AI to predict security threats and disasters, including the spread of COVID-19. And Ghada Zoabi, an Israeli-born Arab journalist, talked about the digital news service she created to unite Arab and Jewish residents and diplomatic leaders striving for peace.

In Tel Aviv, the "White City," I saw thousands of whitewashed Bauhaus-style houses like the one I grew up in, their circular terraces providing shade for the one below. Each neighborhood's character was as different as the women I met along the way. In the Neve Tzedec, a bohemian enclave of narrow streets, I dipped into the boutiques and restaurants. On the tree-lined Rothschild Boulevard, I passed the historic homes of Tel Aviv's founding families and the site of the signing of the Declaration of Independence. I settled in a café at the Habima theater, where I met Colette Avital, a Romanian-born author, former member of Knesset, and former Consul General in New York, the highest position attained by a woman in foreign service. I was treated to a tour of Habima with my friend Ziva Patir, chair of the theater's board, whose influential voice within international standards associations has led to improved corporate and environmental responsibility.

Also in this central area of Israel I met with Orit Adato, a retired brigadier general who successfully advocated for women to hold military roles in combat, technology, and intelligence. She was the first woman commissioner of the Israeli prison system. Orna Berry, an Israeli data technologist, was the first and only woman appointed to the leadership in Israel's Ministry of Industry, Trade, and Labor, and one of the first executives to bring a multinational company to the fledgling Advanced Technologies Park in the Negev. Rony Ross is a software developer and among the first Israeli entrepreneurs to successfully sell technology outside of Israel. Sima Shine, now the head of the Iran program at the Institute for National Security Studies, is the former head of Mossad's Research and Evaluation Division, who has served the Israeli intelligence community for much of her career. And Mina Teicher, PhD, an Israeli-born mathematician and chief government scientist, developed the Playing with Braids conference at the University of Miami to provide female students with an overview of how mathematics influences almost every aspect of life.

In Jerusalem, on a Friday afternoon, I negotiated bustling crowds of Orthodox women pushing strollers and struggling to hold bags of groceries for the family's Shabbat dinner. A sea of men wearing traditional black garments and large furry hats and yarmulkes moved with similar purpose. I was determined to visit the Kotel, the Western Wall, and the archeological excavation of the City of David, where I saw the remains of a three-thousand-year-old kingdom. I made my way to the Knesset and met with Pnina Tamano-Shato, the Israeli Minister of Immigration and Absorption, whose experiences as an Ethiopian refugee inform her work to help newcomers integrate with Israeli society.

Moving south, in the Negev I stood at the edge of one of the makhtesh and saw ribbons of stone in reds, oranges, purples, yellows, and browns. I remembered a childhood gift of a bottle of these many-colored sands. The waves and textures at the bottom of the crater, created hundreds of millions of years ago, danced around in a random fashion. Shadows fell between small, raised formations creating a playground for the sun.

At the Sde Boker kibbutz, I saw the simple rooms where David Ben-Gurion had lived at the end of his life. I was overwhelmed by the serenity and wonder of the desert that unrolled before me. In between the gentle peaks of the Negev's pale mountains, the dry bed of the Zin River made its way like a prehistoric snake before disappearing at the horizon. The bright blue sky and cottony white clouds made me think of the beginning of time in this home of divine miracles.

Here in the Negev, I met Rivka Carmi, a neonatologist, medical geneticist, the first woman president of an Israeli university, and first woman dean of an Israeli medical school. An advocate for women to reach positions of academic leadership, she was integral to the success of the Advanced Technologies Park associated with Ben-Gurion University. Sarah Abu-Kaf, PhD, is an Arab Bedouin and professor at Ben-Gurion University. *Forbes* magazine named her one of the most influential women in all of Israel. Nigist Mengesha, a Jewish Ethiopian refugee and author, is principal of Rosh Ha'ayin's Education Department and combats the isolation, depression, and domestic pressures that plague the Ethiopian refugee community. Tal Ohana, the daughter of Moroccan immigrant, is the mayor of Yeruham and an advocate for equality in education. A proponent of business development, she helps attract investment in Yeruham as an incubator for the medical use of cannabis. I also met with Hana Rado, an Israeli Zionist born to Ukrainian Holocaust survivors. A businesswoman and social entrepreneur, she helps create jobs for women in the so-called periphery—areas in Israel including the Negev in the south, the Galilee in the north, and other more remote locations.

SHINING A LIGHT

These amazing women value education and independence. They are grateful to the Israeli Defense Forces for helping shape their character, grow their intellect, and equip them with leadership experience needed for post-military careers. Their extraordinary skillsets are expressed in industries including high tech, R&D, medicine, education, and international standards, all of which contribute to Israel's worldwide position as a startup nation that brings "light unto others" (Isaiah 42:6).

Another common thread runs through the stories I heard: a desire to fulfill *tikkum olam*, the biblical term for repairing the world. Tikkum olam has been taught for generations, mentioned by Joshua in the Torah, and through the teachings of *halacha* (Jewish law) and Maimonides: "Through wisdom and elevation of character, acts of kindness and observing the Torah's Ten Commandments, one brings tikkum olam, improvement of the world."

Our 24/7 digital world provides a front-seat view of threats to our way of life and the health of the planet. Many of these challenges are being addressed—through science, the arts, medicine, and philanthropy—by the women in this book. Sharon Barak, an entrepreneur and polymers scientist I spoke with, works on solutions to rid the seas of millions of tons of plastics. Sivan Yaari is a nonprofit entrepreneur who brings Israeli technology for clean water, solar power, and agriculture to African villages. Gal Lusky, CEO of Israeli Flying Aid, has, without regard to politics or geography, saved countless lives of people imperiled by natural disasters and military conflict.

Dr. Gili Kenet is an internationally renowned physician specializing in hemophilia and other blood disorders. Judith Richter, born in Czech Karlovy Vary (Carlsbad) to Holocaust survivors, is an entrepreneur, educator, and one of Israel's most distinguished women leaders. She founded a medical device company and the NIR School of the Heart, where high school students learn about the cardiovascular system and work collaboratively with students from other cultures. Chava Shelhav, PhD, is an author and leading practitioner of the world-renowned Feldenkrais method of healing through the integration of body and mind.

Edna Fast, a lawyer, successful real estate agent, and a social entrepreneur supports the arts in Arab communities. Ayelet Ben-Ezer, an Israeli-born lawyer and CEO and vice-president of Israel's first private university, inspires innovative students to embrace cross-cultural partnerships and social responsibility.

MEMORIES VS. REALITY

My early life in Israel was rich and full. I climbed Mount Carmel as a child, cracked pine nuts, and picked anemones. I took wonderful trips with the Scouts to explore archeological sites like Masada and felt enormous pride in my ancestors who stood strong to defend their faith. I can still smell the salt in the air over the Mediterranean and taste the fried fish, hot corn, sabra fruit, and sweet watermelon I consumed in large quantities.

During my recent travels, however, my eyes were opened to a different reality of life, especially for women in the minority communities of the Druze, Bedouins, Israeli Arabs, and Ethiopians. I saw how difficult it is to achieve success while enduring discrimination and negotiating large gaps in educational and economic opportunities. I admired their commitment to create equality for those who are considered "other," and to establish trust between people of different beliefs and philosophies in the name of a more secure state of Israel.

I also realized that the Palestinian-Israeli-Arab conflict and damning media coverage has severely weakened the world's perception of Israel. The children of lifelong Zionist families question once rock-solid ideologies and whether a two-state solution is a dream or a nightmare. People believe Israel is an apartheid country because of the 1967 occupation of the West Bank and the harsh differences in the standards of living between Palestinians there and the growing number of Israeli settlers.

I saw how Israel faces not only these external pressures but intense internal divisions. There are cultural rifts between descendants of European-born Ashkenazi and Mediterranean- and Asian-born Sephardic Jews. Resentment is nothing new among secular Jews who serve in the IDF and pay taxes that support the largely unemployed ultra-Orthodox Jews who do not serve their country.

And divisions between Jewish settlers and non-Jewish people in the West Bank have played out with lethal consequence. I learned about these polarizing views from Tamar Asraf, an Israeli settler, religious Zionist, and former spokesperson for a regional council in Judea and Samaria, and Achinoam Nini, a top Yemeni singer, a Zionist, activist, environmentalist, and United Nations Goodwill Ambassador who adamantly opposes Jewish settlements.

TOMORROW IS TODAY

Since I graduated medical school, the number of women physicians graduating today is almost equal to their male counterparts. More women are participating in industries traditionally dominated by men. Women in all fields take risks. They embrace challenges. They lead with confidence, learn from their failures, and share their successes.

As the complicated story of Israel unfolded for me through the eyes of these women, I saw how a nation divided—by walls, borders, political, religious, and cultural beliefs—can be held together by a single person's love of country and community. I learned that inequality and discrimination can be improved through research, education, art, and employment.

I am hopeful. Peace is a common quest among the women I spoke to, and it is the goal of the Abraham Accords, which in 2020 established diplomatic relations between Israel, Bahrain, the United Arab Emirates, Sudan, and Morocco.

The mosaic that is Israel is, in my mind, an abstract work of art. We can look closely at the individuals who strive to help others and innovate in widely divergent areas. And we can also step back to think, to envision the whole, to see a country where sharp edges and personal ideologies blend and flourish for the benefit of all. My homecoming showed me an Israel different from my youth in many respects, but it also rekindled my feelings of identity and love of the country.

My work will be rewarded if this book starts conversations and drives readers to fully see Israel today and where it can be tomorrow. The beauty of the land and the strength of the women I met inspired my hope that unity will prevail and be a driving guide for tikkum olam.

PART I

THE HEALERS

MICHAL SCHWARTZ,
Professor of Neuroimmunology at the Weizmann
Institute of Science

RIVKA CARMI,
Neonatologist and Medical Geneticist, President of
Ben-Gurion University of the Negev

CHAVA SHELHAV,
author, Head of the Center for the Feldenkrais
Method in Germany

GILI KENET,
Director of the Israel National Hemophilia Center
and Thrombosis Institute in the Sheba Medical Center

MICHAL SCHWARTZ

PROFESSOR OF NEUROIMMUNOLOGY AT THE WEIZMANN INSTITUTE OF SCIENCE

"I thought that since an important organ like the brain cannot be replaced, it did not make sense that it would be excluded from benefiting from the [body's] immune system. This hypothesis led to twenty-four years of research, which I initiated, and which proved that the brain and the immune system do interact."

MICHAL SCHWARTZ HAD A DREAM that took root when she was a ten-year-old girl touring the Weizmann Institute in Rehovot on a class trip. "It impressed me as a tower of knowledge, where golden wisdom resides," she told me. "That was the day I wished to belong."

Now a professor of neuroimmunology at the internationally renowned institute that she visited as a child, Michal has achieved her goals and more. She currently zigzags between overseeing her research group as professor at the Weizmann Institute, and her responsibilities as Chief Scientific Officer at ImmunoBrain Checkpoint, the company she cofounded that is now engaged in clinical trials of immunotherapy treatments that she pioneered for Alzheimer's disease and other neuro-degenerative diseases.

My first attempt to interview Michal was cut short by sirens that shattered our Zoom call. "Sorry, I'm rushing to the shelter," she said calmly, as if the rushing to a safe space, within ninety seconds, had become a routine occurrence since the Hamas massacre on October 7, 2023. When we spoke the following day, our conversation focused on Michal's groundbreaking scientific research and the first treatment for Alzheimer's that targets the immune system instead of the brain.

Though skeptics dismissed her first articles in 1998 and 1999, despite their publication in a high-profile journal, Michal ultimately proved that the brain is tightly dependent on the immune system, a potential interaction that was previously dismissed. Her research further confirmed that the immune system has an important role in repairing degenerative brain diseases, including Alzheimer's disease. She has since published more than three hundred papers in leading journals including *Science, Nature Medicine, Nature Neuroscience, Nature Immunology*, and various perspective and review articles in high-profile journals. As part of Israel's seventy-fifth Independence Day celebration, Michal received the 2023 Israel Prize, the state's highest honor, for her research in the Life in Sciences—only the fourth woman to receive this honor since the prize's inception in 1953.

"It was known for decades that if you put a foreign body into the brain or the eye, it is hardly rejected," she said of the discovery for which Peter Medawar received a Nobel Prize in 1950. Medawar coined the idea that the brain's "immune privilege" isolated the organ from the body's immune system. Based on this finding, the scientific and medical world assumed that the brain cannot tolerate any immune activity.

"It did not make sense to me that such a fragile and such a precious tissue like the brain, an organ that cannot be replaced, has relinquished the opportunity to be assisted by the immune system while many other organs in the body that are irreplaceable—the liver, the kidney, the heart, and the lung—can benefit from immune system support," she said.

In 1998, Schwartz suggested a hypothesis to explain the effects of the brain's immune isolation. After almost any bodily injury, macrophages are needed to first clean the injured tissue and prepare it for rejuvenation. There is a mechanism that orchestrates the initiation and termination of this process. "So, I thought that maybe the brain, once it's injured, doesn't have access to enough macrophages," she said. "That's how I began. My first paper in *Nature Medicine* claimed that macrophages are needed for central nervous system repair. I cannot tell you how many scientists were against me at the time. They claimed 'She doesn't know! She doesn't understand!' I used to come to conferences shaking, wondering who would attack me next, and I couldn't attain any grants to support my work.

"In 1999, we published another paper in *Nature Medicine* where we showed that not only macrophages are needed but so are T-cells that recognize central nervous system antigens. One could say," she continued, "that autoimmune T-cells are needed. It is crucial to distinguish between autoimmune disease and autoimmune T-cells. It is well known that we have self-reactive or autoimmune cells in our body, but these do not imply autoimmune disease. Based on our results I coined the term 'protective autoimmunity' describing the body's own beneficial T-cells that are responsible for immune surveillance.

"It took several years until other scientists joined me, including even those who were against me all along," she said. "But I believe that the major turning point was when we published our data in *Nature Neuroscience, 2006*, showing for the first time that cognitive ability is dependent on the integrity of the immune system, which implies that aging of the brain could reflect aging of the immune system, and not necessarily chronological aging. Using an animal model, we demonstrated that cognitive performance, formation of new neurons in the brain, and coping with mental stress, as well as other aspects of brain plasticity, are dependent on the integrity of the adaptive immunity.

"This was very exciting for us, and this was the first time that the community started to think, 'Wow, she may be right,'" she said. "This was indeed a turning point and the scientific community started searching for the location of such immune cells that can support brain plasticity." Michal's team found them in the blood-cerebrospinal fluid barrier, and a former student of hers found such cells in the meninges. Papers emerged showing that the healthy brain has immune cells in its territories, not inside the brain, but along its borders. "And slowly, slowly but surely many scientists joined us." For the first time, in 2022, *Nature* published an article entitled "The Immune System: The Guardian of the Brain." "This for me, after so many years, provided validation," she said.

Based on the accumulated knowledge and the appreciation that Alzheimer's disease could involve dysfunction of the immune system, not as a primary cause but as escalating factor, Schwartz's team investigated various manipulations to rejuvenate the immune system as a way of treating Alzheimer's disease. In 2016 her team found that they could activate the immune system by targeting an immune checkpoint, similar to a treatment used for cancer. A proof of this concept, published in 2016 in *Nature Medicine*, led to the founding of ImmunoBrain Checkpoint.

BACK TO REALITY

I had some trouble concentrating on the brilliance of Michal's explanations because sirens in the background brought me back to the reality that Israel was at war. I thought about the decades she has dedicated to saving lives and the awful widening chasm between good and evil. Many of her international doctoral students had left the country, driven out by the war, forcing Michal to continue as much of her research as possible via virtual meetings.

"My research group managed very well through COVID. We continued to work nonstop," she said. "I was able to continue working during the recent period of social division in Israeli society due to the proposed judicial reforms, because it was a domestic issue, and my research fellows from abroad didn't care about it. I was traveling almost every week to places all over the world. But now it's the most difficult time, because the foreigners who are among the strongest scientific members of my team have left the country. We are limited in our ability to conduct experiments. My concern is that all of us right now are overwhelmed. I keep telling myself that the world will continue, and we need to strive for a better world for us and for the following generations."

As we discussed the fragility of the world, we agreed that everything is dependent on timing and that our daily struggles are relative. Only weeks ago, we were concerned about an Israeli society divided over the proposed judicial reforms and its effect on academic freedoms and equity. And now we are worried about the consequences of fighting against terrorists who are lacking any moral values. Though resilience and a desire for peace are part of the Jewish people's DNA, as a result of two thousand years of exile and horrors such as the Holocaust, I wondered if people ever get used to war.

Meanwhile, Michal saves lives in her own way and decided to stay in the lab. "What I am doing in science cannot be replaced, and therefore, I am here." The biopharma company that she cofounded is running a clinical trial, developed based on her intellectual property in early Alzheimer's disease patients, where the first concern is to test the safety of the treatment. She and her team are working on the clinical trials in five centers in Israel, five centers in the UK, and one in Amsterdam. They raised enough money to complete Phase 1–Phase 2(a), she said. They expect to determine the optimal dose and frequency for the next clinical trial phase.

FAMILY INFLUENCE

Michal's mother comes from a long line of Israeli-born sabras, and her father is a Holocaust survivor. Her mother lost her dearest brother during the 1948 Israel war of independence and suffered for years over her loss. "Neither of my parents could mentor me academically," Michal said of her thirst for knowledge and long journey in academia. "They never had the benefit of higher education."

She completed a BS degree in chemistry at the acclaimed Hebrew University of Jerusalem and earned her PhD in chemical immunology from the Weizmann Institute. She conceived of the marriage between neuroscience and immunology, which led to the popularization of the now internationally accepted field of neuroimmunology.

Michal pursued her scientific research while caring for her family with the help of babysitters. When the kids were very young, she used to come back home in the afternoon and returned to the laboratory at 9:00 p.m., once her kids were sleeping.

Some of the initial difficulty, beyond scientific skepticism that she faced when trying to alter the dogma regarding the interactions of the brain and the immune system, was exacerbated by hostile male colleagues. "Family obligations or personal health issues were not considered an excuse to minimize one's obligations to the Institute," she said. "It was not accepted at the time to receive any privileges as a mother, and I did not want any justification that could be used against me. I wanted to compete with men without raising any issues. Getting there was not easy."

Michal proudly speaks now about her two sons and two daughters. When I congratulated her on her family, her unbending commitment to her children and her dream, her success, her intelligence, her long hours, beating the odds, and achieving recognition, she responded: "Yes, but with penalties, including the struggle to be supported in the scientific community. Nevertheless, I am gratified, because right now I'm considered worldwide as the guru of the field of neuroimmunology."

Schwartz proved that there is more than one way to contribute to human survival, and I hope that in the future, the world will value peace and choose Michal's way.

———◇•◇———

Michal served as the elected president of the International Society of Neuroimmunology (2016–18). Among her many honors and prizes are the EMET Prize in 2019; the Israel Prize in 2023—the highest prize awarded by the state of Israel for scientific research; and a prize by the Federation of European Neuroscientists, in 2022, for excellence in neuroimmunology.

RIVKA CARMI

FORMER PRESIDENT OF BEN-GURION UNIVERSITY, GENETICIST, AND PEDIATRICIAN

"There's always research and work to be done to advance women's rights for equal opportunities and for fair, important shares in senior leadership positions."

DR. RIVKA CARMI ALREADY HAD a rewarding career as a neonatologist and medical geneticist when she was offered the opportunity to lead Ben-Gurion University of the Negev (BGU). She had just left Israel for a sabbatical in the United States to pursue research sponsored by the National Institutes of Health, and she knew that the presidency would forever alter her carefully orchestrated professional path.

Making the decision took a physical toll; Rivka underwent gastroscopies and swallowed too many antacid tablets to count to alleviate reflux due to her indecisiveness. Eventually, she asked herself three questions:

"Do I care for Ben-Gurion University? The answer was 'yes, very much so.'

"Do I care who would be the next leader of this important institution? This was a sound 'yes' as well.

"Can I point to somebody else who would fit the bill?" Her answer for this one was "no."

She had made up her mind. In 2006, Rivka began her almost thirteen-year tenure as the first woman president of an Israeli university, a position that followed her appointment in 2000 as the first woman dean of an Israeli medical school. Even with those two glass ceilings smashed, she had plenty of important work to do.

Rivka embraced David Ben-Gurion's Zionist vision that Israel's future lies in the Negev: "It is in the Negev where the creativity and the pioneering vigor of Israel will be tested," the late prime minister said. The Negev occupies about 60 percent of Israel, yet less than 10 percent of the desert terrain is populated. About a quarter of residents are Bedouins, including new arrivals and the people who remained when Israel became a state in 1948.

Rivka saw BGU as an incubator for innovation in an economically distressed area, where each student could become an agent of hope for the Negev. Academic research would be grounded in local needs with worldwide applications: solar energy, water treatment, desert agriculture, health, and technology. The Negev would be transformed into an ecosystem for new jobs driven by academic, industry, and government collaborations.

Today, as one of Israel's leading public research universities, BGU has more than twenty thousand students, nearly five thousand faculty and staff, and three campuses, the main one in Be'er Sheva. It is home to six national and international research centers and is a critical partner in the adjacent Advanced Technologies Park, which is populated by pioneering scientific, biotech, and technological companies from around the world. The IDF's new Hi-Tech Center and Communications R&D facility is on track to be built next door.

Avishay Braverman, Rivka's predecessor, initiated the idea for the technology park that came to fruition under Rivka's leadership. To figure out why previous attempts to build the park failed, Rivka assembled a committee of representatives from the university and the municipality of Be'er Sheva, donors, and a conflict-resolution expert. They spent two days analyzing their weaknesses, strengths, the threat of competition, and the unique opportunities. The resulting business partnership including the university, city, and private developers enabled the creation of the Advanced Technologies Park.

ADVANCING THE PARK

A bank loan needed to begin construction, however, required the partners to guarantee a 40 percent occupancy rate. Before she could proceed, Rivka had to convince members of the administration that the occupancy rate would be met by the time the first building was completed. She successfully emphasized the university's Zionistic role in the Negev and the park's potential to create jobs, populate the Negev, and generate profits for BGU in the years to come.

Rivka also teamed up with Dr. Orna Berry, EMC Corporation's vice-president of innovation, to make the company the first multinational to establish an R&D center in the technology park, a move that prompted others to follow suit. Rivka first recruited Berry, whom she had commanded in the IDF, to BGU's for-profit arm that commercializes research products. For three years and until moving to the first building in the technology park, EMC rented a temporary space in Be'er Sheva. Within a year, ten projects involving seventy-five students were established, with great results for the researchers and EMC. Berry and EMC were in.

Partnerships continued to grow after the first couple of years. BGU's strength in cybertechnology attracted industries prone to cyberattacks, including transportation, hospital devices, data, banking, infrastructure, water, defense, and security.

Five buildings went up over the next twelve years. The National Civil CERT (Cybersecurity Emergency Response Team) was moved to the park, along with the establishment of the National Cyber Technology Research Center. A new bridge was built connecting the train station and the university campus to the park, easing the commute time for students and employees.

"Without the university it would never happen," Rivka told me. "The advantage of having the best professors and students in technology and communication working with the industry was the secret to the technology park's success in building a unique, model ecosystem."

A LOVE OF GENETICS

Rivka was born in 1948 and grew up in Zikhron Ya'akov, on the southern slopes of the Carmel mountain range facing the Mediterranean Sea, not far from Haifa. The small town, established in 1882, is known for the winery founded by Baron Edmond James de Rothschild and for the heroism of Sarah Aaronsohn. Aaronsohn established the Nili Jewish underground in 1915 that spied on the Ottomans on behalf of the English to help establish a Jewish state.

Rivka's mother, Zipora, born in Poland, was a social worker and her father, Menachem, born in Germany, was an accountant. Each arrived in Israel in the early 1930s, leaving behind families that perished in the Holocaust. Rivka remembers fondly her childhood years spent biking along the brick road to nature preserves and the seaside.

Her interest in genetics can be traced to her father's death, when she was fourteen, of complications from a gastric ulcer. His suffering prompted her "fascination with cells" and desire to be a genetics researcher. Two years later, she was accepted, along with other students gifted in the sciences, to a summer camp at the Weizmann Institute of Science. She was fascinated with genetics and the phenomenon of cell division that forms sex chromosomes from which a fetus is created. She had the advantage of her own "rebellious and ambitious" genes and wanted to figure out why some diseases are inherited.

After serving in the Israeli Defense Forces, reaching the rank of captain and commanding at the officers' academy training school, Rivka attended Hebrew University of Jerusalem. She did not really like the zoology and botany courses that were required for a degree in biology, so she switched to medicine. In 1975, she graduated from the Hebrew University of Jerusalem Hadassah Medical School.

Every summer vacation throughout medical school she served fifty days with the army reserve, commanding a group of eighty women soldiers who had deferred their service to complete their academic studies. Her command of people only a year or two younger than herself boosted her self-confidence as a leader. During the Yom Kippur War, she worked with a unit that sought persons missing in action. "Looking for missing soldiers was the toughest period in my life," she told me. "Memories were erased to be replaced by a dark hole." Her beloved cousin was one of the missing soldiers whose body was recovered months after the war ended.

Rivka completed her internship and residency at BGU's Soroka Medical Center. She researched genetic diseases among the Bedouin community and provided genetic counseling. During her pediatric residency, she took a two-year break to pursue a fellowship in medical genetics at Boston Children's Hospital and Harvard Medical School. In retrospect, she believes that this unusual track provided the institutional leadership skills that gave her an advantage over her peers. She returned to BGU to complete a fellowship in neonatology and was a lecturer in the Faculty of Health Sciences.

In 1977, her first academic publication of what would be more than 150 papers described an accumulation of carbon dioxide in hoods, infant cots, and incubators, speculated to be associated with sudden infant death syndrome. In 1995, she was promoted to full professor and held the Kreitman Foundation Chair in Pediatric Genetics.

In 2000, at age fifty-two, she was elected dean of the Faculty of Health Sciences, the first woman to hold the position in Israel. Rivka told me that she knew as far back as her late twenties that she wanted to become dean of a medical school and pretty much programmed her life toward her goal. She counseled female medical students, tackled gender issues, systematically wrote scientific papers—all done with the bonus of having Harvard on her resume.

Though she felt secure about the strength of her medical and research experience, she was surprised by what became a challenging campaign. Four men ran against her, one of whom suggested that Rivka's short skirts should exclude her from consideration. She decided not to pursue ethics charges against him; "I wanted to win the position for my professional achievements and capabilities, not because of a side-show drama about discrimination."

When she became dean, she issued a "Ten Commandments" mission statement. The sixth item was a promise to promote women in academic medicine and lessen the "scissor effect," a phenomenon where equal numbers of women and men enter the sciences or medical school, but men vastly surpass women graduates in climbing the academic rank ladder and holding senior positions of academic authority.

Rivka was deeply involved with establishing major biotechnology initiatives, serving as acting director of the nascent National Institute for Biotechnology in the Negev. She also ran the genetic counseling services and was the founder and director of the Genetics Institute at the Soroka Medical Center.

Her genetics research was initially clinical. One of the syndromes she described, where children are born without skin on large areas of their bodies, was later found by her group to be caused by a mutation in the integrin beta 4 gene and is now named after her. She said that the Human Genome Project—which started in 1990, and changed the direction of genetic science in such a dramatic manner by enabling the sequencing and identifying base pairs in the human genetic instruction—fed her own work to find the genetic roots of diseases in the Bedouin-Arab population and to develop prenatal diagnostic tests.

Rivka teamed up with Val Sheffield, a genetic physician-scientist from Iowa, who had the infrastructure in his laboratory to pursue gene sequencing. Their collaboration lasted twenty-five years. They worked together on various genetic diseases in the Bedouin community, among them the BBS (the Bardet-Biedl Syndrome), commonly found among the Bedouins in the Negev. The syndrome appeared in three Bedouin tribes with no apparent connection, suggesting that more than one gene was responsible. There are now more than eighteen known genes involved with the same genetic phenotypic manifestations.

GRAPPLING WITH CRITICISM

After stepping away from her own research, Rivka acclimated to the life of a university president, managing academics, technology researchers, and campus politics. She wasn't immune from criticism. The right wing accused her of brainwashing students by inviting Arab speakers and IDF whistleblowers (from the group Breaking the Silence) as lecturers. At the same time, she was accused of supporting the Boycott, Divestment, Sanctions movement. The accusations prompted her to speak in the Knesset, where she cited the numerous newspaper articles and international lectures in which she criticized BDS and its negative effect on Israel and its universities. She joined an Israeli group of doctors inviting a team from the *Lancet* medical journal to Israel, for them to see that health services were provided without discrimination to all Israeli citizens as well as to patients from the Palestinian Authority, exposing the visitors to the complex and intricate regional conflict.

When one of her left-wing professors supported BDS to "save Israel from itself," Rivka responded that boycotting Israel "is dangerous for the university, which is a Zionist institution that embodies [Ben-Gurion's] dream…to bring development and prosperity to all the residents of the Negev region." Her argument emphasized the university's importance fostering collaborative research by Jewish, Arab Bedouin, and neighboring Jordanian doctors to improve people's lives in the Negev and the region at large. Boycotting Israel, she said, would prevent international collaboration and the exchange of students and professors for the benefit of science and humanity.

"Israel-bashing detracts from the work of the university," she said. "I am strongly committed to freedom of speech for any individual; but when it comes to academic freedom, competing ideas should be discussed in the classroom side by side, so students can enjoy an open and friendly environment to freely exchange ideas and make their own informed judgments and decisions generally, and on controversial issues in particular."

When I asked Rivka about the university's involvement in the Bedouin community and how it tackles social inequality, she mentioned the special gap year offered to Bedouin high school graduates. To prepare for psychometric exams, the students take free courses in English, math, learning, social skills, and university values. Once they complete the gap year, they must pass the psychometric exams for admission, or be exempt based on high scores achieved during the prior year.

A Bedouin graduate's speech during Ben-Gurion Day in 2016 described the university's important position in the Negev and in her life. Naama Elsana thanked Dr. Carmi and her parents—for their belief that the power of education leads to change—and said the university "is a place that gives a lot of strength and possibility to everybody who wants to study and a capability for everybody who wants to make a difference. It gives higher education to those who want to learn."

She continued: "The partnership between Arabs and Israelis is only beneficial for peace and for goodness to live together. In Ben-Gurion University there is no difference between Arabs and Jews; we all get the same thing, and we seek peace." Alsana, who has thirteen siblings, said an education makes possible a wealth of societal improvements: "Our purpose is the employment and education of women which will empower them and encourage our daughters to study. They will be able to open up to the modern world and our Bedouin society will become more independent and not a dependent one. The Bedouin woman has the power to be a mother of four and study at the same time. She doesn't have to have fourteen children. The Bedouin woman should be a modern woman."

Rivka has always fought for women's rights so they can succeed personally and professionally, but stops short of labeling herself a feminist.

As the mother of a daughter, born during an early marriage that ended, Rivka struggled to balance caregiving and her career. "Having a family should not prevent women from aspiring to build meaningful and rewarding careers," she said. "Every woman should find the best solutions that work for her in balancing career and family life."

And as Shira, her daughter, told Rivka later in her life, "Even if I missed you from time to time, you were my role model because of how much you have enjoyed and was committed to your work and career."

I asked Rivka about her post-presidency plans. She said she will return to the world of medicine and health on national levels, specifically medical education, and the promotion of biomedical research by physician-scientists. To that extent, she led a small group of senior physician researchers to found the Israel Academy of Science in Medicine. Her specific interest, she said, has to do with the convergence of interdisciplinary research, bringing together life sciences and medicine with engineering and computation—bioconvergence. She considers this the future of medical innovation, as well as significant developments in addressing unmet needs in fields like food tech, agriculture, energy, environment, defense and more.

"And of course," she said, "there's always research and work to be done to advance women's rights for equal opportunities and for fair, important shares in senior leadership positions."

CHAVA SHELHAV

SENIOR TEACHER OF THE FELDENKRAIS METHOD

"Under certain conditions, every person is able to free herself from her personal and historical background and to make new choices for herself. I came full circle thanks to my profession."

DR. CHAVA SHELHAV'S WORK, CHILD'SPACE Method, has opened new horizons to clinicians and professionals in the field of early childhood development. Child'Space is an integrated approach to infant development based on the ideas and methods of Dr. Moshe Feldenkrais. Her work provides a deeper analysis of movement as an influential factor of emotional and interpersonal development. For example, she looks at how parents hold their babies, how they talk to then, and the way they interact.

A longtime student of renowned educator Feldenkrais, Chava adapted his practice of integrating movement, thought, and awareness to offer a holistic approach to child development. She was the head of the Center for the Feldenkrais Method in Germany, supporting children with developmental delays or illnesses. Using learning through play, Chava was able to help families who came to her with late developmental issues, including motoric, problem-solving, and poor communication skills.

"Learning through play allows you to gain a more holistic perspective on the connections between motoric development, emotion, and cognition," she said. "A playful setting fosters communication, which parents take part in." For example, Jasmin learned how to tie her shoelaces using a rope during mutual play. Then there's the case of Jonathan, who at one year and two months was curious, animated, active, and social. Two months earlier, she said, he began to stand up next to furniture and in his bed, but was unable to let go of support, stand by himself, or take a few steps. "When we look at Jonathan's chronological age, all is well," Chava told me. "Not every infant walks at his age. In a wider observation, in addition to the motor aspect, we could identify that the dynamics between the parents and Jonathan have had an influence on his rate of development. When Jonathan and his mother play together, we notice that the mother takes on the main role." After Chava made contact with Jonathan and interested him in a game, she lowered her voice and slowed the speed of her speech. Jonathan responded in kind.

"In talking with his mom, it became clear that she works every day until late in the afternoon, and when she gets home, she feels the need to make up for lost time with her son. After she observed the process of the session, she understood that she was taking too much space in the interactions with Jonathan, thereby minimizing his opportunities to initiate play and explore his surroundings. After she observed the change in Jonathan, she understood that she must give him time to initiate, explore, and play, and that her very presence contributes to his sense of security and calm."

Chava infuses her lessons and training with a calmness, kindness, and tolerance rooted in her personal history caring for her older sister, Bilha, who had schizophrenia. She was born in Haifa to parents who immigrated to Israel from Europe in 1933. Her mother was an infant caretaker, and her father was an accountant for Haifa's municipal government. Her family was religious, and she studied in Beit Yaakov.

Haifa was a working-class city where it was usual for children to work during the day and attend school at night. During her adolescence, Chava held a job in her father's workplace as a telephone operator and refined her social and communication skills, chatting with people who called in.

At fourteen, Chava took care of her sister after her father passed away a year before. "Gradually, I learned to understand [my sister's] distorted logic," Chava said. "Spending all this time with her, I learned to accept her experiences as it is, not a situation that has to be adjusted to a framework. My sister was my best teacher from the point of view that I realized that there's a different way a damaged person's brain works," Chava said, adding that the sisters had a great friendship. "I had to adapt to her thinking and let her live according to her way of thinking. She couldn't adapt to me. I had to adapt to her. Her version of normal was different from mine. That was a great lesson." Chava told me that despite her sister's illness and having been hospitalized for years in a psychiatric ward, Bilha went to study at university, got married, and published poetry.

In the late 1960s, Chava moved to Tel Aviv and enrolled in Seminar Hakibutzim, where she studied to become a gymnastics teacher and was introduced to the influential work of somatic bodywork pioneer Elsa Gindler. After she graduated, Chava was invited to teach at the college.

In 1968, when Dr. Feldenkrais opened his first course in Tel Aviv, Chava was among the fourteen students chosen to assist him. Over the next three years, Chava took movement lessons at his studio on Alexander Yannai Street. She studied his method, which stated that meaningful action is composed of many movement elements broken down into tiny units.

At first, I was skeptical of this method. But after listening to Chava, I became a follower, and I was convinced of the importance of integrating Feldenkrais into one's daily life.

LEARNING HOW TO HELP

Chava helps people to achieve their mental and physical potential through movement. Each one of us speaks, moves, thinks, and feels in a different way, according to the image of themselves built up over the years. In order to change our mode of action we should change the images we carry of ourselves. "In my own experience practicing Feldenkrais, on my way back home from a lesson, I felt my taller and my mood was better," she said. "I saw my husband in a better light and was more tolerant of my children. I felt that something good happened within me."

Through studying Feldenkrais, Chava said she was also able to see personality behind movement, meaning that there's complexity in working with other people's movements. She added that people could take the awareness they gained from a movement into other aspects of life, such as how you develop communication. A person's movement is not only guided by physical ability, she said, but is driven by an emotional state, a "functional integration of body and mind." Repeated movement, she continued, is not automatic. But by being attentive to the sensations which accompany repeated movement, a person can separate from their automatic moods and change habits.

In 1980, after working with Feldenkrais for ten years, Chava was invited to join him in Amherst, Massachusetts, as a teacher. The experience opened new opportunities for her to lead Feldenkrais workshops around the world. Chava received her master's degree from Boston University in 1989. Her thesis focused on using the Feldenkrais Method in children with cerebral palsy.

She earned her doctorate from Heidelberg University in Germany. Her thesis led to her book *Movement as a Model of Learning* (1999), in which she described her research on school-age children with learning difficulties and how movement helped them concentrate and overcome those developmental challenges. She has been mentoring students, parents, and professionals in Israel and around the world and published several books in Italian, Spanish, Korean, and German. Her latest work, *Child'Space: An Integrated Approach to Child Development Using the Feldenkrais Method* (2019), presents her philosophy relating Feldenkrais's ideology with the goal to "broaden the knowledge for professionals and parents who deal with children who have development issues."

Chava has trained more than a thousand teachers and caregivers in her Child'Space Method. "We all want the best for our children," she said. "Child'Space helps parents understand their babies' development, including new and traditional ways to participate in their child's daily learning, at each stage right from birth.

"Orientation, balance, and sensory systems that develop in infancy influence the development of the infant movement," Chava explained, and her system can address delays in the different stages of infant development from a baby's initial awareness of their environment to the advanced act of walking. Her method entails pre-verbal expressions, touch, and movement to involve an infant's brain and improve their functioning.

With the Child'Space Method, Chava saw improved results in infants who suffer from developmental delays and who have special needs. Chava believes that parents must always participate in the lessons, and she guides them how to communicate with their infants using touch, language, and play.

Awareness of the way a child moves—lifting her head, rolling over, sitting, and walking—can help identify even the slightest delays in early childhood development, she said, adding that each child reaches milestones on different timelines. Her training shows parents how to be observant and identify differences in motor, social, and emotional problems. "Babies are happier and more satisfied with themselves as they discover the vocabulary of activities that belong to the human developmental program," she said. She explained that crawling, rolling, and moving require an understanding of the body's interconnectedness.

A JEWISH WOMAN IN GERMANY

I was fascinated by Chava's explanation of how an Israeli-born daughter of Holocaust survivors studied and worked in Germany. "Under certain conditions, every person is able to free herself from her personal and historical background, and to make new choices for herself," she said. "I came full circle. My parents fled from Germany on the eve of the Nazis' rise to power. They immigrated to the land of Israel as pioneers, and now a center, sponsored by a local German family, is open with their daughter's name [Chava Shelhav], a pioneer center in a field in which she is a forerunner."

Chava joined other professionals to create the first center in integrative medicine at the former Assaf Harofeh Medical Center near Tel Aviv.

It was clear to me how Chava's strong character was molded by the difficulties she encountered as a teenager, her early independence, and the sorrow she felt as a child of Holocaust survivors. Her unique combination of strength, curiosity, flexibility, and the ability to surpass obstacles and be less critical, are all life lessons she learned following Feldenkrais's ideology.

We wrapped up our conversation by remembering Prime Minister David Ben-Gurion, who followed the Feldenkrais Method and is memorialized, standing on his head, in a statue on the boardwalk in Tel Aviv. Chava explained that the pose compresses the vertebra so that when you stand up, you feel taller, as if you have been stretched. I left our wonderful meeting thinking that Ben-Gurion's small stature was inverse to the importance of his Zionistic mission and leadership. He was taller than life.

GILI KENET

DIRECTOR AT THE ISRAELI NATIONAL HEMOPHILIA INSTITUTE, SHEBA MEDICAL CENTER

"The impossible never holds us back.
It is only the possible that holds us back."

DR. GILI KENET SIPPED FRESHLY brewed coffee and then took a deep, cleansing breath. She had just emerged from her clinic at Sheba Hospital. The previous night was spent monitoring an infant with seizures.

"Even though I often don't sleep through the night, I am happy when I go to work every day," said Gili, an internationally renowned physician specializing in hemophilia. She recently became the director of the international PedNet foundation, an independent academic registry and research network in the Netherlands, promoting hemophilia research in pediatric patients. As we sat together, we talked about her favorite subject—her work—including the lengthy research that goes into finding treatments for people with rare genetic diseases, and the nine-month-old Arab girl who was currently on her mind.

She told me that the baby was born two months premature to apparently healthy parents in an Arab village. The parents were cousins, though, and Gili suspected that the baby's brain hemorrhage, causing her seizures, could be the result of a genetic disease. Hemophilia was ruled out through testing, and the baby was diagnosed with a Factor VII (FVII) deficiency, a severe bleeding disorder that occurs once in every half a million children.

"There are very few cases, but we know the disease," said Gili, director of the Israel National Hemophilia Center and Thrombosis Institute, professor and former chair of the Hematology Department at the Sackler Medical School at Tel Aviv University, and chair of the Amalia Biron Research Institute of Thrombosis and Hemostasis at Sheba Medical Center at Tel HaShomer. "We diagnosed her together with the physicians in Afula and we brought her into a tertiary referral center." The medical team started early prophylaxis right after the diagnosis had been confirmed by inserting a central line to give the baby crucial infusions of the missing clotting factor, which is Gili's preferred treatment but not a worldwide practice.

"Usually, physicians treating babies with severe coagulation disorders tend to wait and administer treatment only occasionally, on demand, until these children bleed. Yet some of them bleed severely into the brain, directly," she told me. "I got the notion that in families where the mutation causing FVII deficiency is of high risk, and therefore the clotting factor is completely missing, or where there is severe familial bleeding history—like in this case, where the parents said that the baby had a brother who died in 2011 at the age of five months from intracerebral hemorrhage, and was never diagnosed—there is no time to waste and treatment should start ASAP."

Gili explained that she got a call the evening before from a colleague at Emek Medical Center in Afula, who told her that something was wrong. The infant gets prophylactic FVII injections at the hospital every other day, and as she had received her injection that same day, she should have been fine. Nonetheless, she presented with a seizure, which could have meant bleeding into the brain. At that time, the baby was transferred to a larger referral center in Haifa, and Gili was consulted again. Gili realized that the prophylaxis with FVII did not work, and a blood coagulation profile revealed the presence of factor 7 inhibitors, or antibodies, an extremely rare complication.

"We started treating her with high doses of replacement product (FVII)," Gili said. "Every two to three hours we obtained the coagulation profile to look for a response. We have good experience with hemophilia and inhibitors, and no one in the world has good experience with FVII inhibitors." She said she corresponded that night with colleagues in Italy, Germany, the Netherlands, Sweden, the United States, Canada, and South Africa, and no one could help. "Everyone told me, 'Oh, it's so interesting. If you get something, tell me because we don't know how to deal with this,'" she said.

Gili started the little girl on steroids as a sort of immune modulation and ordered another drug, Rituximab, that would work against her antibodies. She considered a second and third line of treatment and experimental treatments for compassionate use.

"This event started rolling at 11:00 p.m. yesterday. I went to sleep briefly at 3:00 a.m. I woke up at 5:30 a.m., and I'm still running," she said. COVID has depleted her team of physicians, and Gili had to manage the logistics and negotiations for off-label treatment and compassionate use. She also saw twelve patients in the clinic, gave consults, and then came to meet me. "Here I am," she said with a weary smile.

"Physicians know how not to sleep. And this doesn't happen to me every day. But you can understand how I came here for our meeting. I was overwhelmed. But I thought, okay, there is a chance to sit down and have some coffee."

I felt a tremendous closeness to Gili. I remembered the responsibility and sleepless nights to keep newborns alive during my year in a pediatric internship. I remembered having to stay up and monitor blood oxygen levels and chemistry every few hours, and sometimes losing the battle. But there was nothing more satisfying than saving a child's life. At the time, I did not think I could sustain that stressful lifestyle, so I chose radiology, an important specialty that would also allow more time to spend with my family.

Thankfully, and by chance, Gili chose a path that put her at the forefront of working with patients with incurable blood diseases. She served in the army but didn't know what to study at university. "I thought to myself, am I going to become an architect because I like drawing?" she said. "Or am I going to study law because I knew how to express myself very well? Or should I study medicine because it's a very interesting profession and my mom already had multiple sclerosis? Maybe this is the profession for me."

Not knowing how to choose, she sent applications everywhere. She was accepted to the Technion and wondered, "Okay, maybe I like to draw but maybe my clients would not like what I'm drawing. I'm afraid this is too creative for me. I'm not sure if this should be the profession."

When she got accepted by Tel Aviv University law school, she mused that it was too easy a process, so she waited to hear from the faculty of medicine at Hebrew University in Jerusalem. "They do not give you answers until the last moment," she said. "They invite you to another interview and another interview. And Jerusalem was the faculty that gave me the last answer. And I said, 'Okay, let's go get them.' So I went to Jerusalem, I started studying medicine."

EARLY LIFE

Gili was an only child, a "last-chance" baby; when she was born in 1960, her mother was forty-two and her father was fifty. Her parents immigrated to Israel in 1948–49. Her mother avoided the Holocaust, but she was running all the time with her mother and her sister until she ended up in Munich at the Jewish Agency. She worked there for a while, then went to Israel, where she continued to work as a teacher with the Jewish Agency. And she met Gili's father.

"He jumped off a train that took his family to concentration camps, survived in the forests, joined the partisans, and even served for a while in the Russian army, but was such a non-fighter," she told me. "He was a man of books. He hardly knew to hold a stick, let alone a gun. He survived, I think, by writing letters and petitions in the army." After the war, he went back to his village, saw that no one remained, and went to Munich and worked for a while as a journalist for a newspaper called *The Flame*. It was published by a handful of Jewish writers, and he used to sign the paper sheets with different names so no one would know how few people were on the editorial board.

Her father went to Israel and started working for an intelligence agency, Gili said, and then became a teacher. "He felt that not many people actually cared for the education of the new generation," she said. He was introduced to her mother, and they realized they were from the same area in Poland and had been in Munich at the same time. They married in 1956.

Gili grew up in Holon, a small suburb next to Tel Aviv. "My parents were very good people, and they actually never wanted to let me know that they're not allowing me to do things because they're afraid of something, because of all they went through during the war," she told me. "I had a completely normal infancy and childhood. Unfortunately, both my parents died in the nineties because they were old and sick already. But they managed to see me get married, and they managed to see some of my kids getting born. So, I think they were happy."

Gili met her husband, Gabriel, in medical school. He was two years ahead and stood out in a crowd because of his height, but he never looked at the younger girls. Soon they discovered they were both in the Scouts, attended the same high school, and their parents lived two hundred meters apart.

She was smitten. During her first year of medical school, Gili stood with a girlfriend—now the hematology director at Beilinson Hospital/Rabin Medical Center, and still a good friend—and watched this very tall boy on the other side of the room. Gili told her friend that he was from Holon, and that by the end of the year he would get rid of his ridiculous beard, lose twenty pounds, and "crave to become my boyfriend and marry me." It took a few years, but they married during med school.

"We had this small flat in Jerusalem where people came to visit us," she said, "and my husband used to grab them and say, 'I don't know what happened to her. She's such a good student. She's vomiting all the time. She's so uptight.' And then one of our friends told him, 'Listen, don't you think she might be pregnant?'"

That was 1987, and Gili gave birth to their daughter Shira. During her fellowship and residency in pediatrics, she gave birth to her daughter Noa. And when she finished her subspecialty in hematology, she said she felt like she needed another baby. Daniel came next.

The couple lived in Holon, close to their aging parents, and had a communal system for helping each other. A chart on the refrigerator door kept track of comings and goings: "Today I'm on call. Tomorrow you are on call. Take the kids. They are at your mother's. Go to the kindergarten, there is a festivity. They need a white shirt...."

Eventually, Gili and her family moved to Yehud, an Arab town that was captured during the 1948 War of Independence. I found it admirable that one of the main reasons for the move, besides being close to family and the hospitals, was for its scouting activities. Yehud has the third-most-famous Scouts tribe in Israel, I found out, and that choice made sense, considering how much the Scouts contributed to leadership qualities that helped me later in life. I remembered roughing it up in the most beautiful natural areas in Israel, which strengthened my Zionistic feelings and deepened my love for my country. And at the same time, I made lifelong friends.

"We never regretted it. That is our legacy," Gili said, adding that her daughter became one of the five most important people in the country running the Scouts. Shira dedicated her career to caring for thousands of children, including two of her own.

EXTENDED FAMILY

In the 1930s, Gili's grandmother was widowed and brought up a one-year-old, Gili's father, along with seven other children. An older son, Joe, moved to the States before World War II. "She believed that the situation in Europe was not safe and wanted the family to go and visit the older brother," Gili told me. "She took a journey by ship and saw that Uncle Joe was doing well in the sweatshops of New York as a tailor or something like that. And she said, 'Okay, I can bring you the kids.'"

The process of acquiring visas was cumbersome and tiring, Gili said, and though the war had started, her grandmother did not give up. She took the family, including daughters who were already married with kids, and the smaller children, and embarked on the MS *St. Louis*. Unfortunately, this was the ship that many leaders in 1939, including U.S. President Franklin D. Roosevelt, denied entry. "Some of the wiser people got off in Cuba," Gili said. "My family was not among them and went back to Poland, where they got deported and got killed in the German camps. The only one who stayed alive is my father. His mother told him to jump off the train because he was the smallest and had the best chance to survive."

Several years ago, Gili discovered family members who survived the Nazis and lived in the United States. She was attending the American Society of Hematology convention in San Francisco and met her cousin, whose son married a priest's daughter (who converted to Judaism), another second cousin who married a black woman, and one who married a Taiwanese refugee. They connected her with other cousins in New York, North Carolina, and San Francisco.

Gili's children have further extended their unusually cosmopolitan family. Shira's husband is writing his PhD thesis about urban development in a world of global warming. Noa, a lawyer, married a French architect whose religious family settled in Jerusalem outside of Israel's boundaries. Daniel went to college in the States and fell in love with a non-Jewish American girl; they recently married.

THE LIFE OF A PEDIATRIC HEMATOLOGIST

I asked Gili to describe her daily routine as a pediatric hematologist specializing in thrombosis hemostasis and coagulation.

"My work is divided between clinics," she explained. "I see patients almost every day. You cannot anticipate or schedule appointments with patients with bleeding disorders. They come when they need you. It's like an emergency room. You give frontline care. And, of course, you discuss all options and new clinical studies and future therapies and try to educate and become part of their life, because it's a chronic, deep bleeding disorder.

"One is born with the disease, and, as their doctor, you stay in very close acquaintance with the family, the broad family, until they die," she said. "So, you meet these people and you end up being their physician, sometimes their friend, for years."

Of course, Gili said, she does administrative work and research and is most proud of her contributions to gene therapy. "That's the hallmark," she told me. "Hemophilia used to be a devastating condition with no cure."

The disease isn't lethal, but it carries the risk or joint disorders and orthopedic surgeries at a very young age because of repeated joint bleeds, or hemarthrosis, that require intravenous treatment with coagulation concentrates at least three times weekly for prophylaxis, plus extra doses. "Imagine a small kid, the very nice and chubby ones that have actually no venous access," she said. "And imagine the parents having to stick needles into them three, four times weekly. And more if they fall, or they have a head trauma, or something happened in kindergarten. This was awful."

"So, thanks to novelties in medicine, we now have non-replacement therapies that I have brought to Israel, among the first places around the world," she said. "We also have an option to cure these patients, which I'm very, very proud of."

With hemophilia, thousands of mutations are on the same gene, Gili explained. You can go into the lab and synthesize a normal factor VIII or IX gene. Factor IX gene therapy trials started in 2011; factor

VIII trials started in the past five years. Recently, a few gene therapy products were registered as therapeutic drugs in Europe and the United States.

"What's infecting patients? A virus," she said. "So, you take the virus, called a vector. You put a lot of genes into a lot of viruses that are not harmful enough to affect your patient, but harmful enough to give him flu-like symptoms. The patient comes into the center one day after having been checked that he has no antibodies to the specific virus we want to insert the gene into. If he's suitable for this kind of trial, he gets an IV infusion for several hours. In that infusion, he gets a lot of viruses into the blood, and all these viruses contain a normal synthesized factor IX or factor VIII gene. These viruses are targeted to the liver, because that's where coagulation factors are synthesized.

"The process is like what happens in the supermarket," she continued. "The truck comes in, downloads the products, and then goes away. The truck is the delivery vector—the virus. It takes the body several months to get rid of these viruses. But the genes are inserted into the liver cells that were infected by the virus. And the liver is one of the tissues that keep dividing all the time. Therefore, in several months you can get healthy. You can get completely cured of hemophilia, as your replicating liver cells produce healthy genes," she said. "This sounds like science fiction."

TREATMENT OF HEMOPHILIA

The first cases of hemophilia were mentioned in the Talmud, Gili told me. A woman went to the court of rabbis and asked whether to circumcise her newborn. She told the rabbis that two previous sons died at circumcision because no one could stop the bleeding. The rabbis told her not to circumcise her child because "this is something that runs in your family," Gili said. "It's a congenital bleeding disorder, it's a congenital genetic bleeding disorder."

When a blood vessel is injured, platelets and coagulation factors run one after another to the site to stop the bleeding. Gili compared the clotting process to a train moving from station to station to arrive at the destination: clot formation. Like a train's wheels that, when low on air, slow the train, so does the lack of certain clotting factors. If factor VIII is missing, it's called hemophilia A, and if factor IX is missing, it's hemophilia B.

Queen Victoria was the most famous hemophilia carrier in history, Gili said. All European monarchs intermarried, and the disease spread to the Russian and Prussian monarchies. Paintings of young Czar Alexei show him seated and wearing a military uniform to hide the hemarthrosis that caused his knee to swell. Rasputin, Gili scoffed, failed to cure him with hypnosis.

The life expectancy of children with the disease at the beginning of the twentieth century was thirteen years. Today, life expectancy is similar to that of the general population. Mostly males are affected because the genetic disorder is linked to the X chromosome; with only one X chromosome, males can be either affected or healthy. Women, however, can be carriers and pass the disease to the next generation.

Treatment has evolved as practitioners learned which coagulation factor was missing and how to replace it through infusion. Unfortunately, plasma-derived concentrates in the eighties and nineties coinfected hemophilia patients with HIV and with hepatitis C.

"So, with the evolution of hemophilia care and hemophilia centers, came the recognition of the genes of hemophilia," Gili told me. "The genes were cloned and the genetic background was established in families. And then we started to offer families with hemophilia IVF—in vitro fertilization with PGD, pre-genetic determination—in order to select the healthy embryos."

In Gili's treatment center, teams of physicians, orthopedic surgeons, psychologists, specialized nurses, physiotherapists, and social workers are trained in adult and pediatric hemophilia. There are large research labs and study coordinators who bring in the latest developments in medicine. In recent years, the centers started treating hemophilia patients with extended half-life clotting factors, to limit injections to one or two per week. There's also nonfactor replacement therapy, where small molecules are conveniently injected subcutaneously, like insulin. Rather than replace missing factors VIII or IX, the small molecules bypass the missing factor and combine others. For example, if factor

VIII is missing, a molecule is introduced that will combine factors IX and X into the coagulation cascade.

MEDICAL ADVOCACY

Emicizumab, a therapeutic bispecific antibody, was discovered in 2016 by a Japanese group. Israel was among the first countries to introduce the treatment to the care of hemophilia A patients with and without factor VIII inhibitors, improving life expectancy and quality of life.

Gili pushed hard in the Knesset and the Ministry of Health to get emicizumab therapy approved for use in 2018. The treatment is available and fully reimbursed, unlike elsewhere. "This is very unique for Israel," Gili said, "and this is why the care of hemophilia patients in Israel is evolving so well—because we work hand in hand with all the insurers and with the government to provide the most innovative care."

She also mentioned clinical studies of small, interfering RNA that can be injected subcutaneously, targeting the liver in order to block natural coagulation inhibitor proteins. "Instead of putting air into the wheels of the coagulation train, you just take out the brakes," she said, returning to her metaphor. "And then the train keeps running, even without air in the wheels. So, these are very interesting concepts that we study a lot in our laboratory, using thrombin generation, all kind of global coagulation essays, and all sophisticated methods."

Gili was the first physician chosen from an international pool to take part in the gene therapy trials and, in 2019, she used gene therapy to cure five young patients.

Her recent successes still remind her about the time before preventative treatments and other therapies were available. "Twenty years ago, I treated a six-year-old boy," Gili related. "When I first met him, he was a boy in the stage of, 'No, no. I don't want infusions. I don't want prophylaxis. I don't want mommy to give me injections.' And then I sat with him one day and I forced him to sign a very big piece of paper. And it was written in large letters: 'I, this is my name, promise Dr. Kenet that I will give mommy permission to infuse me my factors every week, three times a week or more if needed because it's very important for my health.' I signed it, he signed it. I still have this piece of paper. I showed it to him when he came for this gene therapy trial. He's now a sports instructor."

Gili doesn't take credit for discovering gene therapy but is immensely proud of her success in implementing it, which led her to consider curing other metabolic genetic diseases that affect the Arab population but are rare worldwide. She started research to isolate genes and inject different viruses to find cures for various genetic disorders. She connected a talented young physician with the well-known Dr. Christopher Walsh of Mt. Sinai Hospital in New York, to take the research forward.

"I told her that I need to have someone on my side who knows the routine, knows the technique," Gili said of her persuasive argument. "And whenever I'm presented with a new study or a new option, can tell me, 'Gili, it's bullshit,' or 'Gili, let's go for it.' And you have to learn how to use these techniques."

The young doctor spent almost a year in New York, during COVID, and learned how to put plasmids with special genes into special kinds of viruses that are used in gene therapy trials. When she returned to Israel, they started looking for disorders unique to the Israeli and Arab populations that are not as frequent in the rest of the world. For example, she said, "There are diseases that cause babies to die or to be born with thrombosis or be born blind after perinatal ischemic strokes."

One trial is underway in Gili's lab thanks to a special breed of mice that are carriers for the specific disorders she seeks. "Only one mouse arrived to us from the US alive," she said. "And this mouse was bred with Israeli female mice. We now have our own colony of thirty-five sick Israeli mice. We have the viruses ready. We have the genes inserted into the viruses and we are going to start the trials in February 2022 for a specific disease."

THE POLITICS OF MEDICINE

What I found unusual and admirable about Gili is her availability to her patients. She is always a phone or video call away, and she always answers immediately.

"Whenever you need us, we are there," she said. "Rarely do we tell them to come to the hospital because the treatment improved so much.

It is true for every patient. Some are Palestinians from the Gaza Strip or the West Bank [that] we want to treat equally, but I find it impossible. Many problems stem from corruption. I find the Palestinian patients being neglected where they live, and they arrive with swollen joints filled with blood. It is because their government only gives permits to the privileged patients to come to the Sheba hospital to get treatment. We can put the fire out, but we cannot give them extended prophylaxis. We cannot give them the care they deserve, because they do not have insurance to acquire the drugs. We cannot maintain the standard of care.

"In Israel, we do wonders for these children," Gili went on. "We send them for a week to Jordan River village in the north, dedicated to training debilitated children to take care of themselves. They learn how to care for disease and how to inject the factor coagulates. It is especially for those with inhibitors. It is a fun camp where they ride horses, swim, and play ball. We have a whole crew of volunteers and Arab translators for the Israeli-Arab children at the camp."

Despite the challenges, Gili said she has nothing but praise for Israeli medical care. "I cannot complain because really, the level of medicine and the level of medical care in Israel is very high," she insisted. "Just today, I saw a son of a diplomat who has hemophilia, and he's being taken care of in our center because his father is from an embassy in Israel. He comes to our center occasionally, and we treat him and we guide him. And today they came in and they said, 'Oh, we are so sorry. We are going to India next month.' And I told them, 'Oh, but it's okay, because I know that all the new treatments have been approved in India. I gave lectures to Indian physicians just two months ago. I was on a large Zoom conference with many physicians from Mumbai, from Kerala, from anywhere in India.'

"They said, 'yeah, they are approved, but no one can afford them. They are given to a very limited number of people. And our son, because he got such good care in Israel, is not sick enough. So he's not entitled to the same level of care in India.' And I felt so sorry for them. And this would not happen here. Here, you have choices. You choose to gather with the patient and figure out what is best for them. That's amazing."

Gili developed her love for pediatric hematology/oncology during her residency and declined the opportunity to join an established and financially rewarding pediatric practice run by her father-in-law. Her husband worked long hours as a gastroenterologist, and she was able to follow her passion. At the time, adult and pediatric hematology were combined into one specialty, and she convinced the hospital to separate them. She became a senior pediatric hematology/oncology specialist at Sheba Hospital. She then pursued and created a subspecialty for pediatric thrombosis/hemostasis that she headed, and divided her time between the clinics.

"I started making a name for myself," she said. "I started calling my colleagues, the pediatric hematologists in other hospitals, telling them, 'If you have a special case—a stroke, myocardial infarction, deep venous thrombosis, pulmonary emboli, hemophilia in a child—send them to me, that's my specialty.'" She extended offers for lectures about her extraordinary subspecialty with different treatments, prognoses, and drugs.

Earlier, in 2003, Gili faced a life-altering decision. She was offered a major position in Toronto that was appealing, financially and academically. She would receive an instant professorship, become a citizen within three years, and her husband would get a position in his specialty. She told her children it would be a one-year experiment, but Shira, who was about fifteen, wasn't interested.

"Shira looked at us and said, 'Listen, I will come with you. But only for half a year, then I'm going back to Israel to live with Grandma and Grandpa,'" Gili recounted. When they asked about the short timeframe, Shira said: "I know you. You are both fascinated by your careers, and you are liars. Even if you don't mean it, you will say we're just going for a year to see how it is. When this year finishes, you'll say, oh, a year is nothing. We need to stay another year. Another year. And in several years, I will find myself Canadian, living in Toronto. But after half a year, mark my words, I'm going back."

And so, the family stayed in Israel, and Gili became a full professor after ten years of hard work. "The impossible never holds us back," she said. "It's only the possible that holds us back."

I asked Gili how she reduced the stress in her life, and she cited yoga, meditation, and writing poetry. "Healing through a state of mind, where you can enter an inner place of meditation and find the light within you and send it around," she said. "It works. It relates to Buddhism and nature."

As we chatted, Gili got a phone call about an experimental drug for the infant with the brain hemorrhage. It could help save her life. I watched Gili's face light up, and I felt that the light I was looking for by writing this book was revealed to me through her sunshine.

POSTSCRIPT

Gili shared wonderful news about the baby she was helping when we met. On February 20, 2022, she wrote, "brain [ultrasound] of the baby today completely normal! Had to share the happy news!" And on March 4 she followed up: "The baby went home for the weekend after a very long time!" The little baby happily celebrated her first birthday with the clinic team. Her FVII inhibitor was well controlled, though it relapsed again. In case of another relapse, Gili has already secured a new experimental drug to be supplied for compassionate use, if required. The child continues to receive proper care with FVII prophylactic infusions every other day, which, Gili told me, enables her to lead a normal and active life.

Hearing that, I felt my face light up, just like Gili's.

PART II

THE LEADERS & AMBASSADORS

VARDA GOLDSTEIN,
member of the IDF Special Nachal Division and
longtime member of Kibbutz Kfar Aza

COLETTE AVITAL,
Chair of the Center Organization of Holocaust Survivors, former Member of Knesset

SHIKMA SCHWARTZMANN BRESSLER,
particle physicist, social activist

TAMAR ASRAF,
former Spokesperson for Mateh Binyamin Regional
Council in Judea and Samaria

GHADA ZOABI,
CEO of Bokra.net, Arabic news and social media
platform

GAL LUSKY,
Founder and CEO of Israeli Flying Aid

ORIT ADATO,
former Commissioner of the Israeli Prison Service,
Brigadier General (Retired)

GADEER KAMAL-MREEH,
diplomat, former Member of Knesset

PNINA TAMANO-SHATA,
Minister of Immigrant and Absorption, former
Member of Knesset

TAL OHANA,
Mayor of Yeruham, business development advocate

SIMA SHINE,
intelligence consultant, former
Head of Research for Mossad

VARDA GOLDSTEIN

MEMBER OF THE IDF SPECIAL NACHAL DIVISION AND LONGTIME MEMBER OF KIBBUTZ KFAR AZA

"The Jewish nation is alive and will stay alive forever."

ON OCTOBER 7, 2023, MORE than 1,300 civilians were slaughtered by Hamas terrorists who descended on the Nova music festival in southern Israel and on the small kibbutzim near the Gaza border. The carnage included infants who were burned alive and women who were sexually violated and mutilated before they were executed. Of the 240 people taken hostage that day, more than 138 were still captive as of January 7, 2024: terrified, hungry, in need of urgent medical care, and fearful for their lives three months after the start of the war.

Varda Goldstein and her family are among those whose lives are forever changed. She shared her story via Zoom from her temporary home, a room at the Dan Panorama Tel Aviv Hotel. She spoke of the awful details, the pain her family has endured since Hamas attacked their kibbutz. I could almost see the horrible images in her eyes and gentle face.

Varda relived the devastating moments she learned that her son Nadav, forty-eight, and his oldest daughter, twenty-year-old Yam, were murdered by Hamas in their home, and when she heard that Nadav's wife, Chen, and three other children were in the hands of Hamas being held captive in Gaza.

Then Varda descended into silence. I did not dare interrupt her thoughts. Eventually she said: "There is nothing left there in Kfar Aza. The pictures on the wall, evidence of life, all gone. The mementos and testimony that I once had grandparents who perished in the Holocaust is nothing but a memory with no concrete proof."

On October 7, Varda, her husband, David, and thirty-three fellow kibbutzim were vacationing in Bulgaria. The view of the Musala mountain peak mesmerized the travelers until a cacophony of cellphones announced a Red Alert warning from home. They soon heard about the surprise attack on the music festival and on their home and other kibbutzim within a few miles of Gaza. All communities were invaded and demolished. By the end of the day, one hundred residents of Kfar Aza had been slaughtered.

Wails and a loud cry replaced the initial silence of shock as the events of the Shabbat massacre slowly unfolded. Varda described the suffocating anxiety and confusion that clouded their minds before she and David were able to return to Israel on October 10.

Daughter Naama was safe. Her husband, Shlomi, heard shooting at 6:00 a.m. and quickly gathered Naama and their four children in the car and fled the kibbutz under fire to Naama's sister's home in a near-by town.

Varda and David's home was in rubble, black ash everywhere. Kites that would have filled the sky in celebration of the Simchat Tora holiday were scattered and broken, a forgotten frivolity overshadowed by the multitude of dead bodies still covering the earth.

The family buried Nadav and Yam.

BACK TO THE BEGINNING

Varda Golomb's parents immigrated to Palestine in 1938. They tried to settle on a kibbutz, but instead spent a short while in Jerusalem before settling in Haifa, where Varda's father worked in the flour mills. Her mother and brother, seven years her senior, lived in a storage room in the mill until they were able to move to Kiryat Ata, a small city in the Haifa district. There, they had a common kitchen and bathroom in a shared apartment. Varda was born in that room in 1950, and when the other family vacated, the Golomb family had all the space they needed.

She described growing up in Kiryat Ata, and the tension slipped from her face and her lips widened into a smile. "It was a modest home from one aspect and a very rich home from another," she said. "The sixties were wonderful years." Her father became secretary of the Haifa municipality, the family enjoyed classical music, and reading filled their free time. She remembered her mother with love and gratitude for always being present, providing warmth and a stimulating intellectual environment.

Varda talked about her involvement with youth movements, in-spired by growing up in a Zionist home. She joined the army's special Nachal division, which was known for social action and the type of community care that was fixed in her DNA. The program required thir-ty-five months of service, military training, and eventual residence in a town to promote education programs. Varda's journey to the periphery areas and to kibbutz Kfar Aza aligned with her lifelong ambition and love of her country.

A group of friends who served in Nachal—including Varda Golomb and David Goldstein—arrived at Kfar Aza on a spring day in 1971. It was common for Nachal groups to join kibbutzim together. Most of the *garin* (seed) Nachal members belonged to youth groups during their adolescence and shared nationalist bonds. The natural next step led them to settle in remote southern communities, like Kfar Aza, near Gaza and Egypt, to help develop Israeli agriculture and protect the young country's borders.

Kfar Aza had about one hundred members when Varda and David joined. Luscious greenery and sunflower fields enveloped the relatively young kibbutz. The couple soon married, and Varda worked in various jobs, milking cows, feeding chickens, serving in the dining room, and caring for children who slept together in the so-called kids' house. She loved her work and was devoted to the children, but leaving them alone at night broke her heart.

Eventually, the Goldstein family would include four children, all of whom served in the Israeli Defense Forces (IDF) when they came of age and later and attended university. Naama became a management expert, Nitzan an educator, and Inbar worked in communications.

Nadav, the eldest son, was in love with Chen at the age of fourteen, and their high-school love turned into marriage. He had many friends, was an excellent student, and an accomplished athlete who enjoyed the challenge of Iron Man competitions. After his service, he earned his degree at the university in Be'er Sheba, became an economist, and later worked in technology.

Community life prospered in Kfar Aza, where the main revenue derived from agriculture and later from industrial ventures. "Everybody gives according to their ability, and everybody receives according to their needs," Varda told me. Members shared income equally; the kibbutz covered overhead such as food, education, and health.

Life focused on togetherness, a closeness between parents, children, siblings, and extended family. Varda recalled the Shabbat and holiday gatherings at her home, how she enjoyed seeing her kids devour her schnitzels and matzah balls, and where her eight grandchildren—four from Naama and four from daughter-in-law Chen—developed lasting ties. They shared a devotion to kibbutz life, which is known for providing "formal education to knowledge acquired from life, from the book to the physical work, from a discipline based on blind obedience to a regime of activity and creation, all in an atmosphere of freedom."

LIFE AND DEATH IN THE SHADOW OF GAZA

After fifty-one days in captivity, Chen and her three surviving children—Agam, seventeen, Tal, eleven, and Gal, nine—were returned to Israel during the third ceasefire in exchange for Hamas prisoners. The day they came home and fell into Varda's arms was among the happiest of her life, but she and her family still worry how to console children who endured darkness and terrifying isolation after seeing such unspeakable acts.

Varda briefly introduced me to Agam during our Zoom call. She is an extremely mature, brave young woman who is interested in literature and philosophy. During several interviews that she gave the *New York Times* and other media outlets, she explained how armed guards constantly surveilled the family and moved them to several locations. Agam feared being raped or murdered and never stopped worrying about her younger brothers.

Her mother's skills as a social worker, Agam said, allowed for long and deep conversations with the captors that humanized the hostages and focused on hope. Even Agam had meaningful discussions arguing the merits of war and peace. But most of the time, no one dared make a sound.

"We both look at each other and understand that there will probably never be words," Agam told one of her interviewers about the nonverbal communication with her mother. "There will always be only feelings. Words are too small compared to what the body feels."

When they were about to be released, one of the captors warned them Hamas would be back. Chen, also a talented dancer, runner, and active member of the community, told him she would never abandon her home. "Next time, don't shoot," Chen said in an interview. "Just knock on my door. We will talk."

Reconstruction of Kfar Aza will take two years. Varda expects to move between hotels and another kibbutz while she and David—an economist and the international purchasing manager for the kibbutz—wait for the day the IDF once again protects the border, and her family returns to share the Shabbat table.

In the meantime, Varda cherishes being with her children, in-laws, and grandchildren. Less important now are the clinic she ran to teach people the Alexander Technique for healthy posture, or her positions as kibbutz secretary and president in charge of fundraising.

She thinks a lot about her grandparents, whose lives ended during the Holocaust with no one to bear witness. But when the history of violence against the Jews brutally repeated itself on October 7, Varda was able to speak one last time to her beautiful granddaughter, Yam.

"Hug each other and stay under the window of the shelter," Varda instructed over the telephone, to which Yam responded: "*Savta* (Grandma), do not worry. I'm sure we will get help soon."

Yam was a good student and member of the Scouts who would bring little kids to the kibbutz so they could see what life was like near Gaza. Her military service would have ended in eighty-four days; she planned to move in with her boyfriend and was saving money for a trip to South America. "She had a special connection to her father," Varda said. "She took care of him, to help him walk again for the first time after spending over a month in a wheelchair from an injury during an Iron Man."

While her family watched, Yam was shot to death in the shelter on October 7, as she fainted to the floor. Her mother and siblings were herded into a car bound for Gaza before seeing Nadav shot and killed in his chair.

Varda's life has been molded by Israel and her Jewishness, from the atrocities of the Holocaust, to the slaughter of her family and friends in Kfaf Aza, to her work with the Scouts and service in the IDF. Throughout, her love of country has mirrored the love and care she freely gives to others. Her life is enriched by joyful memories and strengthened by unimaginable sorrow. She is determined to protect her children and grandchildren, who will forever connect her to her dear Nadav and Yam.

As we parted, Varda held up a small metal box that she saved from the wreckage of her home, the box to which she, her brother, and parents steadfastly added pennies to help buy land and trees to build the Jewish state. The nonprofit Keren Hakayemet, now known as the National Jewish Fund, has long distributed these blue-and-white collection boxes, with images of the Israeli map on one side and the Israeli flag on the other.

The map side of Varda's box was completely effaced by the destruction. The flag image was intact, a symbol of hope and a message, the ever-courageous Varda said, that she wanted to me to share: "The Jewish nation is alive and will stay alive forever."

COLETTE AVITAL

DIPLOMAT AND POLITICIAN

"I was overwhelmed. I wondered how a little Romanian girl who grew up away from Jewish culture was chosen to represent the Jewish people in this important moment in history."

COLETTE AVITAL FOUND OUT THAT she was Jewish during a history lesson in Grade Four when one of the students volunteered the information to the teacher. Her family had fled Soviet rule in Romania and made their home in Israel. She was ten and had no memory of the yellow star her parents said she wore during World War II but remembered the Nazi soldiers who took over their home and her flight, with her mother, to Bucharest.

Unable to speak Hebrew in Israel, she was placed in a convent school where all teaching was in French, a language she was fluent in since she was a little girl. Over time, she saw her parents persevere and assimilate into a new land. Colette discovered her own love of Israel. Her extraordinary professional voyage started as an administrative secretary in the Foreign Ministry and led to her career on the team that represented Israel abroad.

Misogyny accompanied Colette's rise to a top-ranking female diplomat with the Israeli Foreign Service, and she often felt vulnerable in her daily life amid potential terrorist threats. But as if negotiating the swells of the ocean, she deftly fought against misperceptions about Israel and unjust philosophical attacks that varied by her postings, the prevailing political winds, and the day's headlines.

Her life-long professional struggle, she told me, was *hasbara*, which in English roughly means to explain and to teach.

When Colette arrived in New York in 1992 as general consul, she became the highest-ranking woman in Israel's Foreign Service, with a successful record of strengthening ties between Israel and diaspora Jews. She also cultivated relations with Israelis living abroad—leading professors, writers, hospital directors, bankers, artists, and journalists—and in the States, the subsequent generation that included assistants to members of Congress.

I was one of the former sabras, born in Israel to Zionist parents. But unable to get into medical school in my homeland, I completed my studies in Italy and then moved to New York. Over the years, I took offense at being one of the Israelis living abroad whom Itzhak Rabin called "fallen weaklings." I felt guilty for leaving my small country to defend itself from enemies on all sides, and always tried my best to speak up for

Israel when world views turned and characterized the 1967 occupation as a violation of human rights.

In 1993, the Israeli government, with the backing of the Foreign Ministry, approved a program to build relationships with Israelis in the diaspora. Colette formed a committee dedicated to the "absorption of returned Israelis," which was instrumental in sending companies to New York to recruit for jobs back in Israel. She created a site for cultural events at the Israeli Consulate in New York to help local Israelis get closer to their roots and the Jewish community. And she helped hundreds of people return to Israel.

CONNECTING WITH ISRAEL

Growing up in Romania, Colette's loving parents provided her with lessons in French, ballet, and sports. Her mother gained degrees in law and in French literature during the prewar period, and her father was a successful businessman. Because of their sophisticated understanding of the fascism and anti-Semitism that had already shattered their lives, they agreed to shelter their little girl from her Jewish identity, the events of World War II, and the threats against her father.

Unaware of the grief and trauma that surrounded her family, Colette remembers a loving grandfather, being an excellent student, and becoming a member of the red-tie-wearing Pioneers, a coveted Soviet-inspired milestone in the life of school children during the communist rule of Romania. Unlike the yellow star, she remembered wearing the red tie that afforded her privileges, including additional food for her family. She wrote in her memoir, *The Girl with the Red Tie* (2021), how she saved her father's life when the Securitatea, the communist militia, knocked on the door looking for a "bourgeois capitalist." Their search ended with a salute to the little girl in the red scarf, a distraction so her father could escape through the back door.

Integration to life in Tel Aviv was difficult for the little rebel, who ached for the days she put on disguises with her girlfriends back home and planned how to overthrow the government. Her mischievous character was apparent when she placed a telephone in the hand of a statue of Jeanne d'Arc listening to celestial voices. After high school, she bristled at the discipline required in the Israel Defense Forces, failing to wear her military hat or be punctual.

Eventually, Colette moved to Jerusalem to join the Hebrew University, and for the first time she felt that she belonged. She studied political science and English literature while, beginning in 1960, she worked as a secretary at the Foreign Ministry to help pay tuition. Colette enjoyed the polite international city where she made friends and played soccer on Friday afternoons in front of the Knesset.

A CAREER IN MINISTERIAL AFFAIRS

At the ministry, she met intelligent, fascinating people and saw how decisions were made—from weighty foreign affairs to personal solutions for individuals in need. Advancing her career took time, even with her BA in political science. All the top officials in the Foreign Service were men, and women served in cultural rather than political positions. "We don't want women. We already have a few of them and they are a problem for us," she was told by her superiors. "Women who don't marry become bitter spinsters, and those who do marry will not ask their husbands to follow them on their assignments." In addition, she was told Israel could not accept additional female diplomats because Asia and Latin America did not.

She wasn't deterred, and in September 1963, Colette passed the exams to become a diplomat. No one told her she succeeded, however, and she was sent to Canada as a chancellor, a minor secretarial position. Even without an official title, she simply worked hard and became a press attaché and a cultural attaché. She also earned her MA in English literature from the University of Montreal.

In her new roles, she reached out to Catholic schools to better acquaint students with Israel. She provided booklets about the "Holy Land," and spoke in churches, social clubs, and Jewish organizations. She arranged guest speakers that included Romanian-born Holocaust survivor Eli Wiesel, whom she convinced to travel to the Soviet Union to raise public concern about the fate of Russian Jews. She organized festivities and invited university students to Israel. And simultaneously, she taught herself Jewish history and cultural traditions.

Israel's victory in the Six-Day War in June 1967 prompted world-wide respect and support.

Two years later, Colette returned to Israel and finally gained full recognition as a diplomat. Student revolts in Europe brought the rise of the New Left, so she asked the ministry to be placed in charge of public information for universities. She advised Israeli students abroad how to handle themselves in confrontational situations and avoid violence over political disagreements. She crafted materials aimed at answering the new leftist ideology, and over the next few years traveled to France, Italy, England, Switzerland, and Greece to share Israel's position on the Palestinian-Israeli conflict.

In 1973, Colette was appointed to her first true diplomatic mission to Brussels, Belgium, as press and cultural attaché. The massacre of Israelis at the Munich Olympics was only a year behind her, and a memorial held in the Brussels Jewish community made Colette feel the pain. Soon after, the Yom Kippur War erupted. Colette told me that the threat to Israel's survival deepened her connection to the nation, as an integral part of her being. She could not understand why her small country was portrayed as the aggressor, given the loss of so many Israeli lives.

Colette confronted a hostile media in Brussels and explained that the Israeli government's need to protect the country did not preclude the goal of peace. She organized an international conference to return Israeli prisoners of war held in Syria, which was attended by well-known dignitaries and mothers of the missing soldiers. The death of David Ben-Gurion at the end of the 1973 compounded a sense of loss.

After two years in Brussels, her posting ended abruptly. Colette was asked to leave because of a brief encounter with a Soviet diplomat, which, she learned after many sleepless nights, raised security concerns and required protection from the Soviet secret service.

Her next posting was to Boston, Massachusetts, as consul. She was thrilled to be part of a vibrant and intellectual community, especially at Harvard's Kennedy School of Government, where she studied in the evenings and deepened her understanding of the political and ideological roots of the Palestinian-Israeli conflict.

While most of the ups and downs during Colette's career abroad reflected international opinion of Israel, they were also the result of her position in a male-dominated profession. She occasionally found herself characterized as a "threat," which was the case in Boston. Her work with the media, campuses, and in cultural endeavors provoked hostility from the consul general. Later accused of financial mismanagement of consulate funds, he took one last swing at Colette's reputation before leaving: he told Massachusetts Governor Michael Dukakis that Colette was a Russian spy.

Despite the rough start, Colette described her time in Boston as an incredible diplomatic and personal experience. She met and worked with Israeli and foreign university students and lectured her way through New England. She organized cultural events that introduced Israeli music and literature to Americans, and had the pleasure of meeting Governor Dukakis and his wife, Kitty, as well as President Jimmy Carter. With pride, she told me how the ministry arranged for six Israeli high school students to be hosted in Jewish-American homes for a month. Each pair of students introduced their American peers to Israeli history and culture. "I was delighted to learn that some of the students went on to become diplomats," Colette said.

She organized a week of festivities at the Boston Public Library dedicated to Israeli poets, archeologists, and writers; hosted the Israeli Philharmonic; and received the governor's backing for a Jerusalem Month, to gain support for Israel's capital while highlighting the best of Israeli art, culture, and food.

In June 1976, an Air France plane was hijacked en route from Israel to Paris and landed in Entebbe, Uganda, where President Idi Amin supported the terrorists. The rescue was victorious, but Yoni Netanyahu was killed, and Colette delivered the news to his brother, Benjamin (Bibi), who was a student in Boston at the time. Together with colleagues in Washington, she suggested to Netanyahu that a center for terror research be created in Israel and dedicated to Yoni's memory.

The next year, Colette had reason to be proud. As an Israeli, she was thrilled by Egyptian President Anwar Sadat's unprecedented visit to Israel and the work that led to the historic peace treaty with Egypt.

She shared the news of the visit with Golda Meir, who was in Boston for medical treatment. Personally, she completed her MA degree at Harvard.

Colette returned to Israel in October 1978 and was appointed to the coveted post of acting head of the Information Division, in charge of communications with Israeli representatives abroad. Once again, Colette went to battle when public opinion turned against Israel. In 1980, a law was enacted that proclaimed Jerusalem the capital of Israel, and resentful countries moved their embassies to Tel Aviv. The following year, Israel bombed and destroyed a nuclear plant near Baghdad, Iraq, and Colette volunteered to brief Israel's representatives abroad. The international community as well as the media were highly critical of the mission.

ESCALATION

Meanwhile, terror attacks around the world escalated. In October 1981, President Sadat was assassinated, and a Paris-Toulouse train was bombed. As she readied for her new diplomatic assignment to Paris, Colette requested training in self-defense and gun handling. The ministry denied her proposal—she was told there was no such training for women—so she asked for permission to carry a small tear gas device. Instead, she was presented with the book of Psalms and a traveler's prayer.

Highly respected early in her position as the Israeli minister counselor, she received many delegations from Israel, among them Shimon Peres and politician Yossi Beilin, and accompanied French President Francois Mitterrand on his historic trip to Israel.

In June 1982, the attempted assassination of Shlomo Argov, the Israeli Ambassador to Britain, triggered the first Israeli-Lebanon war. Colette dealt with a hostile media that compared Israelis to Nazis. She mobilized a group of important public relations firms, "friends of Israel," to her cause. Her fluency in French opened doors, and her essays and opinion pieces appeared in the prestigious *Le Monde* newspaper.

In September 1982, the massacre of Palestinians in Sabra and Shatila, Lebanon, triggered international protests. Mass demonstrations of Israelis in Tel Aviv and the creation of a State Inquiry Committee of judges saved the day. She believed that the best argument that could be made to save Israel's image was to publish the committee's report. To her dismay, the Israeli government blocked her efforts. In the midst of the war, she arranged for the Haifa theater company's production of the play *The Island*, which expressed sympathy for black prisoners in South Africa. The play resonated with the Parisian audience, mainly the hostile left-wing press.

In France, Colette found a supportive Jewish community of six hundred thousand people. Many of the Israeli delegates' children attended an impressive Israeli school, which nurtured their knowledge and feelings about Israel. But the community felt vulnerable and depressed because of the Lebanon war and its consequences. She created a committee of representatives of all the major organizations and put on an event in support of Israel that drew an audience of seven thousand people, among them leading French politicians. The program included expressions of support, as well as music and songs by the well-known Israeli Shlomo Artzi and French Algerian Enrico Macias. The tradition has continued with similar events produced yearly.

"Paris fit me like a glove," said Colette, who loved speaking French, the city's elegance, the abundance of music and theater, and meeting the *Who's Who* of leading journalists, intellectuals, writers, and artists during her stay. She became an influential Israeli representative whose treatment of people with grace and respect endeared her to Jews and non-Jews.

Colette's professional relationship with the new Israeli Ambassador to France, however, became strained. He impeded her work and forbade her from talking to the media. She resigned after three years.

Back in Israel, terror attacks in the occupied territories escalated, as did Israeli retaliation. Colette was promoted to the rank of deputy director general of the ministry and oversaw the departments of public policy, culture, media, public relations, and official guests. She started a school of diplomacy within the ministry to train young diplomats and senior staff in different disciplines, from the art of debate to negotiations and media appearances. She had the task of promoting the status of women in the ministry, with the aim of empowering them.

In February 1988, the ministry sent Colette to Romania to negotiate a cultural agreement between the two countries. She was pleasantly surprised by the warm reception at the airport and presentation of a bouquet of flowers. She recalled how, many years ago, her red tie helped her father escape imprisonment or worse. Her return to Romania was "a moment of sweet revenge" that she wished her father and grandfather were there to enjoy. As the snow fell and darkness enveloped her, she found her former house and school. Seeing one of her old relatives still living in poverty helped her appreciate her parents' courageous decision to escape oppression and move to Israel.

PORTUGAL

Colette was appointed as Israel's ambassador to Portugal at a time when relations were almost nonexistent. She encountered a Jewish community of fewer than four hundred people who were distracted by competition and infighting. Rather than receive help from the community, Colette understood that she needed to help them. By inviting Jewish leaders to holiday and cultural events at her home, she helped unite the small community and foster pride in their new connection with Israel.

"A lot of amazing things happened in Portugal, there was a lot of room to build and to educate," she said. She discovered that cultural diplomacy was a key tool. Because there were no literature or history books about Israel in the Portuguese language, she sought and found willing publishing houses. Along the way she encountered an interesting fellow. Francisco Costa Reich, a self-taught non-Jew who lived in the north of the country, was completely isolated, yet had learned to speak and write perfect literary Hebrew. With the help of the famous Gulbenkian Foundation, she managed to publish for the first time, based on Costa Reich's translations, the poetry of Fernando Pessoa. The foundation, with whose director, Jose Blanco, she became friends, also helped her bring to the Portuguese public noted Israeli musicians and ballet groups.

Barely three months after her arrival in the country, Portuguese President Mario Soares asked Colette to represent Israel at a ceremony in Castelo de Vide, a border town that in 1492 had welcomed Jewish

Spanish refugees of the Inquisition to stay, for a fee. He wanted her to accept his country's apology of its treatment of Jews over the past four hundred years.

"I was overwhelmed," she said. "I wondered how a little Romanian girl who grew up away from Jewish culture was chosen to represent the Jewish people in this important moment in history."

Colette absorbed local culture and history, including information about Portugal's control of its African colonies Angola and Mozambique. She was introduced to the Marrano community of Jews, who were forced to convert to Christianity during the Middle Ages. Outwardly Christian, the community kept Jewish traditions safely hidden at home.

Colette befriended the Marrano community in Belmonte, and gained people's trust despite their longstanding fears of the Inquisition. They asked to be recognized by Israel as Jews. First, Colette told them, they would have to learn Jewish traditions under the guidance of a rabbi. She raised money to bring a Sephardic rabbi to Belmonte, and a local doctor circumcised the men. Not long after, the Marranos were invited to pray at a distinguished synagogue. In 1991, organized by Colette, the Marranos celebrated Israeli Independence Day and declared themselves proud Jews. Two years later, they were recognized as Jews by the Chief Rabbi of Israel.

The ability to forge diplomatic and cultural ties between Israel and Portugal, however, was again influenced by global events. The Gulf War erupted in 1990–91, and the Soviet Union dissolved in December 1991. Saddam Hussein's missiles landed in Israel, and Israelis wore gas masks and feared weapons of mass destruction. Israel's lack of retaliation gained international sympathy and turned opinion away from Hussein's ally, Yasser Arafat and the Palestinian Liberation Organization.

The decision by the president of Portugal to send an emissary to meet Arafat in Tunis nearly derailed Colette's efforts to normalize relations with Portugal. Fortunately, Prime Minister Anibal Cavaco Silva intervened and declared that this outreach was not the policy of his government. At Colette's suggestion, he decided to finally open a Portuguese embassy in Israel, and in February 1991 a young ambassador was entrusted to open the mission. As time passed, Portugal "put Israel on its map," and business and personal relationships flourished.

LIFE IN NEW YORK

For the next several years, as consul general in New York, Colette's mission was to maintain and cultivate relations with one of the most diverse and largest Jewish communities in the world. That was a dramatic period, with a new government in Israel headed by Itzhak Rabin, and Colette immersed herself in the details of the Oslo Accords and Israel's peace negotiations with Arafat. Dramatic divisions in Israel over proposed land compromises and other critical conditions spilled over to American Jews, Colette said, and eroded their long-standing and unwavering support of Israel. In her travels around the country, she outlined to perplexed audiences the provisions in the Accords, the benefits to Israel, and the proviso that occupied land would be transferred to the Palestinians after five years, only if peaceful conditions existed.

Unfortunately, she encountered fierce opposition among Jewish groups. "I had to be guarded when I went to synagogues. And there were many demonstrations that ended in violence in front of the consulate," she said. "It was a dangerous time."

Colette's work in New York was predominantly hasbara, explaining Israel's history and current actions and generating positive vibes to keep the 1.7 million people in the Jewish community—a majority of whom were politically powerful and mostly Democrat—connected and supportive. When Israel's military responded to terror attacks, however, she felt the sting of the United Nations' condemnation and a lack of support from American Jews. Changing American Jewry's opinion on Israeli politics was difficult, she said, and their longstanding financial support was no longer guaranteed. While older American Jews understood Israel's long fight for a secure country and felt a closeness to its people, the new generation needed convincing. Increased mixed marriages also became an important challenge for Israel to ensure "Jewish continuity."

Colette wanted to connect American Jewish youth to their roots and to Israel, and she helped convince the community to embrace a program promoted by Yossi Beilin: a trip to Israel for every youngster. Much-needed help came from Charles Bronfman and Michael Steinhardt of the nonprofit Taglit-Birthright, through which many youngsters developed an affinity to the country and later "made *aliyah*"—that is, immigrated to Israel.

She also believed that exposure to Israeli art, culture, and music were the most effective ways to connect people emotionally to Israel and foster friendships between Jews and non-Jews.

Being in New York and living in a multicultural society, she worked with members of the African American and Latino communities. She learned to understand the plight of the black community and built relationships with community leaders. In her residence, she hosted yearly events to honor the memory of Martin Luther King Jr.

Colette continued traveling the United States to talk about Israel's public policy and lecture at universities. CNN asked her to appear in a debate in Atlanta with Palestinian activist Hanan Ashrawi, a well-respected representative of the Palestinian Liberation Organization and a close associate of Arafat. Colette knew that Ashrawi was talented and charismatic, so she carefully prepared for the debate and gained the support of the media. More invitations followed that successful encounter, during which Colette called for a two-state solution.

On September 13, 1993, President Clinton hosted a ceremony on the White House lawn at which Prime Minister Rabin, Foreign Minister Peres, and President Arafat signed a peace treaty. The gathering was emotional, Colette said, especially listening to Peres say, "Yesterday it was a dream. Today it is a commitment." After shaking Arafat's hand, Rabin said, "Enough is enough, too much blood and too many tears were spilled."

But terrorist attacks continued. Much of the Jewish community lost faith and aligned with Netanyahu and the Orthodox who objected to Rabin's peace deals. Despite nonstop pressure, Colette said she was energized by her time in New York because hope was on the horizon. Being invited to dine with President Clinton and other members of the negotiating teams was another proud moment that she wished she could have shared with her grandfather.

I asked Colette if she felt like she had an impact on New York. "I had some influence here, I am not sure how you measure impact," she said. "But the one thing that I changed is that a woman was finally accepted for the first time in the position of consul general of New York. And they learned that I cannot be marginalized or manipulated and would express Israel's policies without fear."

Rabin's assassination on November 4, 1994, devastated Colette. She attributed his murder to the violent climate in Israel, in which he was compared to Hitler and called a "traitor." Deep in sorrow, she organized flights to attend the funeral ceremonies in Israel, while thousands appeared at the consulate to pay their condolences. She also organized a memorial on the USS *Intrepid* and at Carnegie Hall, which was topped only by the memorial at Madison Square Garden attended by some seventeen thousand mourners.

TURNING TO POLITICS

When Netanyahu defeated Peres in the 1996 elections, Colette decided to end her mission in New York. In 1997 she returned to Israel as deputy director general of the Foreign Ministry, in charge of European affairs. Life in the Foreign Ministry under Netanyahu and Ariel Sharon was not easy, so she turned to politics. When she was sworn in in November 1999 as a Knesset member of Labor, she remembered the road she traveled since her childhood and the brave little girl with the red tie. She looked out at her mother's teary eyes and wished her father, who had passed away a year earlier, could have been there.

In the fifteenth Knesset, Colette served on the Education, Constitution and Law, Defense, Foreign Affairs, and Status of Women committees. She was head of the Ethics Committee. In the sixteenth Knesset she served as chairperson of the Immigration, Absorption, and Diaspora Affairs Committee. In 2000 she formed an inquiry committee for the location and restitution of assets of Holocaust victims in Israel, which in 2005 published a report. Subsequently, a law was enacted, which Colette initiated, to create a state-run company for the restitution of millions of dollars' worth of Holocaust victims' property that had been kept by Israeli banks. Ehud Olmert and Tommy Lapid were among the supporters.

As a member of the seventeenth Knesset, Colette served as the deputy speaker of the house and as a member of the Constitution and Law, and Immigration, Absorption, and Diaspora Affairs committees.

Her interests lay chiefly with the rights of women, Bedouins, and other minorities. Colette was a founding member of the International Women's Commission, supported by the United Nations. The commission included an equal number of Israeli, Palestinian, and international women seeking to achieve peace between Israel and Palestinians. The committee's work was based on the UN Security Council Resolution 1325, voted in 2000, which addressed the impact of war on women and the importance of women's full participation in conflict resolution, peacebuilding, peacekeeping, humanitarian response, and post-conflict reconstruction.

Colette worked with the paternalistic Ethiopian community, trying to solve problems of resentment among the largely unemployed population of men who saw many women with jobs. The imbalance resulted in depression among the men, which at times led to their suicide or violence against women.

She also helped many Russian immigrants in mixed marriages, whose children were not considered Jews in Israel. She devoted much time to the professional problems of new immigrants whose degrees as medical doctors were not recognized. Her ongoing work with Israelis abroad resulted in many returning home.

Nowadays, Colette does "thousands of things" outside of diplomacy and politics to improve Israeli society, including in her role as chairwoman of the Center Organization of Holocaust Survivors in Israel that oversees fifty-eight organizations under its umbrella.

She serves as vice president of the Conference of Material Claims Against Germany and secretary general of the World Jewish Restitution Organization. She is chairperson of the International Harp Contest and a board member of the Schechter Institute of Jewish Studies in Jerusalem. She also is a member of the board of the Gesher Theater and a member of the Executive World Jewish Congress.

After Colette and I spoke, I realized how the challenges she faced as a diplomat enabled her to gain the knowledge and the strength she needed to act on behalf of the state of Israel, and in her future work as an advocate for individuals and for culture. She developed self-confidence as a woman in charge who was scrutinized and judged at every step of the way. Her courage and devotion to the country that she learned to love should inspire us all.

———•◦———

Colette received honorary doctoral degrees from the College of New Rochelle and Wheaton College. She has been awarded the Palmes Académiques and subsequently Officer of the Légion d'Honneur by the French government; the Cavaliere dell'Ordine della Repubblica by the Italian government; and the National Order for Merit with the rank of high officer by the Romanian government. On June 11, 2013, Colette received the highest decoration given by the Portuguese government, Ordem do Infante Dom Henrique. And on May 2, 2022, she was awarded by the president of the Federal Republic of Germany the Order of Merit First Rank.

SHIKMA SCHWARTZMAN BRESSLER

PARTICLE PHYSICIST, SOCIAL ACTIVIST

"History shows that only uncompromising struggle can prevent dictatorial leaders from achieving their goals."

THE HUNDREDS OF THOUSANDS OF demonstrators who gather every Saturday night on Tel Aviv's Kaplan Street chant as one, "De-mo-cra-ti-a. De-mo-cra-tia." They punctuate Dr. Shikma Bressler's energizing speech denouncing the erosion of Israeli democracy and individual rights.

And when she articulates the dangers posed by Prime Minister Benjamin Netanyahu and his far-right cabinet's autocratic rule, the sea of grassroots supporters responds with a resounding chorus: "Shame! Shame! Shame!"

Now a national hero, Shikma is a take-charge, athletic, and naturally beautiful forty-three-year-old particle physicist and mother of five daughters. She has dedicated her life to securing her country's democratic future despite being threatened and arrested. Every week since March 2023—an Israeli flag, and at times, a single pink rose clutched in her right hand—she has spoken fearlessly about the current government's toxic ideology.

"Nobody feels protected under a messianic right-wing government, our most basic human rights no longer will be secure. A situation that will have an economic and social impact!" she shouted. Israeli Arabs are fearful of losing the right to vote. Academics and doctors are worried about their freedom to pursue research. Businesspeople are concerned by the decline in foreign investments and that out migration will take place.

"Most troubling," she said, "is the growling reluctance of soldiers and pilots to participate in military actions that may be ordered by the government that may deviate from international human rights and legal standards.

"We know now that Israeli government's ideology is to change from a democratic country into a theocracy with a very particular religious flavor," Shikma continued. "The mask has been ripped away. They are willing to endanger the country, economy, high tech, security, education, and healthcare systems, for the sake of their own personal political interests.

"We can either fall into a very dark, extreme, racist place where the Israel that we know, in all its social and economic aspects, will be destroyed," she declared, wearing her iconic "We must resist" black T-shirt with its defiant, raised fist. "Or, we can secure democracy for the future!"

The demonstrations target laws that, among other things, limit the Supreme Court judges from using the so-called reasonableness standard to keep the government and parliament in check. But Shikma's initial call to action came during the COVID lockdown in 2020, as Netanyahu's criminal trial on corruption charges was about to begin. Her family discussed the state of Israeli affairs, and she asked whether they thought the courts would be shuttered. Absolutely not, they declared.

"I was naïve," she said. To everyone's surprise, courts were closed two days before the trial, new elections were blocked, and Netanyahu chose his own ministers. "Democracy relies on a balance between the three: the government, the courts, and the parliament. But we were left with just the government and Netanyahu."

The next day, Shikma and her brothers organized a convoy of cars to the Knesset to awaken the passive Israeli populace and prevent Netanyahu's election. The protestors would become known as Black Flags, a reference to the flags that are used to indicate danger at sea and when soldiers are given an illegal command. "We saw the risk to Israeli democracy and brought the call DEMOCRATIA to the streets," Shikma said.

Black Flag members resumed their usual lives after Naftali Bennett formed a government with Yair Lapid, only to reemerge stronger when Netanyahu returned as prime minister after the 2022 election.

"That gave rise to tons of grassroots organizations led by lawyers, doctors, academics, social workers united in their value of democracy," Shikma said. She added that more than two hundred organizations have registered under the umbrella organization that grew out of Black Flags, and more than 70 percent of people in Israel support the protests—"spontaneous gatherings in which people with different politics and philosophies have taken the initiative and come up with their own plans," she said. "It is beautiful and heartwarming. We are backing each other up, so each will be able to speak up for their own rights."

FROM PARTICLE PHYSICS TO PROTESTS

I finally met Shikma in September, over a Zoom call during my daily walk in New York's Central Park. Sirens from passing cars in Israel pierced the park's calm, but Shikma's face on my iPad radiated confidence and intelligence. It didn't take long to see that this charismatic young woman would always be ready with a flag and a galvanizing speech to lead thousands in a united cause.

Shikma was driving from the Weizmann Institute of Science in Rehovot, where she is a leading professor and researcher, to her home in Beit She'arim in the Jezreel Valley. She makes the 150-mile round trip daily, which gives her time to think, plan, and give interviews. I realized that her dual passions—for the Higgs Boson particle and her fight for democracy and justice in Israel—are catalysts for improving life on our planet.

Shikma Schwartzman Bressler was born 1980 in Afula, Israel. She grew up on Kibbutz Gvat and in Timrat, but her family's roots are in a nineteenth-century Jewish community in Tiberias and the green valley in which she chose to raise her family. Blessed with athletic ability and a five-foot-nine-inch stature, Shikma excelled in basketball, joined Maccabi Haifa, the Upper Galilee team of the Hapoel sports association, and even played on the Israeli national women's team. She received an "outstanding athlete" status and continued her training while serving in the Israeli Defense Forces.

She earned her bachelor's degree (2000) in physics and mathematics, her master's degree (2006) in physics, and her PhD (2011) in particle physics, all from the Technion—Israel Institute of Technology, Haifa. The year after her PhD, Shikma joined the faculty at the Weitzmann Institute, and by 2013 she had formed the Particle Detector project in collaboration with the ATLAS experiment at CERN Large Hadron Collider in Switzerland. Shikma and her team gather data from ATLAS to search for what is beyond the standard model of particle physics.

As the first stars twinkled in New York, I asked Shikma about the roots of her interest in particle physics. "It is uncovering the secrets of the universe literally, in the sense that we know that there is so much we don't know," she told me. "We also try to find out what these things that we do not know could be. The links between physics, mathematics, and the laws of nature are unbelievably beautiful. And look at the global collaboration of the human race and its quest for knowledge…it gives a sense that we can discover stuff. That is breathtaking."

NEVER STOP TRYING

Since organizing the initial Black Flag protests in 2020, Shikma said she has learned that "history shows that only uncompromised struggle can prevent dictatorial leaders from achieving their goal." Though the current protests do not guarantee success and Israel's democracy is not perfect, "it is worthwhile to try." She continued: "Having a system of checks and balances for government decisions affords people the room to seek the truth, and that leads to improvement and progress."

Israel's internal social conflicts—the need to improve living conditions and equality for Palestinians in the West Bank, Israeli Arabs, and other minorities—are in danger of remaining unresolved under a government that deviates from the Declaration of Independence. Without a written constitution, she said, "the judicial system now under attack is the only body available to preserve those principles: complete equality of social and political rights for all inhabitants, irrespective of religion, race, or sex, and guaranteed freedom of religion, conscience, language, education, and culture."

I was familiar with Shikma's opinions and writings about democracy and sensed her fear that the unrest would continue. For the protests to end, she said two conditions must be met. First, the elimination of 150 "non-democratic and religious laws proposed by the Netanyahu coalition along with the radical limitation of judicial review. Second, also so far ignored by the government, is that any changes in our constitution framework should be made with broad consent.

"This government is interested in unlimited power and staying in power forever and will do so if there is no resistance," she went on. "We are not protesting just to protest; we are protesting to save Israel. We will act until we succeed, until we solve our problems."

She continued:

"Should we allow our country to become like Poland or Hungary, a modern dictatorship?

"Should we allow a man to become prime minister just to escape trial?

"Should LGBTQIA+ people and women be considered second-class citizens?

"Should the violence between Israelis and Palestinians in the West Bank continue to escalate?"

The adrenaline released by my frustration with Israel's long list of challenges fueled my accelerated pace through the park. I asked Shikma why she thinks that demonstrations will force the Israeli government to change while those in Poland and Hungary failed. "We learn from failures," she replied. "The thing that differentiates us is that Israelis are used to fighting and sacrificing for the country. We are ready to do that again; though this time we are fighting a different enemy, an enemy is an enemy."

NEVER DOING ENOUGH

And fight she does. Shikma was arrested and briefly jailed for allegedly blocking a road and hindering a police officer in March 2023. Demonstrators outside the police station in Tel Aviv chanted "Shame! Shame!" Though Shikma was released on the condition she stay away from the protest site for five days, she immediately returned to press the cause.

I was encouraged by her defiance and let my mind wander for a moment to my parents' ceaseless mission to realize their Zionist dreams. The images of inspirational biblical and modern Jewish heroines—strong and persuasive women like Shikma—popped into my head.

I still had so many questions about Shikma's everyday life and interests, including how she balances the demands of work and social activism with her devotion to her five daughters. She smiled humbly and said: "There are people who do more."

When I asked whether her genetics or sustained involvement in sports have contributed to her leadership qualities, she said both are true. "My brothers are very bright, my mother is a family physician, and father an engineer with Elbit Systems. My grandmothers were housewives, one grandfather was a truck driver and the other worked in a garage. What is common is our love for this country."

Sports is said to foster cooperation and dedication to the goal of winning, she said. "You develop strategies, lessons that can be learned and used in our life, and the competence and communication that are needed to lead a protest."

Shikma refused to take credit for the success of these monumental rallies, including the thirty-one-mile march she and fellow anti-reform leader Moshe Radman led last summer from coastal Tel Aviv to the hills of Jerusalem. Reminiscent of a biblical pilgrimage, the mile-long column of demonstrators swelled with thousands of supporters along the way. "It was almost a spiritual experience" she whispered, with people contributing food, water, and even shoes for participants. "It was a historic moment."

As I was wandering through the hidden trails of Central Park, and the warm hues of the sunset colored the horizon, I felt protected as an Israeli living in the USA, while in Israel the struggle to maintain democracy was going on. From a distance I could only admire the courageous and talented Shikma who became a leader and the symbol of a great story now unfolding in Israel—a movement opposing the regime in order to protect Israel's values of human rights, democracy, and freedom.

TAMAR ASRAF

SETTLER, FORMER SPOKESPERSON FOR
MATEH BINYAMIN REGIONAL COUNCIL

"What I do with my life is to deepen the love and loyalty to Israel and to the Jewish nation in the growing generation. I want to narrow the gap that has been created between religious and secular nationalists."

TAMAR ASRAF WAS BORN IN Haifa in 1972 and grew up in a secular family of Zionist pioneers. She was drawn to helping people through community service, but freely admits that she disliked settlers, people she knew nothing about personally or ideologically. As a teenager, she supported the Oslo Accords and the return of Palestinian territories that were occupied by Israel in the 1967 war.

Today, after service in the IDF and exposure to more people, cultures, and opinions, Tamar is a religious Zionist and one of the very settlers she said she once despised. She believes without a doubt that Judea and Samaria should be part of Israel, the land of the Jewish nation, not a Palestinian state. And as the former spokesperson for Mateh Binyamin Regional Council, a large governing body in Judea and Samaria, she is a frequent contributor to talk shows and opinion platforms.

Tamar wore casual clothes and her ubiquitous head wrap for our meeting. She was warm, engaging, and well-spoken, and we had a frank discussion about the evolution of her views and her commitment to reclaiming Israel.

She recalled attending several meetings between Israeli Arabs and secular Jewish Israelis. "I never knew any Orthodox or religious Zionists, and at the time I didn't even know how to distinguish between the two," she said. She belonged to the Hashomer Hatzair, a Zionist socialist youth movement.

Before joining the IDF, Tamar left home to volunteer for a year of service. She helped children from difficult economic backgrounds with their studies. At one point she aspired to move to Japan to learn about Zen and pottery, but her plans changed when she joined the IDF. In the army, she belonged to a small group of soldier-teachers in the Field Study Center. They organized nature excursions for adolescents, students, and others to foster a love of the land of Israel. Over time, her worldview began to change—about Israel, religion, and the growing settlements in the West Bank.

A NEW WAY OF THINKING

During an intensive course while serving in the IDF, she met religious nationalist settlers, and she realized that she had erroneous preconceptions about them. "For the first time, I was introduced to people who saw the world differently," she said. "Their conviction, which made our discussions interesting, made me realize that while I had a strong Israeli identity, I was lacking in my Jewish identity.

"My conversations with my religious soldier friends revealed to me a whole new world of morals and behaviors," she continued. "This world that I just discovered got me thinking differently. This new world brought truth to my life."

She told me about another experience that convinced her she needed to know what it meant to be Jewish. "On a Saturday night, a group of religious families conducted Havdalah, which looked to me very strange," she said. "They all absorbed the smell of leaves and moved their hands around a lit candle. They appeared to me as a pagan group worshiping fire. When I asked for an explanation, knowing that according to our religious beliefs, we are not supposed to worship idols, they explained that it was a traditional ceremony performed on Saturday night to distinguish the sacred Shabbat from the next six working days. The feeling of shame due to my ignorance about important Jewish traditions was overwhelming."

Soon after, her friends from the Field Study Center traveled from the Dead Sea to Jerusalem by foot to celebrate the end of their IDF service. She told me that they visited churches and the Al-Aqsa Mosque. "I remember sitting on the steps of one of the churches, and I made a decision to learn about Judaism in Jerusalem," she said. She joined a friend at a post-army service college for religious girls and spent two years "slowly learning until I finally identified with my religion and discovered a new truth for my being and adopted a new set of moral values."

In 1996 Tamar married a young religious soldier, a combat parachuter in the IDF whom she met through her rabbi. Her husband was called to active duty in Lebanon, and for the next few years came home once every two weeks. They moved to Eli, a settlement in Judea and Samaria, after Tamar gave birth to five children. There, she found a community of people with similar lifestyles, and women who also had husbands who served in the IDF and who supported each other.

FINDING HER VOICE

She described Eli to me as a settlement of four- to five-thousand people, founded in 1984, and which embraces Israelis of various backgrounds. North of Jerusalem and Ramallah, it is under the jurisdiction of the Mateh Binyamin Regional Council. In addition to a military college, Eli has a pre-military academy that provides military training, leadership skills, education to help students manage the secular world they are about to encounter, and support to make sure they stay faithful to their religion upon discharge. In Israel, there are about 150 of these religious pre-military schools.

Tamar said that the settlers' voices have to counter "the misconceptions spun by the media" that they steal land and mistreat Arabs. And for that reason, Tamar enrolled at Bar-Ilan University twelve years ago to study communication, so she could provide an honest analysis and help decrease the divide between religious settlers and secular Israelis. As the years passed, she committed herself to uniting the country by advocating for love of and loyalty to the land.

She did this in her role as the speaker of Mateh Benjamin and by meeting with groups of young religious and secular children. Through her conversations, she realized that the younger generation eventually lose their connection to the land and to Zionism. She developed a program of boat excursions in Jaffa that recreated the excitement pioneers felt upon their arrival in Israel. By mimicking those early voyages, which run occasionally, she believed the youth would find their Zionist identities and their voices would be heard throughout Israel.

I asked Tamar to explain the ideology of religious nationalists. She said that they follow Rabbi Avraham Kook (1865–1935) and his son Rabbi Zvi Yehuda Kook's (1891–1982) National Religious Belief, which revolves around three pillars: the land of Israel, the people of Israel, and the Torah of Israel.

I asked why she supports the continuous building of homes for Israelis in the settlement in Yehuda and Shomron, which is a dividing question among all people of Israel. To that, Tamar said: "Yehuda and Shomron are a part of Israel, a land that belongs to the Jewish people, and as we build everywhere else in Israel, it is important to build in the rest of the areas that belong to us through our history, as it is described in the Bible.

"The small Arab villages near us use the name Lovan, which is taken from Levona, a village that existed in the prophets' time—the same as Shilo, that was the first capital of Israel," she said. "Our village Eli, for example, is named after the last prophet as it appeared in the prophet book. Those are examples to show how deep a connection the Jewish people have to Judah and Samaria.

"After the Six-Day War," she added, "we came back to our home after thousands of years of exile, and since then we helped deepen the connection and the sense of belonging to the land. It was settled that Area C is for the Jewish settlers, as decided upon in the Oslo agreements, so we build in Area C. Unfortunately, the Arabs are building homes there as well, in an area that was agreed upon to be dedicated to the Jewish settlers. As a result of that, Arab Palestinians own more than 30 percent of the land in Area C, and that is clearly against the rules of the Oslo agreement, and nobody prevents them from doing this.

"For the Jewish nation," she elaborated, "the existence of the state of Israel is a big miracle, and we have not yet achieved all our goals. It's a long process. In order to do that, we all have to take responsibility and be part of the establishment of the state of Israel. And therefore, the spirit of the community of Eli is that of a people on a volunteering mission or community service."

Tamar emphasized the dedication that the Jewish settlers of Judah and Samaria have to the Jewish land: they serve in the IDF, pay taxes, and promote the idea of settling all over Israel, including Judea and Samaria.

"That's the reason why many people in Eli are teachers—because they are a part of that mission," she continued. "Law school graduates don't open private offices to make money. Instead, they join governmental organizations because we have a mission to be a part of the advancement of the state of Israel."

I told her that's all very nice, but it does not explain the detrimental effect on the Palestinians or the international community's overwhelming objection to the settlements.

"The Jewish construction happening in Yehuda and Shamron in Area C is not happening on private Arab land," she answered. "At the end of the day, the total percentage of Jewish homes in Judea and Samaria is about only 2 percent of the total land area. This is not hindering the rights of Arabs who are going to Areas A and B. The international community is acting and reacting without knowing the reality in the region."

She paused a moment, then went on. "The state of Israel has to act based on figuring out what is right for her. After all, it is us who are living under constant terror acts. Our settling in Area C is not against the law, and in fact prevents further terror acts and affords the IDF the opportunity to act against them.

"The price that the Israeli citizens paid from having to leave Gaza is still felt," she continued. "The menacing missiles following the situation in Gaza—and the international criticism of Israel, a country that tries to defend itself—led the Israelis to understand that the international community cannot determine what is right and good for our community. What is good for the country will be decided by the citizens, through democratic elections."

But wait, I said: now that there is a strong Jewish state, isn't it time to consider the rights of the 2.5 million Palestinians living in the West Bank? I reminded Tamar that by becoming a religious Zionist, she had assumed a new worldview filled with truth and moral values. How can displacing Palestinians from the homes they have been living in before the establishment of Israel in 1948 be justified?

"It is true today that most of the Arab citizens in Judea and Samaria live in the Palestinian authority," Tamar replied. "According to the Oslo agreement, 40 percent of Judea and Samaria should be under Palestinian authority, and 98 percent of all Palestinians live in that area. The authority that runs their lives is not Israel, but the Palestinian Authority, which is responsible for their livelihoods.

"Yitzhak Rabin the PM did not permit them to get two things: control of the passages from Judea and Samaria to the rest of the country, and two, the freedom to build their own army. From that time, there has been a status quo. It is not perfect, but it permits for a decent life for both sides in an ongoing conflict.

"All the Jewish settlements that exist today in Judea and Samaria are in Area C," she said. "They were all built on empty land, and not even one Palestinian home was destroyed or taken by the Jews. Presently, and practically, the Palestinians own most of the land in Judea and Samaria; their economic situation is improving year by year; their quality of life also is improving. Every day there are more Palestinian houses being raised.

"If you think that if Israel evacuates the settlements that the Jews have built, there will be an end to the conflict, you are sorely mistaken," she said. "The Palestinians will not be happy having Area C as well. They hope for the day that Israel will cease to exist. They hope to extend their control beyond the Green Line, and finally build themselves a state. I am certainly able to identify with their wish and dream to have their own country/state. But I am absolutely not ready for it to happen at the account of my country.

"If the Palestinians choose to live in peace with Israel, they are invited to stay here, just like all other Israeli Arabs," she said. "But if they choose terror, they will have to leave. The truth is that until today, the state of Israel did not push out any Palestinians from their homes, nor deny them any rights unless they chose the path of terror. Their rights are important, but our right to life is more important. This is where we cross the red line."

THE RIGHT FOR ISRAEL TO EXIST

I told Tamar that the Israeli-Palestinian conflict is aggravated by the growing number of settlements, and she disagreed. "This is not the reason that we have the conflict—because they don't want Eli, because they never lived in Eli," she insisted. "They want Jaffa, Haifa, Accra, Ramallah, and Lod. So, it is not related to the settlements in Judea and Samaria, but the entire existence of the state of Israel."

When I didn't respond, she proceeded.

"The Arab-Jewish conflicts cost the state of Israel a heavy price, and it started a long time before the birth of the country. It also started before the Six-Day War. The organization to free Palestine began in 1964, three years before Israel occupied areas in Judea and Samaria. It is important to remember that there never existed the country called Palestine, and that Arabs lived in Israel under foreign control, like the Turks and the British. The conflict started on the day when the Jews wished to return to their homeland at the end of the nineteenth century, and it will not end until Israel ceases to exist.

"But through all these difficulties and complexities, there is something about this conflict that unites us as Jews," Tamar said. "The great hate of the Arabs against us unites us, and reminds us that this is our land, and that we are all Jews. This conflict, in a paradoxical way, helps our country keep our identity and remember the reason behind building the country: a nation and land for the Jewish people."

I was stunned to hear that Tamar sees benefits to conflict. Settlers live under constant threat, a minority of 450,000 living among 2.5 million Palestinians who want them out. People think of Israel as a colonizing apartheid country that illegitimately takes over other people's lands and freedom. The media describe the Palestinians' horrific living conditions without electricity, water, food, and freedom of movement.

"Does our ancestral history justify ruling over other people in this way?" I asked. "Are we following the Torah's Ten Commandments by having such disparate lifestyles in the West Bank? Aren't we supposed to be better than those who abused us over the years?"

Tamar admitted that I was asking hard questions, but she had answers that she had given countless times before. "We did not invite this conflict," she said. "It existed before 1948. It has been there since the beginning of Zionism. But once it is here, it is not all bad." She said antisemitism "protects our Jewish identity" because Jews are forced to unite against hatred.

PEACE IS ELUSIVE

Tamar said it is important to remember that Palestinians are not the main antagonists, and that the surrounding Arab countries and Iran "are an existential threat." She also dismissed reports of Palestinians' poor living conditions as misinformation and exaggeration by the media. Rather, she said, the lives of Palestinians have improved since 1967.

Finally, I asked how to achieve peace.

"There is no solution presently," she said, and emphasized that she does not support relinquishing any land. She reminded me that the Palestinians have rejected attempts to do so in the past.

"We do not have the right to give up this land," Tamar said. "The facts are that 40 percent of the West Bank is populated by the Palestinians under their own government and authority. They have a parliament and a president. For our safety, they are not allowed to have an army or define clear borders because that would end the existence of the state of Israel."

Tamar described three possibilities for a peaceful solution, considering that 230,000 Palestinians live in Area C: one, for them to become Israeli citizens; two, become Israeli residents like the Palestinians in East Jerusalem; and three, remain under the control of the Palestinian Authority.

"Two thousand years ago, Israelis were exiled for a long time," she said. "The prophets promised that we would come back home, and that day finally arrived. Jeremiah the prophet promised that there will be a day when we are going to plant vineyards in the Shomron mountains. This day, too, thousands of dunams [a measurement of land area] have already been planted in the mountains, similar to the way our ancestors did. We came back home, and we are living each day moving toward realizing the vision of the prophets and achieving the dreams of generations of Jewish people.

"It is not an easy way, and we have many obstacles," she observed. "We also have many other nationalities living with us, and if they are intending peace, they are invited to be part of this amazing country that is called Israel. If, however, they are intending terror, the Israeli government is going to act against them, no different to how it happens everywhere else.

"It is a process," Tamar concluded, "and I know that Judea and Samaria will, in the next few years, become an inseparable part of the state of Israel. I do not know when; it may be fifty years or two hundred years; but it will happen. Just like the prophecy of Jeremiah, the rest of the prophecies will come true."

GHADA ZOABI

FOUNDER AND CEO, BOKRA.NET, PHILANTHROPIST

"I was a pioneer in gathering kippah (yarmulke) and shemagh (keffiyeh) together. The Arabs and the Jews do not have any other solution. We need to strengthen the common denominator we have in order to live together."

I GREW UP IN THE same city as Ghada Zoabi, but our paths would not have crossed even if we were closer in age. In Haifa, Arab Israelis and Jews live peacefully together, yet apart. I had no Arab playmates, and despite the many Arab Israeli patients who frequented my father's dental clinic, we rarely spoke and did not socialize.

Ghada, the founder and CEO of Bokra.net, believes filling those silences and easing the wariness between our communities are critical steps to narrow the gaps in education, safety, and healthcare. And, hopefully, to live together in peace.

There is, however, much to do. In August 2023 Ghada helped lead the "March of the Dead," a protest to mourn the murders of 141 Arab Israelis and chastise the Israeli police for its failure to investigate and punish assailants.

In an emotional speech, Ghada said that guilt over the violence should be shared: by Arabs for deadly infighting and isolationism, and by Israeli society for allowing years of neglect by the government and continued educational and economic inequality between Arab and Jewish society.

There were few dry eyes in the crowd at Habima Square in Tel Aviv, Ghada said, where people held signs with "We seek protection NOW," and "Together we thrive: Safeguard Arab lives, eradicate crime." Women wore long white shrouds and Arab youth carried representative caskets for each of the victims. Some Jews, seeing the exhausted youth on the sweltering day, offered to carry the caskets. While a true feeling of unity filled the air, Ghada said, any positive outcome will depend on more than just words.

"Israel will not be a democratic liberal state without equality for its Arabs citizens," she said to conclude her speech. "Right now, they feel there is no security and they have no life."

GETTING STARTED

In 2006 Ghada launched her Arabic news portal and social platform, in response to rocket strikes in the second Lebanon war that killed eighteen Arab Israelis, most still in their homes. Their lives could have been spared, she said, if a dedicated military division cared for Arabs, and if

Israel's Arabic media did a better job informing people how to protect themselves during wartime.

Bokra.net typically receives 850,000 clicks daily. Unlike most Arabic media outlets, Bokra is not affiliated with a political party or a print newspaper. It attends to Arab society about daily life, social endeavors, and national and international information.

Bokra serves as a bridge between Arab society and Israeli government. Discussions are encouraged, and space is given to all Israeli speakers, not only Arabs, to ensure that Arabs are informed about everything that going on in Israel, and for Israeli society to learn more about Arabs.

"Listen," she told me. "There's a conflict. From one point of view, I want my people to live in peace and equality and to get the rights they deserve as citizens. But on the other hand, the reality is that the entire Palestinian population has been dispersed all over the world, and nobody cared to embrace our people. As of today, they're struggling."

SURVIVING THE NAKBA

Ghada and her nine siblings were born to one of the Arab families that stayed in the newly founded state of Israel in 1948. More than 700,000 Arabs left, but 150,000 became Israeli citizens and settled in villages and mixed cities like Haifa. Ghada asked her father why, in such a state of confusion, her parents kept having children. "He said it was important to build a large family to make up for the Nakba, the Palestinian Catastrophe," she said.

Ghada's soft green eyes filled with tears as she remembered the last conversation her father had with his siblings in Lebanon, a deathbed goodbye by phone instead of a loving embrace. Ghada's grandfather had split up his family after the Nakba to increase their chances of survival. Two sons and a daughter were sent to Lebanon, and her father and his brother stayed in Israel. They lived in Samaria, a small town near Akko, where her father was born and would be buried.

Although the family communicated on the phone and, thirty years after they separated, were allowed to meet near the Lebanese border, they never reunited.

As we spoke, I thought how our ancestors, though worlds apart, lived a similar story. In 1934 when my parents made aliyah to Israel, after years of anti-Semitic pogroms in Ukraine, my father's parents and three siblings went instead to the United States. My father was about fifty years old when he finally had a short visit with his parents in New York. Shortly after he returned to Israel, he received a phone call about his father's passing. My father was my hero, the rock I leaned on, and for me, at the age of twelve, I felt helpless as I heard him sob alone upstairs in his dental clinic.

Like Ghada's parents, mine believed in the importance of bringing children into the world. For them, it was a triumph over the Holocaust and the dark Auschwitz crematorium that claimed my mother's parents and brother. My mother's two sisters were subjected to medical experiments. The memories brought tears to my eyes, and Ghada and I shared the moment, both of us children of parents who struggled to rebuild their families after upheaval and destruction.

Although they were Muslims, Ghada and her siblings went to a Catholic Arab school that provided a good education. Similarly, my parents placed me in the Alliance Francaise, a French-speaking school that enriched my education and foreign language skills and introduced me to a different culture.

Ghada's father worked in agriculture for many years, for a Jewish Israeli named Mordechai in Bait She'an, a village near Afula. The two families accepted each other; they were friends who over the years spent Shabbat and Jewish holidays together. Learning to "love the other" is a lesson that still drives her life.

"We were taught to accept what was inscribed by fate," she told me, and her parents believed that change could occur only through education and communication, not force. Each child received a higher education; when one graduated, they helped the younger siblings get through their studies and, if needed, with financial assistance. They became teachers, worked in healthcare, and some moved to Houston, Texas, Ghada said.

Before becoming a journalist, Ghada was active in youth groups and helped make social connections between Arab Israeli and Jewish

Israeli high school students. The year before attending university, Ghada participated in economic society meetings in Rabbath-Ammon, Jordan, as well as in Egypt. There, she met hostile Arabs who confronted her about living in Israel.

"You can imagine how difficult life was for me," she said, "trying in one hand to integrate and work on achieving equality in the Israeli society with the hope for peace, and in the other hand, to be despised by my own national brothers because I live in Israel."

At the University of Haifa, she studied communication and education, and brought Jewish Israeli children from affluent areas on Mount Carmel to visit the Arab area in Wadi Nisnas. Ghada also joined a women's society that inspired her to strengthen ties between Arab Israelis and Jews.

"I was a pioneer in gathering *kippah* (yarmulke) and *shemagh* (kef-fiyeh), together," she told me. "There is no other way. The Arabs and the Jews do not have any other solution. Nobody is leaving. We need to strengthen the common denominator we have in order to live together."

RAISING CHILDREN AMID DISCRIMINATION

Ghada and husband moved to Nazareth and brought up three children, one of whom is currently studying medical engineering at UCLA. "You'll be surprised to learn that after my three kids frequented St. Joseph Christian Elementary School," she said. "I sent two to high school in Jordan," where they board at the King Abdullah School and are taught in English with other international students.

Almost apologetically, she explained: "I didn't want them to have to digest the same pain and to go through existential struggle that I went through as I had to prove my identity. I did not want my kids to encounter difficulties to find a place to work, or to try to be accepted to universities.

"But truly," she added, "it was mostly because of fear of the conflict intensifying between the two peoples presently. I was truly afraid for my kids to remain in Israel. I brought them up on values to receive the other, to find the common link with the other, as my grandfather and father preached."

When her younger children come home for weekends, they share their experiences in Jordan, and how they often must explain to their peers why they live in Israel, and the difference between Palestinians living in the West Bank. "They were surprised at the misinformation on the subject regarding the Israeli Arabs living in Israel," she told me.

"I was told I am naive in regard to the realization of peace among the two peoples. I believe that one has to be naive and hope for peace, because we do not have another way. Maybe one day the extremists of both sides will calm down. But until then, I will give my children the choice where they want their own life journey to be.

"I do not want them to feel discrimination. We feel this daily. I feel that lately the gap increases, but I do not have my kids participate in my feelings. The opposite. I tell them to go and meet international people and to participate in conversation with them, and demonstrate and emphasize the good side of Jews and Arabs living together."

CONNECTING WORLDS THROUGH JOURNALISM

Ghada started her career at the public radio station Kol Israel, and for four years hosted a weekly program on the Arabic language Channel One. "It is devastating to remember how I got only thirty minutes a month speaking in Arabic to the Arab audience on Israeli radio, talking about road safety."

At Bokra, she controls the agenda and focuses on a range of important geopolitical and social issues. In 2015, when individual terrorists led attacks against Israeli locations, Bokra invited religious, civil, Jewish, and Arab leaders to speak out for peace. The news site also arranged to have Israeli government conventions transmitted to Arab Israelis, to improve information sharing.

The pandemic exposed dangerous gaps in how the two societies were kept informed, a situation made worse because of a lack of computers and cell phones in Arab society, she said. Bokra took over from Israeli Jewish media, shared critical public health information about vaccinations in accordance with Israeli Health Bureau recommendations, and broadcast the locations of doctors who were nearby. Volunteers were organized to provide community outreach.

"It was moving to see Arabs and Jews working together with a purpose to fight the pandemic, without interference of race and religion differences," Ghada said. She was honored by the state health bureau for her work. As difficult as that time was, it also inspired hope for unification.

I clearly heard the pride in her voice when she talked about the increasing number of Arab students attending university, thanks to Bokra's encouragement to use education as tool for progress. I noted that a high percentage of students graduating from the medical field are Arabs.

I told her that I saw reason for hope, but Ghada was more reserved. "There is indeed an uptake in different subjects that can lead the way," she acknowledged. "But we did not come to a situation where we could say that discrimination doesn't exist. Bokra tries to emphasize the Israeli Arab's wish to build a life for themselves and for their family, and to have a united society."

Ghada devotes herself to many organizations that strengthen ties between Jews and Israeli Arabs and that help Arabs with public health, education, safety, disabilities, and other concerns. She helped found the Masira "Journey" Fund, which provides programming for Arab-Israelis with disabilities, and manages its public relations without pay. She is involved with the Mariam Foundation for women with breast cancer, a common disease among Arabic women. Her other commitments include The Next Door Neighbor, which teaches Hebrew and Arabic in Nazareth and Arab villages; a shared community center in Nazareth for Jews and Arabs; Givat Haviva, a center for Arab and Israeli peace; Migdar, to promote women in academia; and Jasmine, an organization for women in business.

She serves on the board of Maala, a nonprofit group of successful business owners who exchange ideas, promote social responsibility, and emphasize that diversity is needed in every company in Israel. She is also on the advisory board of Shomrim—The Center for Media and Democracy.

Ghada also supports the Umm el-Fahem Art Gallery, established by the Shaqra family to promote Arab art education, facilitate meetings between Arab and Israeli artists, and provide lectures and exhibits of Israeli and Arab artwork.

A LACK OF EQUITY

I was curious about the ideology of young Arabs today, and I asked Ghada about the connection between Israeli Arabs with Palestinians in the West Bank and in Gaza. Radicalization among the young Israeli Arabs, I said, intensifies mistrust among the two communities.

"The situation is complex," Ghada said. "The Israeli Arabs carry double identity, a complex identity, and when eruption occurs in Gaza or in the West Bank, it influences the relationship between Israeli Arabs and Jewish Israelis in the land. There are extremists on both sides that incite anger. There are people on both sides that thrive on the conflict, whether in Israel or in the West Bank. But there are also Palestinians that, similarly to the Israeli Arabs, want to live in peace and bring up a family.

"It is the extremists on both sides that caused the problem. It is important to look for people who have common interests and feelings on both sides. The situation in the West Bank influences the Israeli Arabs and provokes those who celebrate the conflict. This is the reality. The ones that thrive on the conflicts are those who do not believe in the solution of two countries for two people, and they increase the tension among us. In fact, the last election shows how the Israeli society moved over to the right."

I asked Ghada why more Arabs didn't turn out to vote in the last election and potentially diminish the weight of the right wing. "Arabs do not like to participate in Israeli elections because they are feeling used and disappointed," she said. "The young generation is asking to be considered, and to be represented in the government. They feel worthless and only needed when elections take place."

The other problem is the fact that there is increasing crime among Arabs, but Israeli police do not get involved.

As for the possibility of Israeli Arab participation in the IDF, Ghada said that "one has to be loyal to the country one lives in, but this is a complex issue in regard to the Israeli Arab." She said the young who do not join should not be judged, because of the complexity of dual nationality. "It has been proven that those who tried to join did not stay for long. The solution is to have them do three years of community service, where they can serve in the police department, in the hospital, and in protecting the Arab villages. They will not join as long as there is tension between the two people."

She also mentioned resentment of Jewish national law because it lacks the word "equality" for all nations. Such a glaring omission fails to motivate Bedouins, the Druze, and Israeli Arabs to join the IDF.

I told her that her work, her care, and her courage could produce significant benefits for Arab society. She agreed. "The Arab woman today goes out and helps to support the family. Due to having exposure to social media on the Internet, they get interested in the outside world. There are many academic Arab women and leaders in the work field. Many of them are building careers today, but the opportunities are not the same as to the Jewish Israelis. Whoever wants to succeed can," she agreed, "but in the Arab reality of life, it is not easy. One has to divide their energy between moving forward along with fighting discrimination. There is a lot to be done."

The Abraham Accords generated controversy in the Arab society, and some objected to having the Emirates make peace with Israel without first having Israel make peace with the Palestinians. Ghada felt differently. The Accords allow members of Arab society to travel to Arab countries and she is now able to see her family. "And besides," she said, "peace has to be grabbed, and may later lead to solve the Palestinian Israeli conflict."

But how, I asked, can there be peace in light of the extremists in Hamas and Hezbollah? "We must find the partners in both sides," she said. "We have to find those who are interested in peace, those who have things in common and want to unite."

So, who are they, our partners that we could talk to? I asked. Ghada said she has heard of moderate voices in the West Bank, but those who celebrate the conflict should be avoided. "I have arranged meetings between West Bank leaders and Jewish leaders to discuss how to strengthen the ties," she said. "Only by talking and communication between both sides can we move forward, along with Bokra spreading information."

Bokra means "tomorrow" in Arabic, Ghada said, and therefore she and her company strive each day to make life more equitable for people who can't advocate for themselves.

GAL LUSKY

FOUNDER AND CEO, ISRAELI FLYING AID,
HUMANITARIAN

———◆———

"The only fear I have that is stronger than the fear of dying is living the rest of my life without compassion."

GAL LUSKY AND HER TEAM of volunteers help survivors of tsunamis, floods, earthquakes, volcanoes, bombings, and civil war. There is nowhere they won't go to ensure that the people caught up in natural disaster sites or conflict zones have the food, medical supplies, and clothing they need.

There are few headlines, however, about the good work done by Israeli Flying Aid (IFA), the humanitarian NGO Gal established in 2005. The life-saving missions are mostly clandestine, operating where local regimes bar organizations like IFA, and in countries that typically lack diplomatic relations with Israel.

"Just as no one asks for permission to kill, we do not ask for permission to save lives," Gal said.

The founder and CEO of IFA lit a torch at the sixty-seventh Independence Day ceremony on Jerusalem's Mount Herzl, an unusual public declaration of honor for someone who runs rescue and relief missions to hostile countries normally off limits to Israelis. She does not ask permission to enter these countries, loading trucks with food and essential medical supplies to ease the suffering of women and children.

The list of life-saving missions is long. IFA saved women and children following Sri Lanka's tsunami, the Darfur-Sudan conflict, flooding in Georgia-Chechnya, Hurricane Katrina in the United States, earthquakes in Pakistan-Kashmir, India-Kashmir, and Indonesia. Gal was there for the cyclone that tore through Myanmar, the Georgia-Russia conflict, the explosion in Beirut, Lebanon, the civil war in Syria. She responded to Myanmar despite its prohibition of foreign aid, and once delivered 3-D printers to a conflict zone and provided training for local doctors so they could print prosthetic limbs. She continues to save lives in the humanitarian crises in Chad and in Khartoum-Sudan.

EMBRACING HARD WORK

Born on a kibbutz in 1968 near the Sea of Galilee, Gal was comfortable with hard labor and understood the importance of community. Sharing and caring for others became a way of life. She was the only girl in a class of youngsters cared for in a communal children's house, and adapted to strenuous physical conditions. She learned to live in the outdoors, sometimes in harsh conditions.

Leadership skills came naturally. She admired her mother, the kibbutz secretary, and saw how masterfully and empathetically she interacted with residents. Independent early in life, Gal paid her university tuition by working as a flight attendant and in a private investigator's office.

Her commitment to humanitarian work—the catalyst for IFA—began in 1992. Gal abandoned her studies in criminology to care for her brother, a paratrooper commander in the Israeli Defense Forces who was wounded in action in Lebanon.

This first-hand encounter with her brother's severe eye and limb wounds, the devastating consequences of human conflict, propelled her to Rwanda in 1994 to join local NGOs working to reunite families. She admitted how foolish she was to jump into a civil war zone with little training and only $5,000 in her pocket.

For the next ten years she volunteered with humanitarian organizations in a seemingly endless list of hotspots. She saw how governments delayed or interfered with the delivery of lifesaving resources, a tool of war that caused the death of political opponents and bystanders.

"I saw a need to help save lives no matter who people are or where they live," Gal told me.

Israeli Flying Aid would have to operate covertly. Gal's nationality could jeopardize her mission to serve people in countries deemed enemies of Israel, including Sudan, Lebanon, and Syria. Israel could also interfere; citizens are prohibited from entering enemy countries. Teams travel below the radar to Muslim countries to ensure the Israeli team members' safety, on the one hand, and on the other hand, for the local victims to be more comfortable receiving and using the aid. IFA is also not absent from the local Israeli-Palestinian dispute.

Early on, during the tsunami in 2004, Gal learned that the Sri Lankan government denied aid to Tamil people who were accused of supporting the Tamil Tiger insurgency, thereby causing their deaths. Over the more than eighteen years since, she and her volunteers have been busy saving lives in areas affected by natural disasters or human conflict.

"When ruling authorities deprive aid, IFA is there," she said. "This is based on Israeli civil society's moral values, and deeply rooted in our Jewish DNA. The sanctity of life is above and beyond any existing law."

Her strategy is to build "helping hands," on-the-ground partnerships that inspire local teams to action. Plans for each operation are extremely detailed in order to lower the risk for all parties. She begins with a deep base of knowledge about her target country, and generates the majority of supplies from local markets or neighboring countries.

By creating a framework for support—that connections are in place and the need for external resources are reduced—IFA ensures success for future emergency situations independent of the United Nations and government approval. Also, generating supplies locally provides local merchants with finances during what is often a critical time. "This empowers them to see the extent to which their needs can be solved locally," she said. Except for professionally trained doctors and trauma experts, Gal's team is composed entirely of local partners and participants, who, through her training and processes, improve their own skills and capabilities delivering and distributing critical aid.

PARTNERING FOR SUCCESS

Local partners are trained in Gal's best practices and scenarios for each type of emergency, which are based on risk assessment and are simple to replicate. Specialized teams address IFA's main goals:

1. Search and rescue
2. Mass feeding centers/aid convoys
3. Medical aid
4. Post-trauma intervention

Responses are further divided based on an aid toolkit that she learned how to assemble with skills she acquired throughout the years. Earthquakes require people trained in search and rescue as well as a multidisciplinary medical team. A burn team and pulmonologists respond to volcano and fire disasters. Additional volunteers are chosen and pulled from reserve IDF elite units who receive additional training by IFA to perform confidential humanitarian missions.

Gal, along with Vice President and Chief Operating Officer Maya Zuckerman, run the organization with more than a thousand volunteers. Donors worldwide provide financial backing and determine which missions to support. Gal is in communication with thousands of contacts around the world and quickly knows where aid is most critically needed.

The Syrian civil war has claimed a million lives over eleven years, including twenty thousand children, and millions of homes were destroyed. From 2011 through 2019, IFA helped people living in areas that were actively bombed by the regime of President Bashar al-Assad. Gal attributes IFA's success to the undercover unit consisting of Muslims, Druze, Christians, and Jews, representing the whole Israeli civil sector. The unit finds its way within crisis areas in creative ways, showing strong dedication to the victims' needs.

Gal shared a few of the many highlights of her adventures, including the time when all the Israeli youth organizations collected blankets, coats, sleeping bags, and other cold-weather items to help the Syrian war victims. This educational mission taught Israeli children to care for innocent victims of the Syrian internal dispute, although Syrians consider themselves Israel's sworn enemy.

One child told her: "I hate Arabs. But I learned my hate is out of fear. When I learned more about the Syrian crisis, and then realized how strong my homeland is, I stopped worrying. We have a strong army, and my president will never kill me unlike what is happening in Syria. I am strong enough to be on the side to help the children of my enemy." In 2014, President Bibi Netanyahu saluted the children at an emotional ceremony honoring their work.

MOVING BEYOND HATE AND FAILURE

While Gal treasures IFA's many successes, she also remembers her failures. When the 2010 earthquake in Haiti destroyed an orphanage of seventy-five girls, IFA provided emergency medical aid, supported the restoration and construction of the orphanage, trained local personnel, and ensured that decent food and medical care was always accessible for the next three years. Toward the end of IFA's mission, young girls started to disappear, and a long investigation revealed that girls were being sold by the head nun responsible for the orphanage to wealthy families, to be sacrificed during religious voodoo ceremonies.

Then there was this bittersweet story, about a local Syrian fighter who was an intermediary for sending supplies across the border. He worked with IFA for years, but always kept his distance and never became a friend, she said. When the Assad government discovered the operation and planned to disrupt it, he asked Gal, perhaps prescient of his death, to send three months' worth of supplies.

Gal set to work to raise the $60,000 and found an unexpected source: a thirteen-year-old boy who wanted to donate his bar mitzvah money to help the people of Syria. She confirmed the offer with the boy's parents, who not only approved but matched the funds.

The Syrian commander, deeply touched by the child's gesture, had recorded a thank you message to the boy, to be played at his bar mitzvah party in Israel. By the time the party took place, the commander had already been killed by the Assad regime. But his poignant message touched everyone present:

> *"Dear _____. As a Syrian and on behalf of my family, and the children, and the people of my town I would like to thank you from the bottom of my heart for your outstanding donation on this special day of your bar mitzvah celebration.*
>
> *"You are truly a model of hope to all children worldwide by deciding to donate all of your personal gifts to the Syrian children. I would also like to thank your parents, who have taught you the importance of giving and raised you as a human and loving child now turning into a young adult on this special day.*
>
> *"It is because of people like you that I continue…I continue hoping for peace in our region and for the possibility of meeting face to face. I hope one day, perhaps through humanitarian aid efforts, the Syrian people will get to the Israel people and be building trust.*

"Dear _____, as our future human generation, thank you for your ongoing kindness. I wish you the best of luck and a very happy bar mitzvah. Thank you."

IFA is a "proud and unapologetic" Zionist organization, Gal said. Some of IFA's volunteers are ex-IDF soldiers suffering from different levels of PTSD. Though their IFA activities may trigger their trauma, she could not refuse their wish to join a life-saving mission. "If they were good enough to fight for the state of Israel, then they are good enough to save lives," she said.

I asked the obvious question. "You are away from your two kids and risking your life. How do you manage, and what drives you?"

She credits her mother for always being available so that Gal could help children who needed her more than her own. "I chose time and time again to do it. Over the years I realized that the only fear I have that is stronger than the fear of dying is the fear of living my life without meaning, leaving the planet without compassion," Gal said. "I have chosen to have children, and my responsibility is to leave the world to them a little better than I got it myself."

ORIT ADATO

FORMER ISRAELI MILITARY COMMANDER AND ISRAEL PRISON SERVICE COMMISSIONER

"Always remember that I was under a magnifying glass being the first woman heading the [Israeli Prison Service]. I was dependent on my staff and looked up to them as much as they looked up to me."

WHEN I HAD THE PLEASURE of meeting Lieutenant General (Ret.) Orit Adato, her sense of justice, strength of character, and dark hair reminded me of the biblical heroine Deborah, a prophetess of the God of the Israelites and the only female judge mentioned in the Bible.

Like Deborah, a leader of victorious battles, Orit's advocacy has led to revolutionary change: for women in the military, for prison systems, and for the underserved and unrepresented people in the periphery. She was the first woman to achieve a three-star general rank, and one of the few to report on the prevalence of sexual harassment in the Israeli military. And as the first female Commissioner of the Israel Prison Service (IPS), she led with authority and deep compassion.

"I brought to the prison system a new worldly perspective, one that integrates and provides care, involves high professional demands, and similar obedience and support when the commanders make mistakes," she told me. "That's how teaching and learning and advancement occur. My mantra is: dream, dare, and do. No one will take your place."

Born in 1955 to a seventh-generation Sephardic Israeli Jewish family in Tivon, a picturesque village near Haifa, Orit was a tomboy who spent more time in the principal's office than the classroom. She said her boredom abated when she advanced to higher, more challenging classes. She looked up to her two elder brothers, who were serving in the Israel Defense Forces (IDF), and she looked forward to joining them. She completed her IDF service as an officer, studied graphic design, married, and became a mother at the age of twenty-two.

But Orit, a natural leader, had tasted the power to make a difference, and she rejoined the army three years after she left. In no time, she became the officer in charge of training for several women's units. At the University of Haifa, she earned her bachelor's degree in educational management in 1987, and a master's degree, with honor, in political science in 1993.

Orit reached the rank of lieutenant colonel in the IDF. She would divorce, remarry, and have two more children. At the age of thirty-eight, Orit said, she was at a crossroads. Then the officer in charge of the Women's Corps suggested she join the exclusive IDF National Security College. She was the only woman in her class with thirty-six men. Their distrust eventually turned to admiration when Orit graduated at the top of her class as a commander colonel, and then became a general, chief officer in charge of the Women's Corps from 1997 to 2000.

SETTING PRECEDENT

She oversaw seven thousand women and quickly sought to remedy the destructive division in the military between women and men. It hadn't been that long since female soldiers were accepted for what were considered men's jobs, such as drivers, mechanics, and electricians. When she learned that the Supreme Court ruled in 1994 in favor of plaintiff Alice Miller, thereby making it unconstitutional to ban female recruits from the IDF's elite pilot's course, Orit seized the opportunity to approach IDF Chief of Staff Shaul Mofaz. She persuaded him to open the navy and combat units to female soldiers, to serve alongside men in Lebanon. The changes led to the acceptance of female soldiers in combat, areas dealing with electronics and technology, and dangerous operations that had been the domain of male soldiers.

Her advocacy helped create roles for women in leadership, and as a result, strengthened the military corps. Her influence helped promote women officers to become colonels—a change in rank that allowed them to prepare soldiers for specific professions, including field intelligence officers, and to be in charge of selection following basic training. She questioned why qualified women had not been promoted, and then assembled a group of nearly thirty exceptional women—her "sack of pearls"—whom she felt could become commanders of battalion brigades.

It was no longer possible to reverse the advancement of women in the military, she proudly told me: "There is no 'them' and 'us.' We are all in it together." Her pearls were promoted to colonels.

When her term of service ended in 2000, the position changed to Officer Advisor to the Chief of Staff Regarding Women's Issues, a transition that expressed the presence of a united army. The care for women soldiers was transferred to direct officers in charge of the different units.

CHANGING ROLES

Orit wanted to become a military attaché, a role given to generals' subordinates who have proven themselves exceptional commanders. The chief of staff persuaded Orit to take a gap year, obtain her doctorate (while collecting a salary from the army), and thereby become the commander of the unit responsible for the IDF military attachés and the international relations with foreign militaries. Orit accepted the proposition, delighted at the idea of rejoining university.

A week later, however, she was offered the position of Commissioner of the Israel Prison Service by the Minister of Public Security, Professor Shlomo Ben Ami. She would be the first woman to hold the prestigious position and would become a three-star general, an elevation from her current one star, which would place her among top leaders.

She was stunned by the offer. She realized that she would be walking into an unfamiliar "dark alley," an outsider in a world where experienced men would doubt her capabilities. She was also concerned that any failure would hurt the status of women that she had worked so hard to improve. Her internal excitement and courage replaced her trepidation, and strengthened when she learned that she, the minister's choice, was backed by the chief of staff of the IDF.

The chief of staff was unaware, however, of Orit's candidacy for prison commissioner; the last conversation she had with him was her desire to become a military attaché. She told me how anxious she was about his reaction to her news. As surprised as he was, she said, he encouraged her to grab the opportunity. He said earning a doctorate and trying to achieve two-star general in the IDF would take about four years, and it would still be just chance, compared to the opportunity to become head of the security organization in Israel.

She was relieved, and in 2000 happily accepted the position, which was announced on the radio at 4:00 p.m. on a Friday. At 3:00 p.m., she called her father and said, "Your daughter is the first female commissioner of the Israeli Prison System." She was also the first leader from the IDF, rather than the police force, and was now in charge of twelve thousand prisoners. She took off her IDF uniform that evening, and the next day wore the IPS uniform and began her term as the Commissioner of Prisons.

BUILDING TRUST

She immediately reassured the six thousand staff members that if they would convince her that they can be trusted, she would not bring in reinforcements from the IDF and would promote qualified staff from inside. Her predecessors came from the police with their personally loyal, high-ranking officers who were mostly police, and they had tapped them for leadership positions. She told the staff they should feel secure in their jobs, but in return, she expected mutual trust and support. "I trust you; give me the option to maintain this trust," she announced.

A change in atmosphere—perhaps a softer touch—was immediately apparent. Orit called the homes of staffers who called in sick to offer her assistance. She made rounds at midnight, unarmed, conversing with the staff and the prisoners, and gained their confidence. She talked with juvenile offenders, female prisoners, and terrorists. "The key is to show no fear," she said.

Orit conceived of the first in-prison rehabilitation system for men convicted of domestic violence. When she presented the concept at the International Corrections and Prison Association (ICPA) as its vice president, she was told there was no need for it. Undaunted, she implemented it in 2001. A year later, Israel was honored for having the program in place, and within a few years it was implemented in prisons worldwide.

During her three years with the prison system, Orit grappled with the steep rise in "security prisoners," those convicted of terrorist crimes, from hundreds to thousands. Terrorist prisoners were classified as "urgent and boiling," and the rest of the prison population was classified according to criminal offense. The Second Intifada started in 2000, following Minister Ariel Sharon's visit to Al Aqsa, and there were nonstop confrontations between Israeli soldiers and Palestinians in Gaza and the West Bank. Many Israeli civilians were killed by suicide bombers, despite attempts at peace negotiations.

Prison staff who lost friends and family in the conflicts felt hostile toward those prisoners. The situation demanded Orit's control with a purely professional approach, while enabling treatment conversations with the staff to overcome their difficulties. At the same time, Orit had to keep prisoners in line, because they were continuously plotting revenge. Though prison security worked 24/7, inmates still received standard care and medical treatment.

"Always remember that I was under a magnifying glass, being the first woman heading the organization," Orit told me. "I believe that a leader is dependent on the staff. They bring the results of your policy. I looked up to them as much as they looked up to me. We achieved our challenges working as a team led by me."

When security prisoners demanded improved conditions, she responded, either directly or through her staff, that inmates were neither eligible to make demands, nor did they have the right to intimidate staff. They can just ask for it, she said, while demands are made by the system toward them. She protected the staff's sovereignty.

Orit continued her mission to advance the position of women, promoting those with merit to the rank of lieutenant colonel and colonel, which made them part of prison management, and she appointed women as wardens of prisons. She cultivated her replacement, who became the second woman to head the Prison Service, who was followed in the job by the woman who is presently in charge. I told her she created quite a legacy.

Orit shared with me a burden she carried, of the suicide of one of her young female soldier officers in training. "I still remember her thanking me for listening to her for three hours before she shot herself," Orit said. "We failed to save her life, despite the team headed by myself. The trauma accompanies me from then, and will forever."

Orit retired from the prison and opened her own company to work with the United Nations and NATO, mostly in Africa. She is chair of Gesher, an NGO of more than three hundred influencers, including ministers, mayors, and journalists, that works to build relationships between Orthodox and secular Israelis. Orthodox youth, for example, visit secular schools to share their thoughts and beliefs. Another project guides women in decision-making for national security issues. She was a member of the Council of Peace and Security, part of an initiative that organizes meetings between retired Israeli and Jordanian generals; has been a board member of the leading organization for autistic children; and promotes governmental aid for disadvantaged communities.

———◦•◦———

Orit was president of the International Women's Forum, and has extended membership in the group to women in Israel's periphery to help them promote themselves. She is active with the American-Israel Friendship League and volunteers with Partnership 2000 to connect the Jewish community in Venezuela with Israel. Orit mentors CEOs from the Bank of Israel and the government's Internal and Foreign Department offices; works with Reichman University on research about terrorism in prisons; and is a frequent international lecturer about prison security, terror inmates, prison intelligence, gangs, prison privatization, and prisoner release. She was Vice president of the ICPA for nine years, and in 2011 was honored with "Outstanding contribution to the ICPA" and life membership.

GADEER KAMAL-MREEH

SENIOR ENVOY OF THE JEWISH AGENCY FOR ISRAEL TO THE JEWISH FEDERATION OF GREATER WASHINGTON

"This is who I am: a complex of identities, of East and Western, Arabic and Hebrew and English, and Washington, DC, and Daliyat al-Karmel, and this is beautiful."

AT TWELVE, GADEER KAMAL-MREEH HAD enough confidence in herself and her skills as a journalist to convince the local cable TV station manager to give her a job. She started as a volunteer and then she hosted her first TV show. Fast-forward two decades, and Gadeer became the first Druze woman to anchor a prime-time Arabic, and then Hebrew-language, news program on Israeli television. She would soon add to her resume another couple of firsts: the first female Druze Knesset member, and the first Druze to serve as a Senior Envoy of the Jewish Agency for Israel to the Jewish Federation of Greater Washington.

Born in 1984 in the Druze town of Daliyat al-Karmel, near Haifa, Gadeer has steadily navigated a path from her upbringing in a conservative, patriarchal society to a series of influential and international positions. Along the way she has mentored young women and is an advocate of equality for all minorities in Israel.

"You don't wake up in the morning and say, okay, what is next— which glass ceiling should I break next?" she told me. "It is rather a way of living. Let's change the system. Let's challenge the society we live in."

In 2021 Gadeer joined The Jewish Agency for Israel, serving as a special liaison to the Jewish Federation of Greater Washington, DC. She worked with Hillel International to share her story, bring the diversity and complexity of Israel's story to America, and discuss issues related to minorities, shared society, potential, and challenges in Israeli society. As one of the few Israelis that the agency has sent periodically to the United States to help Americans better connect with Israel and to strengthen the relationship between these communities, Gadeer believes that "we share the same values and relate to each other by our identities, the way we live, our challenges and our goals."

She attributes her success to her parents' ability to see the potential in their two daughters and two sons, instilling in them, from an early age, self-confidence and the idea that with hard work they could achieve anything.

A SOCIAL CHANGE AGENT

She has always loved to engage with people. She was a Scout, served on various committees in school, and frequently represented her village in discussions about social issues. She earned her bachelor's degree from Bar-Ilan University in social science and medical imaging as an ultrasound technician, and her master's in international relations from the University of Haifa, specializing in negotiation and decision-making in international relations.

Gadeer said she was born to be a journalist, a role through which she could change people's perceptions about individuality, discrimination, and success. She also symbolizes the beauty and complexity of Israeli society. Not only were challenges common in every role she undertook, she also sought to express a modern voice in a conservative society. And, unlike most people who enter politics from the industrial center, from cities like Jerusalem or Tel Aviv, Gadeer came from the periphery of Israel, which suffers from huge gaps in almost every aspect of life, from lack of manufacturing to infrastructure to welfare and education.

Rather than erode Gadeer's determination, that gap drove her to develop social initiatives. She was educated from a very early stage in her life to be a social change agent who must play an active role as an involved citizen. She was a member of student council and municipal education committees. She participated in local and national panels, conferences, and events in order to empower women and minorities, and to share their voices, vision, and challenges on the national and international stages.

Gadeer's ambitions extend well beyond representation of the Druze community. "One of the interesting things that I implement through my work, especially when we are talking about leadership, is not to limit yourself, to box yourself into a stereotype, like 'I am a Druze,' or 'I am an Israeli,' but looking beyond. We are global citizens, too, and must engage at this level, too.

"True leaders have to prioritize, but not work in a narrow prism of serving just one specific sector, in order to highlight issues. We must see the macro perspective and be active through multiple layers. I cannot limit my work saying, 'Okay, I'm Druze, so I am going to serve 150,000 Druze, and that's it.' I am part of the Arab sector, which includes Circassians, Muslims, Bedouins, Christians—the non-Jewish sector in Israel. So I represent and serve them proudly, as well. When working at the national level, I serve the entire Israeli population, too, and beyond. As a human being, I am a citizen of the globe. There are global challenges in the twenty-first century for all of us, and we must see the entire picture and cooperate and work together as global leaders."

Her philosophy about leadership requires an awareness of people's different needs, communicating with everyone, and caring for all. Arab Muslims, she said, face unique challenges that Circassians may not. The northern Bedouins are better off economically compared to the southerners, where some still live in tents. The Arab sector is facing an unprecedented crime wave: in 2021, 126 citizens were killed, half of whom were under the age of thirty. Druze, in recent years, are facing crucial challenges regarding illegal building, economic gaps, sense of belonging, equality, and even questions regarding identity.

"At the national level, Israel is politically divided," Gadeer said. "There is an unprecedented crisis of identity. Israelis are divided fifty-fifty into groups: Jews-Arabs, right-left. We are a polarized society, and history has taught us what happens to polarized societies. This is one of the major challenges that our society is facing and will face in the coming years. After seventy-five years of the establishment of the state of Israel, we are still dealing with the question, 'who are we?'"

SEEKING EQUALITY

The announcement of the Nation-State Law was a major catalyst in Gadeer's decision to enter politics. On August 4, 2018, she was an anchorwoman with the Israeli Public Broadcasting Corporation covering the Druze rally against the Nation-State Law, live from Rabin Square.

People were chanting: "Equality, Equality, Equality."

"Those were their demands. To be equal citizens in the Jewish State," Gadeer said. "Israel has no constitution yet, but we have Basic Laws. Those Basic Laws are going to form the constitution of the future. This law, specifically, is going to be our identity, our opening chapter. The lack of equality as the foundation, as the most important value in a democracy, is problematic. We don't have a problem with the law; we know that this is the historic homeland of the Jewish people. We have a problem with what was not written with the law: equality.

"When I was in Knesset, I ordered for comparative research, and we found that in so many countries around the world, equality was enshrined in their constitutions," she continued. "Twice I tried to include this important value, equality amendment, when I served in the Knesset, but we didn't succeed. I was disappointed to see that, as a Druze woman, I am educating Jewish members of Knesset about the true meaning of Zionism."

Gadeer emphasized that the Druze have proven their loyalty to the state of Israel since its establishment. Roughly 82 percent of men in the small Druze community enlist in the Israel Defense Forces (IDF), a higher rate than in the Jewish community that conscripts at a rate of around 74 percent. "Unlike Jews, it is not written in our religion that we have a promised land, so we are loyal first to the country that we are born in. Therefore, we are loyal to Israel. And seeing the Nation-State Law that came and divided us into A and B, to Jews and non-Jews, is very problematic. It is wrong for us, for our identity in a democratic country."

Civic inequality extends to the national budget as well, she said. "When you are born to a non-Jewish community, you get less. The budget that goes to Jews and non-Jews in Israel, to Jewish towns and non-Jewish towns, to Jewish students and non-Jewish students, and in every other aspect of life, is different."

When Benny Gantz invited Gadeer to join the Blue and White party, she told him in their first meeting about her goal to amend the Nation-State Law. "I explained to him that I know that we cannot cancel this problematic law," she said. "We know that this is the Jewish state. This is a basic law, but we need to make an important amendment to add terms about equality. This is why I agreed to enter politics."

She served with the Blue and White Party and in 2020 was offered to be a minister. But through the new formation of the unity government, Benny Ganz and Bibi Netanyahu refused to make the important amendment in the Nation-State Law, to ensure civic equality for all Israelis and in coalition agreements. She refused to be a minister and moved to the Yesh Atid party. During that time, she chaired the Israel-Switzerland parliamentary friendship group and cochaired the Israel-

Germany friendship group. She was a member of the Interior and Environment Committee, the Advancement of Women's Status and Gender Equality Committee, and the special committee for fighting crime within the Arab sector. Gadeer chaired the Caucus for Planning, Zoning and Industrial Areas, and the Caucus for the Advancement of Druze Women.

She told me a story that helped me understand the conflict she faced about joining the political world as a modern woman from a conservative society. During the month it took her to make the difficult decision, she discussed her internal debate only with her husband, Shadi. Still, the news leaked out. "My husband told me my uncle called," Gadeer said. "It turned out that he knew I was offered to join politics. I didn't know how my relatives were going to react and I was not sure that they will accept it. I didn't know if I'm going to cross a limit or a border or a red line by simply being a candidate. And then my husband said, 'He's very proud of you. Yes, do it!'"

Later, when Gadeer complained of a pain in her elbow, Shadi jokingly said it came from "paving the way."

She also shared the story about the first official visit she made with Gantz to Sheikh Amin Tarif, the Druze community spiritual leader. "It was the first time in which a Druze female entered his home as a political candidate. I was the only woman in the room. I was wearing a white scarf on my neck out of respect to religious women," she said. "Benny Gantz said, 'Can I sit near you on the same sofa?'

"I told him, 'Guess what? I don't know. I am the first to do it.' So, he sat near me," Gadeer said. "And it was okay."

COMMUNITY INFLUENCE

By aspiring to improve the lives of others, and demonstrating to a conservative society that women can be leaders, Gadeer became a role model to Druze women. Although the Druze religion is one of few in the world in which a woman can request a divorce without the consent of her husband, she described the ongoing debate in the Druze community over driver's licenses, which are not allowed for religious women. "In recent months, brave women are having campaigns to say, 'whoa, it's the twenty-first century. You can trust us. We can lead. We can be an independent, mature, responsible component of this society by simply driving,'" Gadeer said. "They say the motive is to protect us [women], but it makes no sense."

Most Druze are secular, Gadeer told me, with less than 15 percent belonging to the religious sector. "But the meaning of secularism in the Western world is totally different from ours," she explained. "I am secular, but I am still conservative in the way of how to act, what to wear, what to say. A woman in our religion is very important and expected to be modest and noble in how she acts, how she speaks. So, although I consider myself secular, you are not entirely and absolutely a secular person. You are still respectful and maintain a unique heritage. It's rooted in the way we live.

"Druze are a very rooted people who don't stray far or move around very much," she pointed out. "If we go out to study, we return to the village. If we go to work, we return to sleep in our homes. Because the village is the heritage, it is the identity. The sense of belonging is very strong and what we seek to maintain."

Daliyat al-Karmel, the largest Druze village in Israel, has seventeen thousand residents and is fifteen kilometers from Haifa, a modern city. Still, the Druze marry within their own community. After meeting her future husband, Shadi, in a Druze internet chat room, they went on a date in the village. "He was in the IDF, I was at university, and we didn't know each other," Gadeer said. "In that way we succeeded in maintaining this beauty. It means you discover the world, you explore the open world as a global citizen, but you also go back home."

DEFINING HER WORLD VIEW

In December 2020, Gadeer decided to take time out from politics. When asked if she would rejoin politics, she didn't rule out a future run. She is part of the Young Global Leaders of the World Economic Forum and declares: "I always seek to improve my skills, knowledge, and experience—initially in my country that I care for, because it is my home. It's my identity. It is who am I. It is important for me as Gadeer to bring leadership skills to my country, and to work in order to build a better future. And then, of course, I am involved and engaged as a responsible leader in the global arena, where I try to solve global challenges.

"Climate change influences our life on many levels," she said. "It is already a huge crisis facing many countries, so this is one example of how united actions must be taken and requires us all to cooperate and work together. It is not a problem of one country, or one nation, or one culture."

Inequality faced by minorities is another passionate topic for Gadeer that extends to the global stage. We talked about democracy in Israel, especially inequality in the periphery, where most minorities live. I quoted the Declaration of Independence, chapter thirteen, where it is written: "Israel will ensure complete equality of all of its inhabitants, irrespective of religion, race, or sex."

To that, Gadeer responded: "Where are we seventy-five years after that? There is a gap between political agendas, and that vision and what our identity means presently. Israel is the historic homeland of the Jewish people. This is the fact. But we must add the important value of equality. I am talking about civil equality. Israel must ensure complete equality of its inhabitants, and be at the same time a Jewish state at the national level."

I saw that Gadeer's love for Israel is beyond question. "It is amazing how much I feel Israeli, sometimes more than Israelis," she told me. "I remember every Independence Day, my father decorated the car with our country's flags. We traveled to Haifa to see the fireworks, to celebrate the state of independence of our state as Israelis."

Her father was a contractor, and his best friends and colleagues were Jews. Almost every Saturday they hosted a Jewish family in their home or were invited out. "We are very integrated," Gadeer said. "We were not raised in a way that said, 'You are a minority in the Jewish state.' No. 'You are an integral part of this state, and this country belongs to you, too.'

"Although I am not a Jew, as a Druze, I feel connected to this nationality, to the collective consciousness of Israelis," she said. "And guess what? I live in peace with that. It's very beautiful to live out these identities on different levels. But when my country took it to the extreme—

to make it the dominant factor of our identity by saying, this is the Jewish state, period, without including me as an equal citizen—this was a problem."

When I asked why the Nation-State Law should not change more dramatically and state that Israel is a country for all its citizens, Gadeer scoffed. Having run three successful campaigns in two years, she said that she's realistic. "We broke records," she said, "25,000 votes just from my sector, the Druze sector. It means I know what we need to do, and I cannot promise things that I know I cannot do. Some people said we should cancel the Nation-State Law. I said nobody will succeed. The Druze sector is 1.8 percent. The Arab sector is something like 21 percent. You must understand your power, your limited power, in this case."

LIFE IN THE UNITED STATES

We turned our discussion to the present chapter of Gadeer's life, as the first non-Jewish senior envoy with the Jewish Agency representing Israel in Washington, DC. She said her work is crucial, especially at this specific time. She collaborates with the Jewish Federation to "represent the diversity, complexity, and beauty of Israeli society," that Gadeer said "is so important, because the majority of Jewish and non-Jewish communities living here in North America are less aware of that."

To illustrate her point, Gadeer told me about the time she and her family took a weekend hike, and she shouted in Arabic to tell her children to slow down. A man approached them and said, "Hi, hello—Arabic, Morocco?" Gadeer told him, "No, Israel," and he said, "Israel? Don't you say Palestine?" Gadeer said, "No, Israel—we are Israelis." He said, "What? Israel? Arabs? Arabic?" Gadeer said, "Yes, we are Arabs living in Israel, almost 21 percent of the population." He said, "What?"

"I was shocked," Gadeer told me. "I looked at my husband. I told him, 'Do you know what? This is why we need to be here.' To educate, at first. It became so trendy to talk about Israel, to criticize Israel, sometimes even without knowing where Israel exists on the map, or who is living in Israel, and what is happening in Israel, and why it is happening in Israel."

She continued: "We are not perfect, but we have to bring those messages of complexity, of diversity, of challenges, of potential, to our brothers and sisters here—the six million Jewish members in North America. The relationship with them is special and important to us all. It relies on mutual values. So, it is very important to bring this diversity, to share our voices, to talk about who we are."

NEW APPROACHES TO OLD CHALLENGES

Part of Gadeer's job is to collaborate with Hillel International at universities and on campuses. She sees how the Boycott, Divestment, Sanctions (BDS) movement is thriving. "I always say I am not here to provide Kim Jong-un advocacy," she told me. "I will not come and teach Americans that we are perfect, that we are absolutely right. That we are pink, gold, and that we are 100 percent right. No, there is a gray zone. Israel is a very, very complicated state. We must be able to bring the whole picture, I say, seeing the 'warts and all.'

"My role is to highlight the beautiful faces of Israel, and to be able to talk about the less beautiful faces of Israel," she said. "Imperfection is part of managing countries. It's intrinsic to the international arena. There isn't one perfect country in this world, including modern Western liberal democracies. Each country is facing its set of domestic challenges and regional problems; and so are we. Israel is a young state and works hard to better itself. We made mistakes in the past, and presently will make more. Our neighbors, too, made and are making mistakes—there is no simple dichotomy of black and white, wrong and right. We are living in a very complicated region with complicated struggles.

"One of my main goals, especially when I meet students at campuses and universities, is to foster meaningful dialogues and constructive discussions," Gadeer said. "Sometimes we open maps, question, think, and rethink our opinions together about what could be done to help resolve these issues. To educate people and to strengthen their involvement as social agents, as involved citizens, instead of doing superficial advocacy. We rely on knowledge to build a better future for us all.

"And guess what?" Gadeer said. "I believe we are mature enough, evolved enough, and robust enough as a nation, as a state, to talk about all of these aspects, and to dive deeper. To ask ourselves who we are, and to trust the process of spiritual growth as a society.

"I don't see many other countries bringing someone from their minority population, who was a former member of Parliament in an opposition party, to deliver this complexity to the rest of the world," she observed. "It's a very powerful statement, in my mind."

By way of challenge, I pointed out that Gadeer is a minority who was able to achieve despite inequality and discrimination. I said that Israel provides the means to become successful. Gadeer agreed: "Of course. Of course. I always say, 'Look at me. I am a walking example of who we are.'

"One day you can be the simple Druze woman, asking your mother in-law how to cook traditional Druze dishes and participate in traditional ceremonies in your village; and the same day I traveled abroad to represent my state in an important conference, as a successful liberal career woman, as a politician." She concluded: "So this, I would not say dissonance or contrast, but this is who I am: a complex of identities, of East and Western, Arabic and Hebrew and English, and Washington, DC, and Daliyat al-Karmel—and this is beautiful."

PNINA TAMANO-SHATA

LAWYER, JOURNALIST, POLITICIAN, FORMER
MEMBER OF KNESSET

"Even though I was only three, I remember being brought up looking toward Jerusalem."

THOUSANDS OF ETHIOPIAN JEWS JOURNEYED north to Sudan in 1984, hoping to fulfill their goal of living in Israel. Three-year-old Pnina Tamano-Shata was among them. Along with her family, she made aliyah to Israel with the help of Operation Moses—and years later became Minister of Aliya and Absorption, the first Ethiopian-born minister in the Israeli government.

Despite her early life in disease-filled refugee camps, a dangerously unsupervised boarding school, and crippling poverty and racism, Pnina successfully integrated into Israeli society. An activist, lawyer, and member of Knesset, she improved the lives of fellow Ethiopians in Israel and—after finding her own—helped give voice to all immigrants. She is the proud mother of two children and lives in Petah Tikvah.

I sat across the desk from this warm and attractive young woman, waiting to hear how she became a valued advocate for *olim* (Jewish immigrants). Pnina read my mind.

"My story is all here," she said, pointing to two pictures on her desk. One was of her receiving an honor named for Prime Minister Menachem Begin, a moment she said she will never forget. The other was of the airplane that carried her to Israel nearly forty years ago.

She described her emotional meeting with the pilot who saved her life. "Benhaim Israel was the son of Holocaust survivors," she said. "On his way to my office, he told me that he mentioned to his mother that he was on his way to meet the three-year-old girl he saved, who is now an Israeli minister." The modest man told Pnina that the real heroes are the thousands of refugees, many of whom died on the journey, not the pilots who merely flew planes out of Sudan in the middle of the night.

Before telling me about her journey, Pnina explained the deep connection that Ethiopian Jews, or members of the Lost Tribe, have to Israel. She described the desire to get to Jerusalem as an Ethiopian Jew's center of living.

"Even though I was only three, I remember being brought up looking toward Jerusalem," she said. "The Qasim, who is our spiritual leader, led the dream and inspired spirit and hope that it will happen. The dream to come to Israel, and the spirit and hope that this will happen, has been carried out for generations."

Pnina's family goes back six generations to Abba Mahari, a Jewish monk and prominent rabbi whose trip to Israel in 1862 was thwarted by the Red Sea that, unlike Moses, he could not part. "Imagine that Abba Mahari tried to reach Israel to fulfill the dream of Jews' desires to live in the homeland when Theodore Hertzl, the father of Zionism, was two years old," she said, adding that her relative was well ahead of his time.

"This is my ancestry," Pnina said. "I am the fifth generation since then. One hundred and twenty years later, I arrived in Israel as part of Operation Moses, and today I am a minister for the government. What an amazing story!"

In 1984 Pnina's grandfather and proud spiritual leader gave the signal to leave Wuzaba in northern Ethiopia and journey to Jerusalem. The family had already lost several children and faced death threats for being Jewish, so they followed their hearts and their faith. They knew that the sacrifices asked of them might be overwhelming and that they might never arrive.

They reached Sudan when Pnina's mother was nine months pregnant. She gave birth at the refugee camp to a little girl, Salamilac-Ariella, who today is called Bracha, or blessing. Pnina remembered having porridge with cinnamon. She was exhausted from the trek, during which people all around her died from dehydration, hunger, and pirate attacks. Unfortunately, the difficulties continued. The camp became a deathtrap filled with disease. Ultimately, four thousand out of fourteen thousand Ethiopian refugees died on the journey and in the camps in Sudan, and many children arrived in Israel without parents.

The refugees were stuck in the camps for many months as a wave of American Jews making aliyah took priority for relocation. One night in November they learned that the Operation Moses airlift had begun. More than seven thousand Ethiopians were to be flown out of Sudan, a covert operation carried out by Israel in collaboration with its national intelligence agency, Mossad, along with the CIA and Sudanese State Security.

Pnina's father decided quickly to split the family between two trucks that pulled into the camp. Pnina's mother, the newborn, and her eleven-year-old sister, Elisa, went one way, and Pnina and the rest of her siblings—sixteen-year-old brother Isaiah and sister Malka, and eight-year-old sister Devora—followed their father. They traveled that night in silence for many hours before arriving at a plane called Hercules that would take them to Israel.

One man, having never seen an aircraft before, took his daughter by the hand and ran into the desert, returning only after he was assured of their safety. Her own father told her that the illuminated plane looked like a big scary bird on fire.

Pnina remembered eating candies and bananas during the flight. Her mother and two sisters, however, were not among the passengers. Their truck had broken down and was taken by Sudanese soldiers. It would be many months before they were reunited.

In Israel, the family reconnected with Pnina's oldest sister, Dina, who had recently given birth and settled in Pardes Hanna's absorption center. But the news about her mother sent Dina into a depression that interfered with caring for her newborn. She was angry that her father neglected to take care of her mother and failed to bring the entire family to Israel. Her dream of living in Jerusalem was broken.

Pnina also felt unbearable loneliness and remembered praying every day with her father to bring her mother safely to Israel. Finally, one year later, the Mossad rescued the remaining refugees. All that time, Pnina learned, little sister Elisa had taken care of her newborn sister and mother while in Sudan.

"I remember a very sick woman and a baby full of wounds," Pnina said about the tearful reunion at the hospital. She kissed the baby, but not her unrecognizable mother. Eventually, Pnina's mother told her she remembered hallucinating from heat stroke in the desert. The vision she had of Pnina—with open arms, calling for her—kept her alive.

LIFE IN ISRAEL

Pnina's parents did not speak Hebrew and had difficulty adjusting. Their very active daughter, however, fell in love with the new language and Israeli songs, and *felt* Israeli right away. Four years later, the family moved to Petah Tikva and started life in the Israeli community. Pnina's parents encouraged her education and helped their bright daughter believe that she could become whatever she wanted. Economically, the family struggled. One after another, the children were sent to a boarding school, and at the age of eleven Pnina was already working menial jobs at an old age home and cleaning hospitals.

She felt independent at the boarding school, happy and very energetic. Though some called her a hyperactive, she was a very good student. She believed she was doing the right thing, but worried about the separation from her family.

Pnina arranged her own bat mitzvah—her parents did not know how, nor were they financially able to do so—and prepared the memorable party. Her mother, who lived her entire life in an Ethiopian village without electricity, did not know how to bake.

Discrimination and racism in Israel plagued Pnina at every turn. She told me about the time when her two white, male companions were allowed into a club, but she and another Ethiopian girl were not. Angry and unwilling to accept rejection, she climbed over the fence. When she went shopping, people eyed her suspiciously, as if her dark skin were the sign of a thief. The most shameful situation, she said, was when she was prevented from donating to a blood drive. At the time, it was falsely believed that Ethiopians in Israel carried the AIDS virus.

Pnina said that those hurtful experiences were meant to be, that the physical and emotional scars of discrimination drove her fight for change. But first she had to resolve the conflict in her heart, between her love for Israel and the treatment she received from her new countrymen. Her need to be heard grew stronger. She loved to sing, but understood that the right way to fulfill her goal was to study law.

After the army, Pnina went to law school at Ono Academic College and worked with children at risk. She was deputy chairman of the national Ethiopian Student Association, and created social-action committees that held demonstrations. Her anger came across in several television interviews as thoughtful advocacy. She believed that the challenges Ethiopians faced to integrate were compounded by active discrimination, including being the target of police violence.

When I asked Pnina how her parents felt about living in Israel, she said: "My parents lived their dream. They wanted to come to Israel, and they achieved it. In their mind, they arrived in paradise, and there was nothing but smiles and thanks to the Creator for reaching their dream."

Then she repeated a quote that her parents would have used, if they were asked the same question: "If the Zadakim dreamt and did not arrive in Jerusalem, who are we to complain?"

"You can see that this generation was a different one—admirable, full of smiles and naivety and love for Israel," Pnina said. "For them, there were no difficulties." Her mother swore that she would never disparage the state of Israel and would continue to be thankful, even when their electricity was disconnected. They would never complain about anything.

Pnina the activist became Pnina the journalist, who turned to politics after five years at Channel One. She was the first Ethiopian-born woman to become a member of the Knesset, in 2013, as a member of the Yesh Atid party.

HONORING ANCESTORS, LOOKING FORWARD

In 2020 she was appointed Minister of Aliya and Absorption, the first Ethiopian-born minister in the Israeli government. She improved education, mental health, medical, and social services programs, increased funding for absorption centers, and developed training initiatives for immigrants. She conceived of a monetary gift program to attract doctors and engineers to settle in the Negev, recruited social workers to the area, and developed a program to attract immigrants to Israel's growing technology field.

At the very beginning, in 2020, she initiated Operation Tzur Israel, which welcomed two thousand immigrants and set the tone for her first term as minister. In her second term in the Thirty-Sixth Israeli government, she allowed three thousand immigrants to enter, an operation that was followed by many other opportunities for immigrants.

Following a long period, when thousands of immigrants were denied the right to be united with their families in Israel, Pnina worked with a Jewish agency to build absorption centers in the country for this purpose.

When events escalated between Russia and Ukraine in 2022, Pnina established requirements for the absorption of a new wave or immigrants, eligible under the Right to Return. She initiated emergency communications with the government, which resulted in the allocation of apartments for rent across Israel. With the severity of the Russia-Ukraine war increasing, Pnina successfully led Operation Coming Home, to rescue and absorb immigrants from Russia, Ukraine, and Belarus. During her two-and-a-half-year term, she was responsible for the aliya of 120,000 newcomers from around the world, a historic record in the past two decades of Israel's history.

At the end of 2022, more than sixty thousand new immigrants had arrived, while Pnina worked with the Minster of Treasury to provide millions of Israeli shekels to absorption efforts and programs that included education, jobs, and housing for the newcomers. She was also active in providing financial aid to the immigrants for their daily needs.

Pnina cooperated with the IDF to absorb the immigrants as they landed and help to place them at hotels across the country. She initiated proceedings for them to get Israeli citizenship, a process that still continues, with the arrival of many more immigrants.

She is responsible for helping pass new laws regarding abused women and representation in family court. She promoted the approval of licensing of immigrant doctors, to be able to help in the medical field in Israel. She produced positions geared toward professionals to come to Israel, especially in the field of medicine.

In June 2021 Pnina received the first Magen Begin Prize for Israeli Leadership, in recognition of her work in the Knesset and promoting the same agenda of equality embraced by Menachem Begin. "Begin knew even then that the most important task is not only to build a state, but also to build a strong, cohesive, and united society," she said at the time. "Most of the struggles I fought against discrimination and racism are because I believe in Israeli society. I believe that only when we learn to create a space of belonging and equal opportunity for all, only then will we become an exemplary society."

In 2022, on behalf of the Nefesh B'Nefesh organization, Pnina received a certificate of appreciation, named after Sylvan Adams, from the Zion Builders Award, for her efforts for new *olim* (immigrants on aliyah) over the years. In 2023, with the election to the Twenty-Fifth Knesset, Pnina was appointed chairwoman of the Committee for the Advancement of Women's Status and Gender Equality.

TAL OHANA

MAYOR OF YERUHAM

———◦—◦———

"In the desert, we can try different ideas. We can be innovative and wild. We can bring new blood into Yeruham."

AFTER TRAVELING HOURS UPON HOURS across the Negev desert, I passed the sign for Yeruham, with its iconic image of the Desert Twins monument. This was no mirage. Neither was the "well of mercy" I saw upon entering Yeruham Lake Park, where Hagar and Ishmael were said to have satisfied their thirst after being expelled from the home of Abraham.

Even more extraordinary than the geologic formations and ancient history would be the town's diverse community of eleven thousand Romanian, North African, Indian, and Persian immigrants, as well as Orthodox Jews and National Zionists. There are twenty-five synagogues, and multiple schools to satisfy the different cultures and religions in the periphery—people who are united by their Zionism and their respect for each other.

The town of Yeruham was founded in 1951, but in 641 CE the Byzantines had used its dusty spice road through the Negev. Now the road leads to Sde Boker, the home of the late prime minister David Ben-Gurion, and the oil road leads to Be'er Sheva. Yeruham is bordered by the Bedouin village Rakhma and is blessed by the presence of one of nature's marvels, a *makhtesh*, or crater, that is a smaller version of Mitzpe Ramon but considered by locals to be superior in beauty.

Mayor Tal Ohana, the first woman to hold the position in the town's history, leads with a vision shared by Ben-Gurion, who said that "Israel's capacity for science and research will be tested in the Negev and this effort will determine the fate of the state of Israel and the standing of our people in the history of mankind."

Tal greeted me at her home with a newborn girl in her arms. To my delight, I discovered a young woman who, despite her fatigue, radiated enormous love as she introduced her baby to a new visitor. I looked around, and the view of a sandy desert mountain transported me to biblical times. There was a striking difference that day between Tal the mother, and Tal the mayor and businesswoman I had met months earlier, and I was happy to get to know both.

Tal was born in 1984 to a poor Moroccan family that had immigrated to Israel. Her mother cared for five children by herself and worked as a teacher, while her father worked hard as the owner of a bus company, after serving in the Israel Defense Forces. He recognized the need to lift his family out of poverty but overextended himself, and after thirty years of operation, had to shut down his business.

"I inherited from both of them," Tal told me. "One, to be very sensitive to people, and two, to never stop. To be very ambitious, to work hard, to dream big, to be innovative, creative, and never to give up, even if I fail along the way."

She dreamed of becoming a successful businesswoman, like her father, but also loved working shoulder to shoulder with his Bedouin employees, and the relationships she developed. After serving in the army, where she cared for soldiers from broken homes and lower economic backgrounds, she realized her preference for more human-focused work. She visited Morocco for the first time when she was twenty-four, and she saw the villages where her parents and relatives lived. Upon returning home, she organized many trips for groups of fifteen students from Yeruham to visit Morocco. She has visited Morocco thirty-five times.

Tal drew on the social and leadership skills she developed as a teenager, and over many years she brought more than a hundred Moroccan Jews to visit her beloved country. She earned her BA degree in organizational sociology from the Max Stern Yezreel Valley College in the north, and a master's from the Lauder School of Government, Diplomacy and Strategy at Reichman University in Herzliya.

"Tal Ohana is an Israeli hero," said Professor Uriel Reichman, a legal scholar and the founder of Reichman University. "She took it upon herself to lead a difficult area in the south of Israel with a mixed population and tremendous economic pressure. She needed the support of the population while fighting the authorities and the non-modern attitudes of some of the community.

"She is a great example of what I would like all our graduates to take this level of leadership upon themselves," Reichman continued. "Tal devotes her life to Israeli society, bringing people together and uniting different parts of the country. A young person undertaking such a mission is remarkable."

Between 2004 and 2009, Tal held managerial positions at the Rashi Foundation, the ISEF Foundation, and the Yeruham Community

Center. From 2009 to 2010, she served as the director of the Young People's Association in Yeruham and focused on youth at risk, leadership, and settlement. In 2011 she established a movement for Zionist activities in Morocco, in which hundreds of youths from the Jewish communities of Casablanca, Marrakech, Tangier, Agadir, and Rabat participated in several programs in Israel and abroad. This was in addition to encouraging the immigration and absorption of families, as well as fundraising and support for welfare, health, and relationships between Jews and Muslims in Morocco, supported by Keren Leyedidut, an international fellowship for Christians and Jews that supports aliyah.

FINDING MEANING, MAKING CHANGES

Tal settled in Yeruham, she said, because that's where she found meaning. She felt that if she did not take responsibility for Yeruham's future, nothing would happen and nothing would change. She also came to the realization that to create change as a social entrepreneur, she needed to be a part of the government and get involved in politics.

She became deputy mayor at the age of twenty-six, at the request of then-Mayor Michal Biton, then became acting mayor. "I didn't understand what he saw in me," she said. "But he believed in my potential and told me that I had a lot to give back to this community." As deputy mayor, Tal tackled such issues as employment, education, culture, welfare, health, and early childhood. When she was elected mayor in 2018, her agenda expanded to improve the quality of life and encourage development and social mobility. She aspired to think differently, rather than repeat what was done in the past, so she worked to gain people's trust and built a team that shared her goals. "I wished to be a leader of the people, not a leader of missions," she said.

She spent time at Harvard in the States, where she met Rabbi Jonathan Sachs, who said: "Every Jewish leader must tell the story in the way that everyone feels like they belong." When she asked herself if her community felt part of the story she was telling, her answer was no.

So, she pivoted. Rather than focus on the town's poor, she focused on the privileged newcomers to help build a bridge between the two communities. For example, she told educators she would not approve budgets if underprivileged children were barred from a special robotics program and other after-school activities that help with social mobility.

Tal strove to improve Yeruham's economy, and she proudly told me that the town is no longer known just for its supply services but is a valued business and technology hub. She is chairwoman of a committee representing Yeruham for economic development. There is a great interest in creating an infrastructure to develop drones in Yeruham, in partnership with the business sector and the government, she said.

ECONOMIC STRENGTH THROUGH CANNABIS, TECHNOLOGY

The young mayor gained national attention when she proposed that Yeruham develop cannabis for pharmaceutical purposes. The idea came to her during a sleepless night, having read that half of the workforce at Yeruham's glass factory were being fired and operations partially shuttered.

The next morning, she walked to the site, where reporters asked her how the employees would be compensated. She realized that unemployment was reaching a level where she needed to find a way to create jobs, perhaps in a new sector.

Tal said she first heard about the cannabis business from a Russian man who called with a proposal to build a cannabis factory in Yeruham. Even though she refused the offer, she researched the cannabis industry and found a market for it in Israel. She contacted the Ministry of Health to familiarize herself with the rules and regulations, and requested that ministry officials refer to her those businesses applying for cannabis licenses, at which point she would invite them to consider locating in Yeruham. She would offer the new businesses a chance to be involved in making Yerhuam the capital town for medical cannabis in Israel. Yeruham already had a pharmaceutical factory that employed seven hundred, and another one hundred people for R&D. In her mind, Yeruham was the perfect place to develop medical cannabis in different forms.

Yeruham became the site for incubators for agriculture, industry, and academics. At a recent conference they were classified as "Economic Commandos," she said. Tal realized that from a social entrepreneur she had become an economic one, and spent much of her time in business meetings.

Under Tal's leadership, Yeruham has also become a site for innovation and "hackathons." MindCET, for example, is an edtech center that brings together entrepreneurs, educators, and researchers to develop educational technology in Israel and beyond. One of its goals is to reduce the gap between high tech and education.

The participating groups stay in Yeruham for a few days to brainstorm ideas and solutions, and Yeruham and its students participate in the beta testing. Accelerated programs are being provided, dedicated to startups in their early stages. They come up with software solutions for children in kindergarten through high school, and sometimes into higher education. In one of the many unrecognized Bedouin villages, for example, a special education design was tested to accommodate Bedouin children who often live in poverty, are undereducated, and drop out. The children who arrive for accelerated studies complain about their own education system and having to be taught by Arab teachers from the north, who are culturally different.

"In the desert, we can try different ideas," Tal said. "We can be innovative and wild. We can bring new blood into Yeruham."

Her mission is to create a thousand technology jobs in Yeruham over the next five years. There are currently five companies in the technology incubator, and she has the license to build two pharmaceutical factories, with the aim of becoming functional by 2024.

One aspect of her plan to increase employment was to provide a site in Yeruham for Tech19, a technology-focused outsourcing center run by Inbar Cohen and funded by Hana Rado's Group19. I met Cohen, an impressive woman who worked for Intel and was the only woman in her division. She laughed when she told me how being laid off from Intel, and then joining Group19 to help to provide jobs in the periphery, was the best decision she ever made. Now she has a crew of five women and two men, all of whom were born in the Negev, who provide solutions in mechanical engineering, software solutions, and augmented (AR) and virtual reality solutions. Juniors on her team are trained and given courses to provide high-end solutions that Tech19 is known for. To illustrate an AR experience, Cohen explained how a team with a mechanical engineer, doctor, and chemistry professor worked to simulate the chemical reactions a pill undergoes in the mouth for it to work slowly over time. Tech19 developed the mechanical design under Cohen's leadership.

Tech19 launched in 2022, and Cohen said her customers include some of the popular companies in the center of Israel, like SynTech and crypto companies. When I asked her why companies from the center look for mechanical engineers or software developers in the periphery, she recited three reasons: "One: Zionism, to provide jobs for people in the periphery. Two: you will not find a team as dedicated as we are. And three: because of the high school here in Yeruham that provides a three-year program in mechatronics, in cooperation with the army, which provides students with the background needed to become excellent engineers."

As I left Tal and continued traveling over sandy roads, I smiled at the memory of the movie *Turn Left at the End of the World*. I had found out that it featured Yeruham and was produced by a resident. The film, about an Indian family trying to integrate into a town at the edge of the desert, portrays the hardship of the integration of multiple families of different ethnic backgrounds.

I realized that the actual residents of Yeruham have a wonderful advocate in their young mayor, a woman committed to her constituency and their economic security.

SIMA SHINE

FORMER MOSSAD HEAD OF RESEARCH AND EVALUATION, SENIOR RESEARCH FELLOW AT THE INSS

"Iran must be stopped from developing a nuclear bomb, which is the biggest strategic threat to Israel and the Middle East. Not an existential one, in the sense that I am not willing to give any outside player the ability to threaten our existence."

FOR HER STEADFAST DEDICATION TO national intelligence research, Sima Shine had the honor of lighting a torch at the sixty-seventh Independence Day ceremony at Mount Zion in 2015. She was thrilled to be there, to publicly share with the crowd of thousands her pride in Israel and shine a light on her colleagues, who work day and night to warn of any arriving danger to the security of the state. The fanfare was unusual, since Sima's crucial role in Israel's national security had always played out in secret.

During the ceremony, Knesset member Yuli Edelstein blessed the participants. "Each time we rediscover the human treasure that is latent in our nation," he said. "You are the proof that we are a startup nation."

Sima served as the head of the Research and Evaluation Division of the Mossad from 2003 to 2007, the first time this position was held by a woman. She oversaw daily and periodic evaluations of Middle Eastern and international issues, led security and intelligence dialogues with her counterparts in the international community, and was involved with political and military decision-making. She also presented the annual assessment to the Israeli president's cabinet, alongside intelligence representatives from other organizations.

Sima often joined the head of the Mossad in meetings with the prime minister, and during security deliberations she was responsible for gauging an evaluation's influence on decision-makers.

Her division was deeply involved in the activity before and after the bombing of the Syrian nuclear reactor that was built secretly with the help of North Korea. Operation Outside the Box, an airstrike against a threat to Israel's national security, was carried out on September 6, 2007, but not officially acknowledged by Israel until 2018. That was the last project Sima was involved with before retiring from the Mossad. She related to me that Meir Dagan, the director of the Mossad, jokingly told her, "What a wonderful end of career I arranged for you."

During an interview with *Israel Hayom*, Sima was asked about the similarities between her work and the television thriller *Tehran*, in which a female Israeli agent is sent to disable Iran's nuclear reactor. First, she admitted she liked the thriller, but even though she personally wasn't in operations, some of the scenes were, to her understanding, too imaginary. Then she added: "I was on assignment, of course, in a country with which we didn't have diplomatic relations, but with the knowledge and assent of the local authorities, which of course is different from the situation in the series.

"It was a strange feeling," she continued. "I flew somewhere that in other circumstances I wouldn't, and obviously, I couldn't speak Hebrew. I didn't say a word the entire flight, and sometimes I preferred to pretend I was sleeping. When I saw what countries we were flying over, it was stressful."

After her retirement from Mossad, Sima was deputy head of Strategic Affairs of Israel's National Security Council (2008–2009), and then the head of the Iranian Division as deputy director general of Israel's Ministry of Strategic Affairs (2009–2016). In this position, she was part of the Israeli interagency delegation dealing with the negotiations of the P5+1 (the UN Security Council's permanent members + Germany) with Iran on the nuclear agreement, known as the Joint Comprehensive Plan of Action (JCPOA). In recent years, Sima has been a senior research fellow at the Institute for National Security Studies (INSS). She holds an MA in political science and security studies and is a graduate of the National Security College.

FINDING HER WAY TO THE INTELLIGENCE COMMUNITY

Sima's parents arrived in Israel from the Soviet Union in 1948, during the War of Independence. They had been detained by British Mandate authorities and sent to a camp in Cyprus for more than a year. In 1949, Sima was born in Haifa, and then the family moved to Tel-Aviv. She told me how, as a young girl growing up, her grandmother always asked her to turn off the radio when piano music was played. Eventually, Sima learned that her grandmother had lost her son and daughter during World War II in a German Nazi bombing in the Soviet Union, and that Sima's aunt was such a talented pianist that she was accepted to a prestigious conservatory in Moscow, despite being Jewish. "She couldn't listen to piano music without crying," Sima said of her grandmother, who always listened to a radio channel that announced the names of

Holocaust survivors. "She had the hope to hear the names of her daughter and son that perished, but she never heard those names."

As Sima told me how these memories stayed with her, I realized how the powerful untold stories of the Holocaust continue to affect the lives of the generation of people who lived with survivors.

Sima said her school years were usual, except for two experiences she wanted to share with me. One was her very meaningful membership for many years in a youth movement, where she was also a counselor responsible for educating younger children. The work, she said, gave her the chance to emphasize values related to personal relations, as well as love and dedication to the state of Israel. The second was the Six-Day War in 1967. It was her last year in secondary school, and the first war she experienced as a grown-up—she was a child during the Sinai War in 1956. Sima remembered filling sacks with sand to protect windows, writing letters to soldiers at the front, and the difficulty she had studying for matriculation exams.

Joining military service two months later, as part of Israel's conscription, seemed the natural step. After serving as a soldier in the office of the chief of staff, Sima enrolled at Tel Aviv University in 1970 for her BA in Middle Eastern studies. Her interests led her to join "Aman"—Israeli Military Intelligence, which along with the Mossad and Shin Bet comprise Israel's intelligence community. Aman generates national intelligence reports for the prime minister and cabinet, gauges the risk of war, and produces targeted studies on nearby Arab countries.

She had been a year on the job in 1973, a junior member in Aman dealing with the Soviet Union and its presence in the Arab States, when the Yom Kippur War broke out. She was aware of the tension among the researchers as to the meaning of the military preparations on Israel's borders. Only later, with the rest of the country, did she learn that warnings about the Egyptian-Syrian military preparations were not given their due attention, because of the dangerous combination of the intelligence community's erroneous conceptions as well as political hubris. This traumatic war and the very high price paid in Israeli lives became a lasting lesson through her career in the intelligence establishment.

The war in Lebanon in 1982, against the presence of Palestinians in South Lebanon attacking the civilian population in the north of Israel, started because of the assassination attempt on the Israeli ambassador in the UK. Sima was already ten years with the Intelligence Division in Aman and followed the deepening process of Israeli involvement in Lebanon that lasted for "eighteen too-long years."

WOMEN IN THE MOSSAD

In 1990 Sima joined the Mossad, climbing the ladder from deputy head of department to the head of the Research Division, the function of which was to combine different pieces of information into a coherent picture for different purposes. "It started with the operational level to the higher political one—where to go, what will cause major damages, where are the weak spots, and what will be the political ramifications," she explained.

Sima told me about the special personnel of the Mossad, and explained that recruits are people with different skills needed for operations or the research teams. In her Research Division, roughly half of the positions were performed by women, who, Sima said, have a very important combination of professional knowledge as well as skills to deal simultaneously with different variables. There aren't enough women in top positions, Sima believes, and women are important to operations because they bring a sensitivity to the job, they can more easily fly under the radar, and they are also inherently more attuned to safety. I wondered how women deal with their seclusion from the outside world and the need, depending on their job, to live in secrecy. Sima said she felt lucky that her husband, Uri, was retired from the Mossad and she could freely talk with him about her work.

Though Sima could not disclose details about operations, I got a sense of how women were involved with the nuclear facility bombing by reading *The Mossad Amazons* by Michael Bar-Zohar and Nissim Mishal. It tells the story of a female Mossad operative who obtained the key to the room of a Syrian scientist while another female agent kept him busy in a restaurant. In the meantime, the operative duplicated and photographed information about the nuclear facility, confirming its existence.

IRAN

Given Sima's position as head of the Iranian program at the INSS in Tel Aviv, our conversation shifted to more current events, such as Israel's relationship with Iran, Iran's nuclear program, its presence in Syria, and its overall effect on Israeli security.

As difficult as it may be to deal with militant groups like Hezbollah, Hamas, and the Palestinian Islamic Jihad (PIJ), Sima told me, the real strategic threat comes from Iran's nuclear program. The joint agreement between the P5+1 and Iran, confirmed under the Obama administration in 2015, rolled back parts of the program, but had faults, Sima said. The main one was the legitimacy it gave to a comprehensive enrichment program in Iran, at any scale, as the agreement would sunset. The second, she said, was that it allowed Iran to continue research and development on advanced centrifuges, and the third related to inspection that could be more intrusive. Despite those faults, Sima told me she supported the JCPOA.

Following the departure of the United States from the nuclear agreement in May 2018 under the Trump administration, Iran began reducing gradually its commitments to the agreement and is already now a threshold nuclear state. It's only a question of political decision if and when Iran will finish the extra mile to produce a nuclear device or warhead, she said. "I hope, that in that situation, there will be an American administration that would be willing to use its military power, and Israel won't have to do it on its own," Sima said.

"I think Iran must be stopped from developing a nuclear bomb, which is the biggest strategic threat to Israel and the Middle East," she continued. "Not an existential one, in the sense that I am not willing to give any outside player the ability to threaten our existence. Iran should be worried about its own existence if it has a bomb, not the opposite."

Meanwhile, Sima said, Iran strengthens its proxies in Lebanon, Iraq, and Yemen, and establishes its military presence in Syria after coming to the support of President Assad in the civil war against him. "By doing that, Iran wants to create a territorial continuity from Iran through Iraq to Syria and Lebanon and the Mediterranean," she said. "This would allow for a land corridor that directly links Iran to Hezbollah in Lebanon. This could be a dangerous situation for Israel, alongside other fronts. Iran is a common threat to Israel and the Gulf states, and that was for a long time the basis for secret security cooperation with those countries, until the normalization agreements that were concluded with the UAE and Bahrain in 2021."

There are many more stories and conclusions from her years in the intelligence community, but Sima said there is no place for conjecture in the delicate framework of nuclear threats.

Back in 2015, during the Independence Day celebration, Jerusalem mayor Nir Barkat told the torch-lighters they were "role models whose work would positively affect many generations to come… [O]n that day the entire nation remembers the debts and expresses eternal gratitude to its sons and daughters who gave their life for the country's independence and continued existence."

Sima's important work, which was carried out largely in secret, has had a lasting impact on Israel's security and will continue to for generations to come.

PART III

THE ACADEMICS

AYELET BEN-EZER,
CEO and Vice President of Reichman University

MINA TEICHER,
Director, Emmy Noether Research Institute for Mathematics, Bar-Ilan University

SARAH ABU-KAF,
Senior Lecturer in Cross-Cultural Psychology,
Ben-Gurion University of the Negev

NIGIST MENGESHA,
Principal, Education Department of Rosh
Ha'ayin, Founder and Executive Director of the
Fidel Association

AYELET BEN-EZER

CEO AND VICE PRESIDENT OF REICHMAN
UNIVERSITY

"[Students] are our full partners. We want them to fulfill their dream in academic innovation, in social science, and the inter-woven social sciences with advanced technology."

I MET DR. AYELET BEN-EZER at noon on a day when the sun was winning its quarrel with the winter chill. The scent of lemon trees accompanied me as I walked toward her office at Reichman University. The campus looked like a quaint village where old and new coexist. Twittering birds landed on perches in a garden populated by statues, Roman artifacts, and modern sculptures. A giant eucalyptus tree drew my gaze upward, and I wondered how this abandoned military base just north of Tel Aviv became a mecca for Israel's future leaders.

Ayelet was involved from the start. A courageous young lawyer, Doctor of Law, and lecturer, she shared founder Uriel Reichman's vision for an academic institution that, over the last nearly thirty years, has produced skilled, innovative students who embrace social responsibility. The private university, the first in Israel, also created a model for the state to develop a higher education system that does not rely on public funding.

I visited on a holiday, and the campus was almost empty. A few Israelis chatted with international students during a coffee break. I heard them trying to convince their friends to extend their temporary educational visits into permanent residency in Israel. Every day, Reichman students sees themselves as ambassadors, working not only toward their degrees but helping fulfill the mission of the university: to embody Zionism and nourish humanity.

My destination was ahead of me: red, wooden cottages blanketed with ivy and surrounded by indigenous trees. What were previously homes for military officers were now populated by the university's administrative staff. The door opened, and Ayelet invited me in.

Ayelet was born in Tel Aviv in June 1963. Her parents—highly educated, intellectual, and driven—were also born in Israel. Her father's family came from Russia, and her mother's from Poland and Austria. Ayelet never knew most of her relatives from her mother's side; they were killed in the Holocaust.

AN ADVOCATE AND PIONEER FROM A YOUNG AGE

Ayelet's parents instilled an appreciation for literature, culture, and theater. "It was a house that pushed us very hard to achieve and to excel. It has its own price as well, but you can see the fruits." Ayelet is the eldest of three; one sister is a former CEO of Bank Leumi, and the youngest, also a lawyer, just completed a documentary about surrogacy and founded the surrogacy agency New Life.

When she was five, Ayelet started to play piano at a conservatory. She excelled, and for a decade performed in prestigious concerts. She understood justice and was always eager to advocate for others. At twelve, she successfully represented her peers by making the case for additional study time before an exam.

"But it's not only that," she said of her drive to make a difference. "I was a leader in the Scouts, different kinds of clubs, I took dance and jazz lessons, I participated in the track team of my high school, I played piano, learned languages. I always had the urge to lead, to excel—for doing the best I can."

I asked how she ascended to CEO and vice president of a prestigious, internationally renowned university, and she cited her involvement in many youth activities, an exchange program to the United States, and her service in the Israeli Defense Forces. And, she said, she and her sisters were shaped by her parents' encouragement for excellence. "If I got a ninety-nine," she said, "he'd ask why we didn't get one hundred."

Her journey to Reichman University began even before she knew it; she attended high school at Tichon Hadash in Tel Aviv, where Uriel Reichman had studied decades earlier.

Ayelet would become professionally entwined with Reichman and his dreams for a university when she met him at the University of Tel Aviv law school, where she was a student and Reichman was dean of faculty. "That encounter directed my life path," she said.

At sixteen, she traveled alone to the United States as an exchange student with the American Field Service. Ayelet lived with a family in Monterey, California, and a girl from North Carolina stayed in her parents' home.

"The purpose was for me to introduce Israel to my new friends in class, to tell an Israeli's story from the point of view of an adolescent," she said. She always started her lectures with an image of people riding a camel in the desert. "I said, 'This is my family,' and they believed me in the beginning. The kids in America at the time were unaware of Israel. In 1979, there was no internet exposure, no cell phone, no computer."

Because telephone calls were prohibitively expensive, Ayelet's only communication with the world, including her family, was via the postman. "He came and brought me letters every once in a while," she said.

Ayelet's English was very basic before going to America. Technically a sophomore, she was assigned to senior classes because of impressive test scores in math and other subjects. She went to two proms.

"I really felt the American experience," she said. "I think this half-year was crucial to whoever I became, because I learned to be independent."

Ayelet's family didn't have much when she was a child, all three sisters living in one room until their economic circumstances improved. "I spent a lot of time with my mom in different libraries and taking out books and swallowing them," she said. Her parents—her mother was a teacher and her father, an accountant—worked hard, and she came to understand the importance of a good education and perseverance.

Always an outstanding student, Ayelet was drafted into the army's elite intelligence Unit 8200, or "Shmone-Matayim" in Hebrew. She proudly told me that her son serves in the same unit.

LAW AND REICHMAN

She left the IDF with distinction after two years and enrolled in Tel Aviv University law school, where she got to know Reichman. She also met her now ex-husband, and the couple moved to London, where he attended business school and she worked as a solicitor. In London, barristers wear wigs and are involved in courtroom litigation. The solicitors, she said, do everything else; they prepare the other aspects of casework. At the same time, she completed her Master of Laws and finished her thesis at London University, in cooperation with Tel Aviv University. She graduated summa cum laude.

After London and a year in Switzerland, they returned to Israel. Ayelet taught Private International Law in Ramot Mishpat, which was established by Reichman. She was acknowledged as an excellent teacher, and thereafter was approached by Haifa University. There, she was a faculty member and a law teacher for five years, during which she worked on her PhD and was awarded prizes for distinction and excellence in law teaching.

The new Ramot Mishpat school, she said, would increase enrollment opportunities and accessibility at a time when it was extremely difficult to be accepted by an Israeli law school, and when many students left the country in search of an education. A few years later, Reichman asked Ayelet to join him at the Interdisciplinary Center Herzliya (IDC), the college he created in 1994 that today is known as Reichman University.

She recalled their tour of the undeveloped site in the pouring rain. "As we were walking in a muddy field, my umbrella broken, he was explaining his dream, which at the time seemed like madness," Ayelet told me. "But again, his passion was overwhelming. He said to me, 'You know, this going to be an international university. People will come to study here. It'll be the best in the Middle East, one of the best in the world. It will be different, and it will be wonderful. It would be like the Ivy League in United States.'

"God only knows what made me join this crazy man, but there was something in his eyes that expressed conviction, and I went for it," she said. "I became a part of his dream."

If Reichman had the courage to fail and to take the risk to succeed, so did Ayelet. They both champion the words of Zionist Theodor Herzl: "If you will it, it is no dream."

In the beginning, about three hundred people were studying for a law degree at IDC. "We didn't even know if we would be approved by the Council of Higher Education," she said. "It was a very high risk."

The IDC received accreditation as a university in 2021 and was renamed Reichman University, in honor of its founder and newly retired president, who today serves as chairman of the board. It offers PhD programs in computer science, law, and psychology. More than 34,000 graduates have come from its ten schools: in government, diplomacy, and strategy; international studies; business; computer science; communications; psychology; economics; sustainability; law; and entrepreneurship.

A NEW DIRECTION

When Ayelet arrived in 1999 as a lecturer at the Law School, there was also a business administration school and school of government. "I had a passion for it," she said. "I wrote a book, and I wrote many articles, publications, which was very important in order to become a professor. I realized that I liked teaching, I like to work with people, but I was not passionate enough regarding the writing. The life of a professor, in that respect, is a very lonely life.

"It was very difficult for me, being so close to being a professor, to change direction," she said, "and to admit it to my father. I told him that I wanted something else, something that will make me happy." Many years later, she still reflects on her decision. "Was I brave or stupid to take this turn?" she asked herself back then. Today, she knows the answer.

Ayelet approached Reichman in 2004 and told him she needed a break. Her marriage was failing, she was unhappy, and it affected her physically. "I told him I needed a change, that I do not want to spend the rest of my life writing articles and sitting in front of a computer."

Reichman told her to take the time to do what she needed. "But, he said, 'you're not going anywhere,' and that they would wait for me, and when I was ready to come back, we'd think about it together."

So Ayelet took a break. While thinking about her next step, Prime Minister Sharon asked Reichman, then a Knesset member, to be the minister of education. Ayelet was ready to help him on his journey, but Sharon became ill, and instead of education, Reichman was offered minister of justice, which he turned down. "He wanted to make a difference for the education of children of Israel," Ayelet said. "He wasn't interested in the politics; he had a vision; and he came back to the university, this man who is a national asset."

Ayelet also returned, in 2006, as vice president for student affairs. She advanced to vice president for administration, and in 2018 she was appointed CEO and vice president. The overriding goal, she said, is to promote personal excellence and social responsibility—to prepare students with the knowledge, research data, and tools to adapt in a rapidly changing international marketplace.

"We are here for the students," she said. "They are our full partners. We want them to fulfill their dreams in academic innovation, in social science, and the interwoven social sciences, with advanced technology."

Reichman University promotes interdisciplinary studies, often a mix of law, business, communications, and more. For example, a student of computer science will review business management plans to ensure technology is adequately funded. She said the approach is substantiated by the growing importance of combining technology and brain research with social sciences.

"It is my job to attract the students to study in our university," she said, "to show that once they graduate, they have so many tools, because they are exposed and encouraged to do volunteer work and participate in many workshops."

I told Ayelet that it must be a privilege to be able to learn different disciplines, and that as a physician, I am intrigued by the studies of brain research, studies of communication that include technology based on artificial intelligence, and survival issues related to climate change and world hunger. I am especially interested in the new academy to fight terror that also looks at research and preventive strategies, given the rise of anti-Semitism.

The university receives no government funding and relies on tuition fees and private donations. The tuition is high, to cover the salaries of distinguished faculty and top lecturers in their field. "Our aim was to develop a generation of leaders, even though some could not afford the tuition," she said. "We support students that are motivated and have a chance to succeed, no matter what their social or monetary background."

The university gives preference of admission to leaders and combat soldiers in the IDF reserves, and accommodations are made when they are called to duty.

Reichman's thousands of students come from 90 countries; exchange students benefit from partnerships with 130 universities, including many in the Ivy League. The campus is bilingual; 30 percent of students learn in English. Most of the students are Jewish and driven by Zionist ideals. And 70 percent of graduates stay in Israel to build their homes. Many volunteer with the IDF, Ayelet said, and those who return to their countries become ambassadors for Israel.

Ayelet understands the value of Reichman University and what it has fought to accomplish over the twenty-seven years before it was accredited as a university by the Council of Higher Education. And recently, she said, Reichman was recognized for generating the country's highest number of student-led startups and unicorns, compared to other graduates in Israel.

To keep the university at the forefront, Ayelet has visited campuses in the United States, Singapore, Hong Kong, Korea, and Europe, where she observes innovation in operations, takes tours, talks to the most senior people, and brings back the best ideas and practices for application. "We never freeze in our tracks," she said. "We are always thinking ahead."

Ayelet has had the privilege of being a substantial partner in achieving Professor Reichman's vision and transforming the university into an international, innovative, and pioneering smart campus. She works for the welfare of students and faculty members, with the benefit of having been faculty herself.

Professor Reichman illustrated a small example of Ayelet's dedication by recounting the time when excruciating back pain left her unable to stand or sit. Undaunted, Ayelet lay on the floor and continued to work, to the amazement of the others in the room. Overall, he said, the university's success owes much to Ayelet's hard work, particularly during the COVID-19 pandemic.

INNOVATION

To meet the immense challenge of maintaining Reichman's unique, village-like environment and collaborative focus without students on campus, Ayelet established a committee tasked with developing student-focused options and creating a unique student experience, despite the closed campus. For example, students from the School of Computer Science were trained to help lecturers teach on Zoom when the campus was shut down, and orientation week was conducted virtually, to allow students to get to know their peers and lecturers from afar and meet with the deans of their schools.

Ayelet's team also established virtual study rooms, online mindfulness activities for the entire RU community, online sport activities

(Zoom tournaments with a university in Abu Dhabi), and students interviewing each other on the university's radio station. For guidance support, the team had a "panic button" installed on the university app, and the dean of Student Affairs offered financial, mental, and academic assistance, and consulting services on financial matters.

For the administrative faculty members, because of the severe global crisis in the job market after COVID, Ayelet promoted a strategic plan for improving employee experience and dealing with the serious problem of staff recruitment and retention. Several significant steps were taken to increase employees' satisfaction and their personal happiness: employees transitioned to a hybrid work model; additional vacation days were allotted; development and enrichment programs were devised for managers, employees, and their children; a program was developed for enhancing employees' wellbeing and resilience; welfare conditions were improved; and employees or their family members were given the option to study for an academic degree funded by the university.

Ayelet also established an innovative career center, modeled on the Ivy League, with a team of consultants specializing in the fields of study offered at Reichman. "The center is constantly updated with what's happening in the industry, and its services accompany students from the first day of their studies onwards, even after graduation," Ayelet said. Free services include a Coffee Chat mobile app for scheduling on-campus meetings with potential employers, assistance finding jobs, internships, research opportunities after graduation, job fairs, and simulations of interviews.

The focus over the last few years was not only crisis management, Ayelet said, but on strategic thinking for whatever comes next. Her team enhanced cybersecurity protocols; adapted platforms to support remote work, including a call center in all departments; and digitized many processes, including budgets.

Ayelet paused to gather her thoughts about the importance of face-to-face exchanges that foster logic and reasoning.

"A student of the past did not ask for an experience. He used to receive a lecture, write it down, and learn it by heart. The student of today is different.

"The thing I most pay attention to is the importance of bringing the student to a place where they want to be, which is to come back to the Aristotelian experience," she said. "That is to think together in groups and to exchange ideas, despite the digital world of today."

MINA TEICHER

MATHEMATICIAN AND DIRECTOR, EMMY NOETHER INSTITUTE

"I named the institute I built after her, because I felt so close to [mathematician Emmy Noether], following her footsteps in geometry and algebra, having a similar Jewish-German ancestry, and having the love of sharing our knowledge."

THERE ARE ONLY A FEW world-famous female mathematicians, and Emmy Noether (1882–1935) was one of them. Her work formed the basis for abstract algebra and theoretical physics, and continues to help explain the behavior of black holes and the existence of dark matter.

Noether's scientific achievements and struggles to succeed in the predominantly male world of mathematics would become a road map for Mina Teicher—since 1999 the director of the Emmy Noether Research Institute for Mathematics at Bar-Ilan University, and the university's former vice president for research and development.

Now, Mina combines her considerable skills as a researcher, policymaker, international consultant, and advocate for the participation of women in the field of mathematics. Like Noether, Mina feels very close to her students and follows their careers, nurturing them until they become professors. She also shares her knowledge internationally.

Born in Tel Aviv in 1950, Mina learned about Noether during her studies. In Noether, Mina found a role model for mathematical insight, perseverance, and graciousness.

"I named the institute I built after her, because I felt so close to her, following her footsteps in geometry and algebra, having a similar Jewish-German ancestry, and having a love of sharing our knowledge," Mina told me when I visited her in the spring of 2022. "My mother is from Jerusalem, and the Jerusalem spirit is to share one's knowledge."

The institute invites international scholars to work with local researchers to participate in conferences and give community lectures. International PhD graduates are eligible for one-year postdoctoral fellowships.

Mina said she was practically born a mathematician. She fell in love with the magical quality of numbers at the age of four and chose to devote her life to mathematics, despite developing interest in many other fields. Her father, whom she described as a bookworm, one day lifted his eyes from his reading to give Mina important advice: "If somebody wants to study, he doesn't look for reasons not to study."

Rather than heed his words immediately, she joined the army after high school graduation, like most young women in Israel. She declined the opportunity granted to gifted high school students to do a BSC and postpone service until graduating from college. After serving in the army in the Shin Bet (the Israeli version of the CIA), she started her academic studies and received her bachelor's, master's, and doctoral degrees from Tel Aviv University. Her father proudly attended her PhD ceremony.

THE LANGUAGE OF MATH

Mina's doctoral fellowship brought her for a year to the Institute for Advanced Study (IAS) in Princeton, New Jersey, where she was honored to work in Albert Einstein's former office—he was there thirty years prior. "What a privilege it used to be, just fulfilling the obligation of sitting with your colleagues, talking and exchanging ideas in mathematics, while enjoying the food prepared by a French chef," she said.

During this Year of Algebraic Geometry at the IAS, about thirty established mathematicians and PhD graduates specializing in algebraic geometry were chosen to present developments in the field. Mina would develop lifetime friendships with about twenty colleagues from IAS.

"I still collaborate with them anytime I come up with an idea or a question," she said. The tight-knit group of specialists in algebraic geometry consult each other and promote each other's discoveries. The algorithms they have developed are used in all aspects of everyday life, including science, music, art, and social sciences.

While most people are invited once, Mina accepted four invitations to join the mathematicians at Princeton, a distinction that helped her advance in academia despite the prevalence of gender discrimination.

She became a lecturer at Bar-Ilan and received funds to build a visitor program. Every year, she invited twenty-four researchers—a mix of senior mathematicians, young collaborators, and friends she made internationally—to spend a month at the university. There, they brainstormed and shared their work using a model like the one at the IAS. The visitor program was a key point in her career, Mina told me.

When Bar-Ilan could no longer support the program, Mina approached the German government to subsidize the institute she would name after Noether, the Jewish-German mathematician, who fled to the United States in 1932, when the Nazis introduced laws that prevented Jews from working in a university.

IMMORTALIZING A ROLE MODEL

The connection to Germany made sense. Solomon Elbe, Mina's great-great-grandfather, arrived in Israel in 1856 from Hamburg, Germany. In 1864, he married Hanehinke Weinstein, whose family came from Belarus. Solomon is considered the family founder, and in history books is referred to as The Fabricant, Mina said. Nearly one thousand offspring are spread around the globe, mostly in Israel and the United States. The family kept German citizenship for generations, and thus in 1915, Mina's grandfather was drafted into the German army in WWI.

Mina explains that "I took this opportunity to immortalize Emmy Noether, my role model." The inaugural conference was held at the home of the Israeli ambassador in Germany, which was still in Bonn in 1992. Every seven years, a committee from Germany visits to evaluate the institute and its adherence to its mission. Representatives are typically amazed by the papers produced and the knowledge shared, Mina said.

Noether's struggle to achieve as a mathematician made a lasting impression on Mina, who couldn't understand how a great mathematician was denied recognition in her own town of Gottingen, the shrine of mathematics. Noether was only allowed to lecture there because she used a pseudonym. A sign on the lecture room door said: "Professor David Hilbert room—a lecture given by Emmy Noether." Noether repeatedly tried and failed to secure herself a professor position, despite having Hilbert campaign for her using the famous sentiment: "Why don't you give her a professorship; the senate is not a bathhouse. What does it matter that she is a woman? How does it matter that she is a woman?" At this time the senate had reserved professor positions for men only.

In 2001–02, Mina was the inaugural Emmy Noether Visiting Professor at the University of Gottingen, where she lectured about "braid" groups.

Mina became a full professor at Bar-Ilan and said she felt very lucky and fulfilled by her accomplishments. One day, colleague Eli Merzbach approached her to become chairwoman of the Department of Mathematics and Computer Science. Because Mina preferred research to administration, she only reluctantly considered the two-year term—until an old-school and older religious man declared his candidacy. Mina became the chairwoman and was elected to a second term, which she happily accepted to bring to fruition many projects she launched. One defining success was keeping mathematics and computer science together as one department.

OPENING INTERNATIONAL DOORS

The next phase of her career began when the university president asked her to be vice president for research. He told Mina he was tired of fighting with her for money for her department, and instead proposed that she work with him. "I was amazed. I was not a dean, a rector, or a vice rector," she said of her less-than-lofty status. "I jumped directly [to the new position] because the president said I have to be on his side.

"It was a dream position for me," she said, because "my face was outside toward the funding agencies for research, and toward investors interested in commercialization of patents. I created numerous technological startups that resulted from Bar-Ilan University research. I was in charge of commercialization for the entire university, including chemistry, physics, archeology, life science, mathematics, and computer science."

It was then that she became passionate about applying mathematics to other fields, including neuroscience.

She served as VP for four years. The position gave her visibility as she negotiated with the government on behalf of the university, and went to the Israeli parliament to resolve issues and fight against the boycott of Israeli academia.

The next stage of her life story began when the president of the Israel Academy of Science offered her the position of chief scientist of the government. Her work from 2005 to 2007 opened international doors.

Mina consulted with governments on how to become a start-up nation like Israel, and her discussions with small countries and universities were largely about establishing policies and strategies for commercialization. "I am clever—I learn fast and am able to adapt my knowledge quickly," she told me about her skillsets. "Using my analytical and logical skills from my experience in the world of mathematics, I was able to help commercialize technologies in fields not related to my scientific expertise. I also mastered the governmental duties in research."

When Mina was chief scientist, she oversaw three main areas:

* the relationship of Israel, as a government, with other countries, which helped her establish relationships with policymakers across the world

* all the public research done outside the universities in the periphery, like the Negev and the Galilee

* research on topics that benefited people, but were not monetarily attractive to private companies or academics

Mina was invited to take leadership positions in policy-making for international nonprofits, such as being the chair of the board of governors of the United States-Israel Binational Science Foundation, and vice president of the International Commission for Mathematical Instruction. She sits on advisory boards of US-based startup companies in artificial intelligence, blockchain, and cyber security.

She took a sabbatical, using the time she accumulated during her administrative and public service in policymaking in Israel, and became a visiting professor at the IAS in Princeton, at Columbia University, and at New York University. She continued doing research predominantly at NYU for several years, where she concentrated on mathematical finance, or translating brain function into mathematical models that could be used in financial markets. This opened new doors for Mina, and she was offered consulting work in the finance space.

Her neuro-finance research is aimed at using her patented algorithm to predict a financial crisis, based on how the human brain creates and solves a neurological trauma.

Simultaneously in Israel, one of Mina's math PhD students, an Israeli Arab whom she advised and supported, mastered magnetoencephalography (MEG) scans, a new brain imaging technique. The MEG measures the small magnetic fields induced by the brain's electrical activity, cognitive functions of the brain, and the concept of numbers.

On behalf of the University of Miami, Mina leads a campaign to increase the presence of women in mathematics. Similar to a program she ran in Israel and China, talented girls in the last two years of high school in Miami are taught higher-level math and earn twelve college credits at the university. The partnership allows the recruited students to graduate college in three rather than four years. Students find the program attractive, Mina said, because of the potential for an early graduation, access to exclusive events, and opportunities for employment.

In 2021 Mina created the Playing with Braids event at the University of Miami, a two-day conference to provide female students with an overview of how mathematics influences almost every aspect of life. They also got a basic understanding of "braids" in mathematical applications, including machine learning, topology, and cryptography.

"Based on the data we see today, women are dropping out of mathematics throughout their academic careers, for all the wrong reasons," Mina said after the Braids conference. "It's called the 'leaking pipeline,' because they start on the path but then drop off at different stages of their academic career. One of the reasons is that they are intimidated by the idea that men are better in math than women and, of course, this idea is incorrect. This special, female-only weekend event was tailored to overcome this obstacle and encourage young women who are talented in mathematics to pursue a career in academia, or in knowledge-based industries, and ensure they obtain fulfilling careers and economical independence."

Mina is also planning to create the first museum of mathematics in the southern United States, to present exhibits, mathematical sculptures, and images of graphs, and to host lectures about how to present phenomena with math backgrounds. For example, the museum would sponsor an exhibit to show how COVID spread across the world, or mathematics competitions to create beautiful objects with math software, and more. The museum would provide jobs for female undergraduates and would be supported by the University of Miami, as well. Mina's main goal is to build a museum that will raise awareness of mathematics being everywhere, and make sure that its leadership is comprised of female mathematicians—both young women interested in mathematics, as well as more senior mathematicians.

As our conversation wound down, I asked Mina a question I often ask myself: "How do you feel as an Israeli living abroad?" Despite having spent a significant portion of her life in Israel, Mina said it's important for her to have more than one passport, a safeguard against the existential threat against Israel. Mostly, she is concerned about a nuclear attack by Iran and its support of Palestinian terrorists.

She recalled an exchange with one of her students, an Israeli Arab, who expressed his opinion favoring a one-state solution with a Palestinian majority. Though she understood his viewpoint as an Arab in a Jewish state, she told him: "That is not a good solution, because we [Jews] have been a minority for two thousand years. I want someplace where I can be in the majority. If I wanted to be a minority, I would live in New York permanently."

I got the sense that, just like most Israelis who live abroad, Mina and I love, appreciate, and are thankful for the countries that supported our advancement. The spirit of Israel, the place where we were born and grew up, is the strength that enables us to overcome obstacles. Israel is home.

SARAH ABU-KAF

SENIOR LECTURER AT BEN-GURION UNIVERSITY

"Since I come from a collective culture, I pursue my dreams while respecting the cultural values of my society where I grew up, but I am working to change some of them."

I CAUGHT UP WITH SARAH Abu-Kaf in her office at Ben-Gurion University of the Negev (BGU). She was dressed in traditional black Bedouin attire and a black hijab covered her hair. My gaze went directly to her brown eyes and her inviting and kind smile. For the first time in my life, I, an Israeli sabra, was completely at ease talking with an Arab Bedouin.

Named by *Forbes* magazine in 2018 as one of the most influential women in Israel, Sarah is a professor in cross-cultural psychology in BGU's conflict management and resolution program, and she serves as the head of the Department of Multidisciplinary Studies. She earned her PhD in clinical psychology there, and completed her post-doctoral studies at Harvard University's Department of Anthropology. Informed by her own challenges, she researches sources of stress and coping strategies among mostly minority students in Israel, and helps Bedouin students struggling to make the transition to academic life without forsaking their ancestral culture.

Later, she extended her interest to different sources of stress, coping resources and strategies, conflict-management strategies. She examined in particular different idioms of psychological distress among women, youth, and students from different cultural backgrounds in Israeli society, with special attention on the Arabs and the Bedouin Arabs.

Born in 1976, Sarah grew up in Umm Batin, one of the so-called "unrecognized" Bedouin villages populated by Bedouin Arabs, who, for hundreds of years, have cultivated the Negev and raised livestock.

She attended primary school in her village and told me about her happy childhood, which included playing with bottles and stones as sophisticated toys. Mature and responsible for her age, she became the teacher's assistant and helped other preschool children with their homework. She credited her parents for supporting her academic achievements, as well as those of her four siblings. Her family was highly regarded among the four thousand members of their community.

There was no middle or high school in her village, so for seventh grade she went every day to the nearby Tel Sheva, a recognized village, to continue her study there. Sarah majored in biology and science and graduated with high scores. Her classes were taught in Arabic, except for two taught in Hebrew and English. The latter was taught by a Jewish teacher.

At eighteen, she married a man of her choosing to avoid extended family pressure to wed someone she didn't want or care for. "He was very educated and a very nice person," Sarah told me. "I felt that if I want to lead the life I choose, then I should marry him. I knew him since the age of fifteen, and I realized with him I will be able to develop and grow, that he will support and advise me about higher education, since he was the first young man in our village with a BA degree."

A year later, she had her first daughter and prepared for the psychometric exams required to enter university. The exams, which draw on Israeli daily and cultural experiences, present significant challenges to almost all Israeli minorities, including ultra-Orthodox, Ethiopian, Bedouin, Arab, and Druze.

"My own community, we have a different way of thinking and solving problems," Sarah told me. "We think differently about how to arrive at a solution to solve a problem. And so psychometric exams contain hidden Western knowledge that the system assumes we have."

COLLECTIVISM VS. INDIVIDUALISM

The differences between Western society and Sarah's are many. Bedouin culture is more collective than the individualism championed in Western culture, she said. Individualistic people work to distinguish themselves, achieve their own goals, and gain power rather than work in harmony with others.

"The Arab culture," she continued, "has a lot of collectivism—being affiliated with the entire social group, [people] make decisions and/or change their goals according to the need of the group. When a Bedouin wishes to make an individual decision, they consider the opinion of the group, how they will be viewed, and how the group will react. Collective goals can sometimes interfere with a person's individual goals and become an obstacle to the individual's success."

Sarah took a diplomatic approach to pursue her dream by using the right argument with her community. "I convinced the village that I am the village's daughter, whose success in academia will drive change and betterment in the village," she said. "That I represent a collective goal, providing research and knowledge that is required to help Bedouin society."

Sarah believes that she is an individual with different experiences from her family and community, yet with a goal others might share: "to narrow the distance between the collective and individuals so they don't counteract one another," she said. "Since I come from a collective culture, I pursue my dreams while respecting the cultural values of my society where I grew up, but I am working to change some of them. For example, giving priority for education, especially females' education, and sex roles in the family."

As a role model for village daughters, she reassures her community that the girls will remain faithful to their cultural values. They can be educated, she said, while still wearing a hijab and continuing to participate and contribute to community life. "I have always been aware that my appropriate behavior will affect those who follow me." And there's the positive effect on the village and village youth when Bedouin students who graduate return home as professionals, including physicians, psychologists, and social workers.

In 1995, when Sarah enrolled at BGU, she was one of five female Bedouin students and needed time to adapt to university life. Most students had served in the IDF, took a year off to travel, and came to school with rich life experiences she couldn't imagine. Sarah joined university one year after high school and was already a mother. She made the decision to dedicate quality time to her children while at home, dedicate herself to her studies while at university, get help from her husband and family members, and accept the mistakes she would make along the path.

I asked Sarah how she manages to care for her six children while working full time. She admitted that it was and is difficult, physically and mentally. It weighs on her because she had an internal conflict— that in addition to wanting to succeed and fulfill herself, she believed that it was important to be near her daughters and raise them, the most common practice in her society. With the oldest children she relied on her mother's help. When her sisters, a teacher and a physician, had children and asked for their mother's help, Sarah turned to her mother-in-law. Her husband, Jazi, was extremely supportive throughout these very challenging periods and helped a lot, emotionally and instrumentally. Later, the older children became great helpers for her.

CONFLICTING GOALS

Her life has been pulled between conflicting goals. Sarah believed that her education would ultimately lift her family, but she hated leaving her children in the village's poor living conditions when she went off to school. At school, meanwhile, she felt like a minority, almost invisible in the Western culture, while at home she was made to feel important.

As an Israeli who went to medical school in Italy, I could identify with Sarah's difficulties learning Hebrew and working extra hard to keep up with her classes. We sat silently for a while and shared a knowing smile about those days and how our efforts led to successful lives and careers.

I felt pride in my homeland when Sarah described her gratitude for being a student at a university in Israel, who enjoyed respect and kindness from students and professors. When she enrolled in a master's program in BGU's psychology department in 2000, she was the only Bedouin Arab female, with two Arab male students, among three hundred Jewish students. She received help from a group tasked with teaching Bedouin Arabs and other minorities how to write and express themselves in Hebrew, as well as how to deal with academic challenges. She proudly told me about her high achievements in tough courses.

By the end of her second year, Sarah said, she felt comfortable enough to invite her peers to her village and help them with their anthropological research. "I can bring enrichment to their learning experience by introducing them to my life," she said. She also started to participate more fully in discussions about cross-cultural psychology.

CROSS-CULTURAL PSYCHOLOGY

In 2010, already equipped with her master's, she earned her PhD in clinical psychology. Her doctoral thesis addressed depression among

Bedouin students compared to their Jewish peers. I asked her about the social and academic integration of Bedouin Arab students at BGU, considering their high dropout rate. "During a decade of research for my PhD," she answered, "I tried to go step by step to understand what difficulties they faced—how they dealt with these difficulties, and what adjustments had they made to succeed in their academic mission and improve their mental health."

Most of those difficulties in the early stage stemmed from the language barrier. "Though they are excellent students in high school, when they come to the university, in the best scenario they are on par with the average Jewish student," she said. "Many of them experience a lot of failures in the first year and feel that they cannot reconcile the experience. I called it a 'dropout in academic self-esteem.' I found it was very important to prepare them, and tell them that there is a big difference between high school and the life they would experience in university. We are talking about different levels of materials and challenges. The mental preparation for that is very important."

For the last few years, she said, the university has offered a pre-academic year to prepare students for these higher expectations. Sarah also successfully proposed that the university stretch the first year to two, to give Bedouin students time to concentrate on learning to speak, write, and read Hebrew fluently. Students who made good progress are allowed to take more courses in the second semester of the first year. "We convinced the students that taking it slow in the beginning was a wise decision for them to succeed and excel later," she said.

The differences between a student's home culture and the university's also needed to be understood and addressed. For example, some of the Bedouin Arab girls who volunteer at Soroka Medical Center wait to be asked to do something or to help, a hesitancy that is misinterpreted as laziness, Sarah said. She met with the medical staff and explained the need to explicitly ask the girls to do tasks and to provide instructions. Then she told the girls to offer their help to the staff and to ask for help when faced with difficulties. "I found that the dropout rate is higher among those who do not adopt an active position and hesitate to ask for help, a position that may be encouraged by the collectivistic cultural context such as the Bedouin Arab society," she said. "This is how a lack of mediation between the different cultures could have caused a failure."

IMPROVING MENTAL HEALTH

Meanwhile, the Bedouin Arab villages need psychologists, because they were found to have elevated levels of emotional distress that affects a significant number of community members, Sarah said. "It relates to living circumstances and daily difficulties. It is not a mental illness. It is the daily stressors and distress that cause common mental health problems, for example, depression. Common mental-health problems require help, and it is difficult to get it because there is only one center for adults in Rahat, the main Bedouin Arab city, and a very limited number of mental-health professionals. There is a very long wait list. Untreated mental health problems can get worse and lead to severe social and economic consequences, and to heavy burdens on the health and welfare system."

In addition to challenges from the scarcity of mental-health services, Bedouin Arabs in general, and especially those in the unrecognized villages, have very limited knowledge about mental health, and stigmatize mental illness to the point where many are afraid or don't know where to seek professional care. Instead, they turn to family members who often don't recognize mental-health issues, or to healers whose attempts to "get the evil spirit out" can result in injury or death.

Sarah said that it is important to encourage the patient's family to accompany them to treatment, a practice found to correlate with improved results and compliance with care, raised community awareness of mental illnesses, and increases in the patient's support system.

While at Harvard for her post-doctoral fellowship in 2011–12, Sarah said she had an amazing experience working with Professor Arthur Kleinman—an expert in depression in the context of collectivistic populations, like Bedouin Arabs in Israel and Chinese society. They developed a program to provide mental-health support in towns with no mental-health professionals, by integrating the services with the daily work of other professionals, such as nurses, physicians, educational psychologists, and counselors. The objective was to provide them with basic knowledge about mental-health problems, and increase their awareness about mental-health services available for the Arab minority.

"I have a very fruitful and interesting cooperation with ultra-Orthodox female colleagues doing research projects related to higher education and employment of Bedouin Arab women and ultra-Orthodox women," Sarah said. "We found similarities and differences, because each minority group in Israel is unique. The similarities and differences help inform us on how best to provide mental-health support for these women."

SEEKING RECOGNITION

I decided to ask Sarah some difficult questions—about the Bedouin community's opposition to service in the IDF, the prevalence of radicalization, increased violence within and outside the Bedouin community, involvement with drug trafficking, and the criminal practice of extorting protection money from non-Bedouin businesses.

She told me that the worse the living conditions are for Bedouin Arabs in all the villages and the towns—including the large city of Rahat, and the unrecognized villages especially—the more open they are to being identified with Palestinian Arabs and refusing to join the IDF. Bedouin Arabs in the northern recognized towns, she said, have better living conditions, more recognition and development in the villages, and thus experience less violence and are more likely to join the IDF.

"In the south, in the Negev, we feel discriminated against," she said. "Since we are Israeli citizens, why are our villages unrecognized, not developed, and lack basic essential services?" Joining the IDF, she said, does not bring any reward or provide good-paying jobs.

Additionally, Israeli police do not intervene in the violence or protect the community. But it's not all the government's fault, she said, because elder family members no longer have the power to prohibit the use of violence. "They have lost control over the youth. The Bedouins have lost their traditional family authority, and there is a lack of guidance from a leader. So, there is no social control of criminal activity."

In fact, because she feels that the increased violence among Bedouins relates to living conditions, she organizes student trips to recognized and unrecognized villages. The purpose of these trips is to increase awareness in the Jewish Israeli society to the real difficulties and challenges facing the Bedouin Arab community. The visits are made without the media coverage that she said usually incites negative public opinion against Bedouin Arab society, and does not care to present the discriminatory policy toward this community.

Though her village was recognized from 2005, conditions did not improve; there is still no electricity, and especially in the winter, Sarah cannot use her computer at home. Not only do Bedouin Arabs have to struggle to survive, but, she also added, their villages are threatened with destruction and replacement by Jewish Israeli communities. "We want to be recognized as people living in the place we are."

In 1948, with the establishment of the state of Israel, most Bedouins were driven off their land or restricted to Siyag, a recognized triangular area of seven modernized towns north of Be'er Sheva. The forty-five villages outside of the triangle are unrecognized by the state of Israel and lack electricity and paved roads. Since 2003, thirteen out of the forty-five villages were recognized, but still not developed. Sarah's village, Umm Batin, is one of the thirteen.

Like all Israeli citizens, Bedouin Arabs are supposed to receive welfare and unemployment benefits and are rewarded for every child born. The Israeli government provides education, medical care, social benefits, and national insurance, along with basic needs for a sustainable life. But Sarah disagreed, and said that Rahat, the largest Arab city in Israel, has limited health, education, and welfare facilities and services compared to the nearby Jewish cities. As a result, she said, Rahat and the other old Bedouin Arab cities endure a high rate of violence.

I asked Sarah why Bedouins don't move to the cities built for them, if living conditions elsewhere are so bad. "The local municipalities are suffering from many problems including difficult living conditions," she told me. "And they do not have enough resources and services for their local communities." I asked if villagers would give up their land and move if conditions improved in the cities. "If the conditions were really better," she said, "I believe that many people would consider moving to them."

We wound up our conversation with a walk through the campus, and Sarah pointed to the Women's Center, which was built for Bedouin women students as a private place for support, talking, and studying. This center is operated by the dean of services for students. The Bedouin female students spend many hours on the campus and do not feel comfortable to lie and rest in public places, she said. Funds for the center came from the Arnow family from New York, foreign donors who met Sarah in her early stages and were impressed by her and her achievements. They also helped her get additional financial help from the American Associates, Ben-Gurion University, for her post-doctorate work at Harvard. The family wanted to contribute to Bedouin Arab female students, Sarah said, and they still do.

As I parted with Sarah, I thought about the dichotomy she experiences: between the university's welcoming environment that fosters her academic and professional goals, and the harsh reality of life in a recognized but not developed village.

I told her I admired her courage to step out of cultural stereotypes and remain faithful to her community. She became a role model by applying her studies in cross-cultural psychology to the mental-health needs of Bedouin Arab students specifically, and to the community.

NIGIST MENGESHA

ETHIOPIAN ISRAELI COMMUNITY ACTIVIST, SOCIAL WORKER

"I believe the only key to be integrated into Israeli society is through education. It is the key to penetrate into Israeli society and reach into equality."

NIGIST MENGESHA WAS A MOTHER of four in 1984 when she arrived alone in Israel from Gonder in Ethiopia. Her successful aliyah, after several failed attempts, immersed her in the racism and cultural challenges Ethiopian immigrants confront in their chosen home.

Ever since, Nigist has used her skills as a social worker and activist to help families assimilate to new cultural expectations. She fights to improve life for many of the 160,000 Ethiopian Israelis who struggle to navigate the school system and gain access to higher paying careers, or cope with the depression born of isolation.

"I believe the only key to be integrated into Israeli society is through education," Nigist told me. "It is the key to penetrate into Israeli society and reach into equality."

Nigist founded the Fidel Association in 1997 to addresses problems in education for Ethiopian Israelis and empower local communities to enact change. She is now the executive director of Fidel, and trains teams of Ethiopian Israelis and non-Ethiopians to be mediators in the education system, and to be aware of cultural and educational differences that can sabotage success.

Fidel workers go to areas where there is a "vacuum of support," where the needs of Ethiopian Israeli children and their parents are not being met. They focus on prevention, organize parent workshops, and set up centers for at-risk youth. As a result, more parents get involved in school and take those opportunities to ask questions, a bold practice unheard of in Ethiopia. Nigist also sees growing support from other organizations and government institutions, and increased access to higher education that has led to new Ethiopian Israeli doctors, teachers, engineers, social workers, university lecturers, and researchers.

"My experience as a social worker and the decision to keep developing in this field was instrumental to my integration into Israel cultural society," she said. "My role is to inspire others. I came here as an immigrant, educated with three degrees, and as a mother of four kids, and a grandmother. I tell my story to everybody."

In her book, *Here I Am*, Nigist explores her road to success and how *olim*, the term for an immigrant in Israeli society, can navigate life in the Holy Land.

THE HISTORIC DREAM OF ALIYAH

Few Ethiopians were allowed to leave their country before Operation Moses, when up to eight thousand immigrants arrived in Israel from Sudan in 1984, and Operation Shlomo (Solomon), when fourteen thousand arrived from the Ethiopian capital Addis Ababa in 1991. Even so, and despite the prohibitions during the forty-four-year reign of Ethiopian Emperor Haile Selassie, the Beta Israel community (Ethiopian diaspora Jews) kept dreaming of aliyah, imagining a life in Jerusalem. In 1973 Israel's Chief Sephardic Rabbi, Ovadia Yosef, recognized Beta Israel as Jews. He legalized as citizens those who were in Israel, and, like all citizens, they were drafted into the Israel Defense Forces.

Nigist belonged to a loving, upper-class Ethiopian family and the quest to make aliyah to Jerusalem was deeply embedded in daily life. She said that she and her friends "went to sleep at night and woke up in the morning with thoughts of Jerusalem." After her cousin Rachel visited from Jerusalem, Nigist's dream was strengthened. "In Ethiopia, it felt as if we were living in a foreign country."

Her parents had a loving relationship, Nigist said, but she was determined not to follow in her mother's path of marriage at the age of nine to a man nineteen years older. Her mother gave birth to only Nigist, but she was adored for her wisdom and dedication to the three children her father had with another woman.

While Nigist's mother expected her to marry young and have many children, her father encouraged her to continue her studies. Unlike his brothers, her father refused to be a farmer and educated himself throughout his life. Nigist's grandfather was a leader who developed a village and built a synagogue, where on Saturdays, using the ancient languages of Ethiopia, Jerusalem was always a central prayer theme. Nigist said her grandmother somehow knew that she would wind up in Jerusalem.

Nigist decided to realize her dream at age thirty, and with friends took a two-day bus ride north from Gondar, their small village in Ethiopia, to Asmara in Eritrea, and stayed at a cousin's house. They had hoped to take a ten-day trip to Israel in a fishing boat but, after the complicated and costly process, the government closed all the exits. Nigist tried again to leave, this time from Addis Ababa, after adding years to her actual age to get a passport. She was refused by the Israeli consulate for not having a letter from a guardian in Israel.

On the ride back home, she told her father she was too ashamed to face her friends, who expected her to be in Jerusalem. Her father shared his own painful experience of seeing his professor, who taught him Hebrew, beaten and forced to disrobe to show his "jackal's tail." The horrifying event and comparison of Jews to animals had a permanent impact on him. He told Nigist how he decided to pursue education and enrolled in school, despite being married and having a family.

Her father became a judge who traveled to Ethiopian towns to protect the weak, and he established health reforms that benefited women giving birth locally. He believed in equality and freedom of religion. Nigist said his attempt to join the Ethiopian parliament failed by seventeen votes.

Their conversation encouraged Nigist to persevere in her studies and work to save money for her next attempt at aliyah. She adored her father, a leader in the country who supported aliyah, and who repeatedly told her, "You will be a light." His encouragement gave her strength even when she failed in her studies or in attempting aliyah, situations where most people would have given up.

Jerusalem never left her mind, and Nigist frequented the post office to get news about Israel. In the meantime, she was assigned as a volunteer to help in Wolo, a region in northern Ethiopia where 25,000 people had died in the 1970s from widespread hunger and disease. Nigist and each of her four friends, along with one doctor and nurse, were responsible for a hundred people. Babies arrived in cardboard boxes and, if they survived, disappeared the same way to adoption centers. She told me about her unimaginable joy when she saw a smile on the face of a baby who made it. She also realized the cruelty of the Selassie government, despite his visits to the region and faked compassion for the victims.

At college, Nigist befriended her future husband, Assefa. After graduating, students were sent to work in remote areas, and Nigist landed in Metekal, a region that lacked basic infrastructure. The surprise arrival of Assefa brought her joy, and they decided to marry. They lived together and avoided all the cultural habits of traditional ceremonies required before marriage. She was so in love with this "intelligent, strong man filled with charisma."

In 1976 revolution brought communist leader Mengistu Haile Mariam to power, and the couple escaped to Addis Ababa with their first baby, Mentuab (Mimi). Nigist continued as a social worker and had three more children—Amy, Samuel, and Benny—over the next few years. In 1980 Nigist again attempted aliyah. She obtained the required letter from Hebrew University, which explained that she was accepted and sponsored to be a student in social work, but the Ethiopian government denied her request. There would be no need for educated social workers in Ethiopia upon her return, she was told.

Finally, Ben-Gurion University sponsored her study of computer science, with the condition to leave her family behind as a guarantee for her return. Her parents moved in with her family and helped take care of the children. "11 November 1984 was the most important day in my life," she said.

In Israel, family members greeted her, and she was placed in the Nazareth Elite absorption center with Ethiopians from Operation Moses who were sick and debilitated from the long journey from Sudan. She didn't speak the language and missed her husband and children terribly. Immense changes greeted her at the supermarket, where rows of milk cartons and an array of frozen meats represented a new world.

Her family arrived a few months later, and they all moved to a three-bedroom apartment. The children were sent to school, and Nigist began to study at Bar-Ilan University, where she would earn her BA in social work. On Saturdays, she worked with Ethiopians who lost dear ones on their way to Israel and suffered from PTSD. She remembered the difficult days when, like other immigrants, parents needed their children's help to translate the challenges of daily life. Youngsters were forced to mature quickly.

On top of her own sadness and loneliness at university, Nigist had to deal with her children's frustrations as they integrated into a new society. She was grateful for her husband's gregariousness and ability to make friends while working long hours in a gas station to put food on the table.

Her children adapted to Israeli culture and started to speak their minds, which Nigist at first found disrespectful but later learned to appreciate. She involved herself in their lives by organizing birthday parties and, when they all moved to Rosh Ha'ayin, she joined various school committees.

Nigist also worked in a social welfare department at Bat Yam municipality, where she felt discriminated against when her offers of assistance were rejected by clients in need of help. Ethiopian Jews, she said, were stereotyped as ignorant and judged by their looks. Eventually, there was a joyous breakthrough when Israeli friends invited her to celebrate the High Holy Days.

CULTURAL DIFFERENCES

Nigist understood that depression was common among Ethiopian immigrants, and that it could lead to abandoning one's education, violence against women, and suicide. She largely blamed socialization differences between Ethiopian and Israeli students, and expanded on her theory in her thesis for her MA in social work from Hebrew University of Jerusalem.

Ethiopians, she said, are raised to respect their elders, tell the truth, and keep their promises. Privacy was of utmost importance, and helping the community came before individual needs. When problems arose, Ethiopians sought out their elders for help and avoided involving the legal system, especially with domestic issues. And, unlike more egalitarian Israeli families, Ethiopians lived in a patriarchy.

In Israel, Ethiopian women went to work and found employment more easily than men. They achieved financial independence, and their status improved in contrast to the men, which stressed traditional hierarchies and caused family conflicts that sometimes ended with violence or murder.

For Israeli professionals to solve these problems was impossible, Nigist explained, because they didn't understand Ethiopian behavioral codes or self-expression. And it didn't help that Ethiopians would not reveal personal family information to a stranger. It took time for Israelis to understand that Ethiopian elders needed to become involved before victims would accept professional help.

This lack of understanding also existed in the school system, where teachers failed to understand students' ways of thinking or motivation. For example, she said, immigrants accustomed to a different system for time and date were often late for school or appointments or missed them completely, actions that were misinterpreted as lazy or uncaring. Nigist said her father summed up the change in expectations when he declared, "In Ethiopia, I was big. In Israel, I am like a cat."

TURNING TO ADVOCACY

After four years at another relief center in Bat Yam, Nigist recognized her strengths and understood the social dynamics of Israeli society. She was ready to confront the challenges and help with the absorption of immigrants from Operation Shlomo in May 1991. The new arrivals, she said, were placed in 27,000 caravans and dispersed through the country, disconnected from the Israeli society they wanted to be part of. They were ostracized by the media, which spread misinformation that the Ethiopian immigrants were carriers of AIDS/HIV.

Nigist believed they needed one of their own to communicate and care for them, and she joined Shatil, an organization for empowerment and social change. She translated immigrants' rights into Amharic and found volunteer lawyers. With the media, she represented new immigrants' voices about the inequity of life in the centers and caravans, and thereby developed her leadership skills. For three years, she fought to get basic needs met, supported demonstrations, pressed the government to bring over the immigrants still left behind, and tried to form a parliament lobby for immigrants.

In 1994 Nigist was accepted to the prestigious Mandel School for Educational Leadership in Jerusalem, where she studied education, public government, legal and social work, Jewish philosophy, and humanism. She had some difficulties with Hebrew but got help from friends. "Everybody was nice and friendly," she said. "I had a strong connection with my colleagues." Her thesis, which would become the basis for her Fidel Association, offered two options to help Ethiopian students, their parents, and their teachers. One was to cultivate Ethiopians in education and social work who understood the cultural differences between communities. The second was to empower Ethiopian teachers to speak Amharic or Tigrinya or both. The government, she said, was struggling to handle the absorption of children from Operation Moses and then the children from Operation Shlomo, and was forced to open new classes in need of educators.

The Ministry of Education in Jerusalem, Department of Immigrant Students from Ethiopia, asked Nigist to be a guide for teachers and explain the cultural habits of Ethiopian immigrants. Principals, she told me, typically allocated two-and-a-half hours each week for teachers to tutor immigrant students to get on par with their peers. The time, however, was used by the principals for other purposes and, out of fear that their wrongdoing would be revealed, her visits were not always well received.

After a year, Nigist asked to leave to establish her own foundation, the Fidel Association. The time she spent working closely with teachers and schools gave her a glimpse into a system where some educators were supportive of immigrants while others belittled them, she said. In some cities and towns, mayors committed larger-scale discrimination by refusing to register immigrant children, barring them from school, and prevented Ethiopians from purchasing homes—actions extremely destructive to the integration of the Ethiopian immigrants.

Her discoveries led to discussions between the Immigration and the Education Departments at the parliamentary level, and Ethiopian immigrant organizations demanded that Ethiopian children be allowed to register in the educational system.

The search for strong Ethiopian educators continued, and Nigist needed to secure financial backing for Fidel. The first supporter was Mary Ann Stein, the president of the Moriah Fund, which supported social justice and equality in Israeli society. She was followed by Arielle Landau, who had read an article Nigist wrote about the difficulties Operation Shlomo refugees were facing, their disconnect from Israeli society, their suicides, and the failure of Ethiopian students in schools.

Stein taught Nigist how to fundraise and Fidel was formally established in 1997 with Israeli and Ethiopian members.

Nigist believes that her own experiences and her children's frustrations to integrate helped her envision and build educational and social bridges for immigrants. Without a doubt, she said, having the help of someone from an organization like the Fidel Association when she first arrived would have greatly eased the absorption process.

People who act as social and educational mediators to bridge the gap between Israeli society and immigrants help students pursue higher education and reveal the hidden potential in the Ethiopian people that the Israeli education was not able to identify, she said. In addition, for example, a Fidel volunteer who drives parents to a late-night meeting at school creates a bridge by helping parents learn how to support their children with their studies, and also teaches students about patience and understanding.

For her work to narrow the gap and prevent scholastic and social failure for other Ethiopian immigrant students, Israel's government granted Nigist the honor of lighting a torch at the fiftieth Independence Day celebration, a recognition of how an individual's actions can enrich an entire community. "I was born in Ethiopia," she said she told herself. "I dreamed from a young age about holy Jerusalem. I went through failed attempts to make aliyah to Israel. Now I have been blessed to light the torch for the fiftieth birthday of Israel, and that is the biggest gift, besides the tremendous pride I feel."

Nigist earned her PhD in education from the University of Sussex, England, in 2007. In October 2008, after nineteen years of being away, she and her family went back to Ethiopia to explore their roots. Many things unfortunately had changed, but the visit helped close the circle. All that is left are photos of their memories.

Beginning in 2014, Nigist was the director of the Education Division in the municipality of Rosh Ha'ayin. She served more than 60,000 citizens, among them kindergarteners through adolescents in a high-quality education system, and she was grateful for the support of Mayor Shalom Ben Moshe.

"Do not run away from challenges—rather, wrestle with them," she said, her advice to young immigrants. "And when failing, do not give up until you win."

———◦•◦———

Nigist received the Bar-Ilan Award for Leadership in 2015, the Open University Award in 2013, and the Hebrew University Samuel Rothberg Prize for Jewish Education in 2010. In 2001, she represented Israel at the United Nations World Conference against Racism, Racial Discrimination, Xenophobia and Related Intolerance in Durban, South Africa. In 2002, she helped found the Ethiopian National Project (ENP), a partnership between the Israeli government, the Jewish diaspora, and the Ethiopian Israeli community. She served as the ENP's director-general between 2003 and 2011.

PART IV

THE ARTISTS

ACHINOAM "NOA" NINI,
international singer, composer, and
human rights activist

BOTHAINA HALABI,
visual artist, owner of
Druze Holocaust Art Gallery

ACHINOAM "NOA" NINI

ISRAELI SINGER-SONGWRITER, HUMAN RIGHTS ACTIVIST

"I am sure that decisions and actions that come from the heart, from care and human solidarity, love of nature, and a dedication to higher values, are the right ones, even if in the short term it may not seem so. As artists we are visionaries, and I try my best to see far into the horizon and strive always for the light."

DRESSED IN A FLOWING BLOUSE adorned with brilliant oranges and purples characteristic of Yemenite embroidery, Achinoam Nini,
known internationally by her stage name, Noa, faced a full house in the
two-hundred-year-old B'nai Jeshurun synagogue on Manhattan's West
Side. It was her first singing and percussion performance in the United
States after a two-year hiatus because of the pandemic.

The excitement was overwhelming and the sense of freedom and
joy, in getting back to normal times, was evident. The crowd stood
and applauded as she entered. Lights danced on the intricate Torah ark
behind her, and she sang without introduction as if her performance
were a continuation of an earlier concert. So natural and comfortable
in public despite abundant COVID masks in the audience, she and her
musical partner, guitarist Gil Dor, launched into a bravura set. Soon, we
fell into a meditative mood, inspired by the music Noa composed to the
words of her favorite poet, and adapted to a classical Bach-like fugue.

Our eyes filled with tears when she performed a song dedicated to
a dying friend. Noa's voice moved with ease from soprano to mezzo-so-
prano and to the lower range of the musical scale. She opened her arms
in prayer and an embrace, transporting us to an angelic world of beauty
and peace.

At fifty-two, Noa is a top Israeli singer, a Zionist, activist, environmentalist, and United Nations Goodwill Ambassador. She has performed in more than fifty countries and enjoys a full career, but her
criticism of the Israeli government's policies regarding the occupation,
and her belief in a two-state solution, has led to canceled concerts and
threats against her life.

"In Israel, we're very good at going to war. Israel is a strong country
that can defend itself," said Noa, who supports a strong IDF and considers herself a Zionist. "But we are less eager to go to lengths and take
risks to achieve peace. We have tried, but I believe we must try again
and again, leave no stone unturned, and come with goodwill, respect,
great courage, and the knowledge that compromise on both sides is un-
avoidable, until we find a way to ensure a future of peace and prosperity for our children. This is the essence of what I have been saying for
twenty-five years. From my point of view, everything I'm doing is to

glorify Israel, by strengthening and highlighting the endless people and organizations in Israel working indefatigably for peace.

"I know that for many, many people around the world, I am their only outlet or inlet in Israel," Noa said. "They don't have anything else Israeli but me, except maybe the evening news! I am their connection to the soul of Israel. So, I take that responsibility very seriously."

ENVIRONMENTAL ACTIVISM

I talked with Noa in an apartment in Tel Aviv, then again in New York after the March 2022 concert. We started with a lesser-known aspect of her life—her passion for coral reefs and her work with marine biologist Maoz Fine of the Hebrew University in Jerusalem.

"I wanted to be a marine biologist when I was a kid," she told me. "Incredible!" Through many discussions, she learned about Professor Fine's research into the coral reefs in the Gulf of Aqaba, and their unique resilience to the bleaching that is common in other places in the world. The work fascinates her, she said, as protecting these reefs would connect Israel with neighboring Arab countries in a common goal.

"This is my favorite general subject—bridge-building, cultural diplomacy, and environmental protection is a major issue and challenge today," Noa said. "I'm really loving it and very excited about it. And I feel that it's a mission. It's a tikun olam, which is what I love to do, and there can definitely be a synergistic triangle of science, diplomacy, and art that can be extremely important in materializing this vision."

Noa was born in Tel Aviv in 1969 to a fourth-generation Yemenite Israeli family that immigrated to Palestine between 1890 and 1895. They arrived by foot, plane, and boat, and settled in areas between Jerusalem and Tel Aviv. Her father, whom she describes as a "very talented and wise human being," studied in Technion under a scholarship. A chemical engineer, he also earned a scholarship to the University of Rochester. The family moved to New York when Noa was one-and-a-half. Her father earned his PhD from Columbia University, so they moved to the Bronx and Noa was sent to modern Orthodox Yeshivas.

"We were a totally secular family, so a paradox was created between home and school," she told me. "I was the only dark-skinned kid in the entire school. Fortunately, I was a gifted student." Her mother taught at the school, so Noa was further driven to succeed. "I wanted to prove myself," she said, "and I did."

Noa had a clear talent for music from the age of four. "Despite my talent for music, I saw myself doing other things," she said. "I was interested in math and science, I wanted to study English literature at Harvard. I had all kinds of ideas. But music was so clearly my calling, it was overpowering. I say that music chose me even more than I chose her. Finally, I fell in love with her. Now we're inseparable."

FINDING ISRAEL

The summer when she was sixteen, Noa visited an aunt in Israel. She met a young man on a hiking trip and, as she told me, "totally fell in love with him." When she returned to the United States she kept her boyfriend a secret, afraid her family would "freak out," but declared her Zionist orientation and her intention to return to Israel.

She told her parents: "You raised me with all these ideas. I'm going back to Israel. You guys can stay here, and come when you're ready."

She made aliyah by herself and went to a boarding school in Jerusalem. The boyfriend, Asher Barak, roughly seven years her elder, was studying medicine on campus next to her school. "I was totally crazy about him. The good news is that I married him and we're together to this day, with three beautiful children. Sometimes romantic stuff like that really does happen."

Noa finished high school and went into the army for two years of mandatory service. She then considered pursuing music at Juilliard in New York…until she thought of Asher. Instead, she found the Rimon School of Music near Tel Aviv, a newly built school for jazz and contemporary music modeled after the Berklee College of Music in Boston. There, she met Gil Dor, the school's cofounder and her future musical partner.

After a year at Rimon, Noa left and took Dor with her. "I wanted to be like Sting," said Noa, who eventually got to sing with the front man for the Police. Her role models were Paul Simon, Joni Mitchell, and Leonard Cohen.

Dor is now Noa's musical director, arranger, producer, and co-writer. She is a songwriter and plays several instruments. "I'm a total autodidact," she told me. "Everything that I know I've taught myself...except all the wonderful things I've learned from Gil in all our years together on the road!"

The duo had international success almost immediately. An encounter with guitarist Pat Metheny, a multi-Grammy-Award winner who loved Noa's music and voice, led to his production of an album for Noa. They also signed with Geffen Records just before David Geffen started DreamWorks.

At twenty-three, Noa had a record contract with an impressive label, an international career, and released a "live in concert" album in Israel. She is more fluent in English than Hebrew and writes almost exclusively in English because, she said, her English vocabulary is richer. But when in Israel, she wanted to sing and write in Hebrew. "I needed words," she said. "That's when I discovered the poetry of Leah Goldberg and fell in love with her writing. I felt that if I could write Hebrew, this is exactly what I would write. So, I started composing music to her poetry."

A few years later, in 1995, Noa received a life-changing invitation from Pope John Paul II to sing "Ave Maria" at the Vatican. The song would appear on her first international album. "I wrote lyrics to the piece, which was sort of an ecumenical prayer for peace. Gil arranged it upon my request like a folk song, because I wanted it to be accessible to people."

She was the first Jewish performer to sing at the Vatican and has performed there several times since. "I thought it was crazy that a Yemenite Jewish Israeli girl from the Bronx would perform for the pope," she said. "You can imagine, in my mid-twenties, my parents came, maybe a million people in St. Peter's Square, and I made a little speech in Italian saying that we are so proud to be able to break the walls between religions and culture." She would later sing at Pope John Paul's funeral.

She also sang for Pope Benedict and then Pope Francis, whom she said is "the coolest and the most amazing human being." She wanted his blessing for one of her projects, so she met with him and then performed for him many times.

Also in the nineties, she was invited to write the lyrics and sing the theme song from *Life Is Beautiful* (*La Vita è Bella*), the Oscar-winning Roberto Benigni film: "Beautiful That Way." "I think the song touches right to the soul," she said. "That's always our goal as artists. We take the entire universe of emotions and feelings and we condense it. It's fascinating work."

RAISING HER VOICE

On November 4, 1995, Noa was invited to sing at the fateful rally in Tel Aviv's Kings Square. She would be one of the only major artists who agreed to perform. "I was very proud to sing at the peace rally," she said. "About five minutes after I sang, [Yitzhak Rabin] was murdered. And I was devastated and traumatized. That bullet changed my life."

After the shooting, Noa decided to speak out and has been doing so ever since. But her advocacy for a two-state solution created a rift with the once-adoring Israeli public. Her life was threatened, and her concerts were canceled.

I said to Noa that many people in Israel believe in the two-state solution and asked why she thinks she is being singled out. Noa believes one of the reasons is her ongoing refusal to sing in the settlements until a sustainable agreement is reached. "I said that anybody living in the settlements was more than welcome to come to see my shows within the Green Line. That really did not go over well with the settlements." In addition, Noa said "there was racism and misogyny involved: how dare a Yemenite woman speak her mind, going so clearly against the grain? One guy tried to run me over. I'm laughing, but it was not fun at all." She continued, "Maybe I didn't always know exactly the right way to say things. I'm not a politician or a diplomat. I'm very much an intuitive and gut-oriented person. But I was 100 percent honest and listened to the voice in my heart."

Noa demonstrated against Benjamin "Bibi" Netanyahu, performing a version of the Queen song, "We Will Rock You," with her lyrics about democracy. She said she was proud to be active and "serving Israel," and criticized her performance peers for failing to step up. "They always seem to have something better to do when there's anything that demands actually taking a side," she said, adding that the protest movement helped convince many people to vote in such a way that would not enable Netanyahu to return to power.

FAMILY AND MUSIC

Noa and Asher—the military officer she met in Israel—have three children: a twenty-one-year-old son in the army in computer science; an eighteen-year-old daughter volunteering for a "service year" in the Oranim boarding school for youth suffering from post-traumatic psychiatric disorders; and a twelve-year-old daughter.

"I dragged them around the world," she told me. "It was a traveling circus. It was the hardest thing in my life to do, but I couldn't see myself living without music or without having children, so I just had to find a way to balance both." Noa said she nursed them on trains, buses, planes, and in the middle of a show. "I'm doing half the show, I go to change my dress, and nurse the baby while the guys play. If I was not finished, the tour manager signals to the band from the sidelines: 'Wait, she's not finished, play some more!' It was crazy and exhausting but worth it."

Asher traveled with her at the beginning, but then stayed mostly in Israel while Noa was joined by her mother, aunt, and nannies—anyone she could get to help with the kids, even band members.

In 2009 Noa was approached by Eurovision Song Contest to represent Israel at the international musical bonanza. After initially refusing, she came to see the contest as a platform to reach millions of people and convey a message. She agreed after ensuring that she would write the song and be joined by Mira Awad, her Palestinian friend, singer, and actress. "It was the first time that Israel was represented with a song that had Arabic in it and where a Palestinian Israeli was representing Israel," she said.

She and Awad reached the finals, made the album *There Must Be Another Way*, and collaborated on other projects. The title song became an international hit and is still taught in schools, Noa told me. Their performance also generated inspiring emails from throughout the Arab world, in Israel, and in the West, and they were interviewed by *The New York Times*, BBC Iran, and Al Jazeera.

In 2019 Noa and Dor made an album dedicated to Johann Sebastian Bach that was executive produced by Quincy Jones. Twelve pieces of Bach's instrumental music are accompanied by Noa's lyrics, inspired by "subjects as diverse as technology and religion, global warming and feminism, euthanasia, the Palestinian-Israeli conflict, and relationships in the age of social media," according to one reviewer.

Noa sings beautifully in Italian, which deeply impressed me! She learned to sing Neapolitan and won Italy's prestigious Caruso Prize, given annually to the finest performances of Neapolitan music, for her album *Noapolis*.

After Israel, she said, Italy is her favorite place in the world and the site of most of the amazing experiences in her life. She has performed "under every tree and in every village," including jails, and enjoys the work she does with inmates and in mental health institutions. "I've discovered that I have a deep connection with people who are distressed in any way. I reach them, and I love doing it."

AN ARTIST'S ROLE

What pains Noa is the way she's perceived. "Most people don't know what my opinions really are. That, I think, is one of the biggest problems," she said. "Very few artists speak out in Israel. We don't have that culture. And it's understandable in some ways, in the sense that it's such a small country, a small market. Artists are aware that if they express their opinions, they'll be jeopardizing their careers in many ways, and risk a large portion of their audience. Israelis do not react favorably to performers who are activists. They want artists to stay mild and nice, not be outspoken or controversial."

Noa said that in her opinion, the role of an artist goes beyond entertainment and helping people feel good. "It is to make them think, and sometimes to confront them, force them to review their own opinions and go deeply into themselves," like Joan Baez and other influential artists from the 1960s.

Noa believes that if Rabin paid with his life for peace, then she can also pay a price for what she believes is right. "I'm very much a Zionist. Everything I do and say comes from a place of great care and love for my home, Israel. I think Israel must be an open-minded place, a place of peace, a place of equal rights and opportunities, a place where people can flourish, develop, and grow, and where all the many talents that we have in Israel can flower. And I truly believe our well-being in Israel depends, intrinsically, on the well-being of our neighbors."

Her biggest argument with the worldwide Jewish community is the tendency to justify whatever Israel does, regardless of the essence and consequence. "On the way to fulfilling our great dream of establishing a homeland for the Jewish people, we hurt others," she said. "There is no shame in admitting that and apologizing. On the contrary, the act of coming to terms with your actions and past, and facing the truth, demands enormous courage and strength. We often over-protect Israeli policy, even when in our deepest heart of hearts we know that there are problems. The way that Israel has been handling itself the last couple of decades is very harmful to her reputation and future."

Noa said the solution lies in three simple words: recognize, apologize, and share. "You must recognize the pain and the rights of others just like you demand to be recognized yourself. We also have wronged, and we have to recognize that and apologize. And then we have to share. Nobody is going to get it all, compromise is the name of the game.

"The Palestinians are not going to throw us into the sea," she said. "We're here to stay. On the other hand, we are not going to be able to overtake the entire land. We will not be able to survive that way. We're going to finally lose our country if we annex millions of people and attempt to force our language and culture on them. The two-state solution is in the best interest of the Israeli people and Jewish people. And all of that has always been my philosophy. I don't see it as a non-Zionist philosophy."

What Israel should be worried about, she said, is the number of Palestinians who support the one-state solution. "It's a problem we brought upon ourselves," she said. "We knew we would have to dismantle some settlements but never had the courage and political gumption to do so. The settlers have become so powerful, choking Israel with their messianic philosophy. As a result, we back away from every possible solution."

She said agreements were reached to allow many settlements to remain, with only the "more radical" places dismantled. There should be land swaps to compensate the Palestinians. "We were so close to that with Prime Minister [Ehud] Olmert. If he did not get himself jailed, we might have already reached a compromise solution."

I asked her how we should handle other disputes, like who should control Jerusalem and the right of return. She believes Jerusalem should remain the capital of Israel, but that it should be a joint capital, an international city of peace, shedding a light upon nations. "Why can't we think of it in those terms?" she said. And regarding the right of return, "I don't think that it's possible to manifest the right of return in the fullest way, it's too late. The Palestinians will have to come to terms with that, compromising, just like we would dismantle some settlements and stop building new ones."

Noa said she is consistent in her beliefs and doesn't try to please everyone. "I spend a lot of time talking and learning," she said. "I visited the settlements several times and I talked to people, [but] we often speak a different language. I make great efforts trying to find common ground.

"The Palestinians have their story, and we have our history, and we have our rights, and we're implanted in the land of Israel. We recognize the Palestinians' pain, and we expect them to recognize ours. We're going to have to live together in compromise."

When I asked Noa if she would give back the West Bank, she responded that she would, in order for the Palestinian state to be established. But, she said, Jews should always be able to visit their holy places. That is just one of the reasons friendly relations are so important.

"I wish for peace with our neighbors, security, and safety for my children and theirs, a future for Israel and Palestine that is not constantly riddled with violence and fear. I am happy and proud to work for this goal, even if it does not happen in my lifetime. The price of speaking is high, but the price of silence is higher! I am sure that decisions and actions that come from the heart—from care and human solidarity, love of nature, and a dedication to higher values—are the right ones, even if in the short term it may not seem so. As artists we are visionaries, and I try my best to see far into the horizon and strive always for the light."

BOTHAINA HALABI

ISRAELI DRUZE ARTIST

"If you want to change the world, first, we need to change ourselves and educate our children to love, not to hate, to respect the others and the different, to be patient and tolerant, and not to judge anyone according to his faith or religion. It doesn't matter if you are Jewish, Christian, Muslim, or Druze."

ON MY WAY TO VISIT painter Bothaina Halabi in Daliyat al-Karmel, my childhood memories were awakened by the sight of forests and the scent of peppermint from the trees along Mount Carmel's serpentine roads. I had enjoyed many summer vacations collecting anemones on the sloped terrain, and I remembered the colorful bushes from my time with the Scouts and paramilitary training during high school.

A Druze city, Daliyat al-Karmel is part of the large Haifa district where I grew up. Strangely, it took decades of living abroad to finally visit the town. I wondered why I had never gone there before. Perhaps it was the Druze community's secluded way of life. Or was it my parents' erroneous belief that the Druze were Arabs? As the years passed and the Druze became "blood brothers" of the state, and their sons sacrificed their lives in the Israeli Defense Forces, I learned that the ethnic community I was about to encounter was unique, brave, and moral.

I arrived at Daliyat al-Karmel on a sunny Saturday and immediately noticed the locals: the men had long mustaches and wore long black robes and cylindrical headdresses made of tightly wound white cloth; the women covered their hair with long white veils.

I would soon learn that white, one of the colors of the Druze flag, stands for peace and purity. Each of the flag's colors symbolize one of the five prophets and a corresponding way of life. Green is for nature, red for courage and love, yellow for wheat and knowledge, and blue for the sea and the sky.

Bothaina greeted me with a smile at the entrance to the quaint stone home that also serves as her gallery. Sweets of all kinds dotted the living room coffee table, accompanied by the aroma of the cardamom-spiced, freshly brewed coffee. Bothaina and her husband wore modern attire and looked Israeli in every way. In perfectly spoken Hebrew she told me about her life in the Druze community, her outreach efforts, and her commitment to educate people about the Holocaust through her paintings.

Born in 1975 and now a mother of three, Bothaina took courses in office systems management and legal administration, and trained as a medic. She and her husband are heavily involved in community service, volunteering at kindergartens and schools in Daliyat al-Karmel and Isfiya, another Druze-majority town. She spends time with children with disabilities and students in need of special education.

Bothaina said she painted as a child but had no formal training. It wasn't until about fifteen years ago, when she saw in the newspaper an archival photograph of the forced death marches, that she started learning about the Holocaust, beyond her limited knowledge of the number of lives lost. At that point she hadn't met any Holocaust survivors or heard how they existed in the death camps. "The stories and the picture [in the paper] affected me," she said, "and I decided that I must think about the pain and the despair that I saw on the faces of the Holocaust victims."

She developed her skills to create haunting black-and-white, and then color, oil paintings of people in the extermination camps. Her first exhibition, at the Community Center in Daliyat-al-Karmel, attracted many neighbors, none of whom knew about her thematic choice. "I was surprised by their reaction," she said, "that they supported and sympathized with the Holocaust [survivors]."

EMPATHY THROUGH ART

Bothaina named her first painting "Reflection." "You see them walking toward death, but there are no faces, because to the Nazis they were only numbers," she said. "The plants at the bottom of the prisoners symbolize a new life after the Holocaust. I believe that I push some of my [Druze] belief of reincarnation into this painting."

In concert with another exhibition, at the Western Galilee College in Acre, she brought Druze students from sixth through tenth grades from Daliyat al-Karmel and Isfiya to the Beit Terezin Holocaust Museum in Kibbutz Givat Haim. "We did it so they, too, can learn about [the Holocaust] and how they should learn to accept 'the other,'" Bothaina said.

In addition to Bothaina's Dialogue Between Neighbors project, the directors of Beit Terezin annually bring Jewish students from across Israel to visit Daliyat el-Karmel, to learn about the Druze community.

"At the end," she said, "they come to my gallery, and we do a dialogue about the Holocaust together." Another of her projects, Windows for Memory, invites tenth-grade Druze students to express in writing how they feel after learning about the more than one million Jewish children who died during the Holocaust.

About ten years ago, Bothaina donated one of her paintings, "The Last Letter," to the art museum at Yad Vashem. "This was the first time they accepted from me, a non-Jew, a painting."

A copy of "The Last Letter," which hung on her gallery wall, caught my eye. In it, a woman sits on rich, red ground and writes a letter before the Nazis send her to the gas chambers. "And they don't know for whom she's writing this letter," Bothaina explained. "Is it for her family? Is it for her friends? Is it to the world to let them know what happened in the Holocaust?"

Bothaina continued to tell me her story, remembering how she lighted a candle for the Holocaust victims when she traveled to Romania, and how the subject of Holocaust denial came up when she returned. In 2014 she traveled to Poland to take part in the March of the Living, a trek between Auschwitz and Birkenau. This was her first visit to an extermination camp.

"In the march, I didn't feel that I was different from anyone," she said. "All that I felt was that I am a human being, a human being who goes to the unknown. I didn't know what to expect. When we arrived at Birkenau, I was afraid to enter the gate. And when I did, I was struck by the large number of pavilions and felt the chemicals.

"I didn't believe what I saw. That was very scary. I entered one of the pavilions, and I had many thoughts and many unanswered questions. I thought to myself, 'How can it be that the human being loses all humanity and becomes a monster whose only goal is to destroy and kill? Why? How could such a thing happen, and nobody did anything, exactly like what's happening today in the world, with the killing of innocent, and the world is watching? Everyone is talking about peace, but no one is doing it.'"

Bothaina said she returned from her journey stronger and more determined to continue her work. She involved her children, who also traveled to the extermination camp. "They were extremely affected and their view on life changed," she said.

Bothaina has been honored for her work by the University of Haifa and received an ambassador award that is given to people who fight against antisemitism, racism, and the BDS (Boycott, Divestment, and Sanctions) movement. She also received the education prize from the Massuah Art Institute for her commitment to universal acceptance and education, which she summarized for me: "If you want to change the world, first, we need to change ourselves and educate our children to love, not to hate, to respect the others and the different, to be patient and tolerant, and not to judge anyone according to his faith or religion. It doesn't matter if you are Jewish, Christian, Muslim, or Druze. First of all, we are all human beings, and we need to respect each other."

Among her other projects, she holds video meetings with international students at Ryerson University in Canada, and has secured funding from the university for Yad Vashem, the Holocaust memorial.

In addition to international and Muslim visitors, Bothaina's small Druze Holocaust Art Gallery welcomes survivors who often cry, bare their hearts, and share their stories. She said they find solace in the love they feel from a non-Jew: "They say, 'we can die in peace because you, Bothaina, commemorate what happened.'"

I told Bothaina that my grandmother died in Auschwitz, and that I am named after her. And though I don't believe in reincarnation, I feel like part of my grandmother resides in me. Bothaina said that survivors who visit her gallery tell her that she gave them hope. "And a lot of them told me that when they were in the Holocaust, they didn't believe in God. And now, after they hear me, they believe in God again."

DRUZE IN ISRAEL

Bothaina's family lived in Daliyat al-Karmel several generations before the birth of the state of Israel in 1948. Her recently deceased father, who was an electrician and encouraged her to pursue her education, followed his father's mission to connect faiths and bring Jews and Muslims together. Her father, she told me, took a great risk when he thwarted a potential act of revenge after a Druze was killed by a Muslim. Her father "adopted" the Muslim family for three months, giving them shelter and providing financial and emotional support. The generosity is typical of the Druze in general, she said, and then told me more about the Druze community's culture and religion.

There are roughly two million Druze worldwide, most of whom live in Syria, Lebanon, and Israel, including the Golan Heights. More than 100,000 Druze live in Israel, comprising roughly 2 percent of the country's population. They have been farmers for generations. They are united by a monotheist religion that is an offshoot of Islam, they speak Arabic, and they have guarded their unique culture and customs for about one thousand years by isolating themselves from the non-Druze. Since just after their religion's founding in the eleventh century, Druze have not accepted converts and intermarriage.

The Druze accept the prophets of Islam and Christianity and have incorporated elements of Greek philosophy. The main religious book is the Kitab al-Hikma, which means "book of wisdom," and the most important prophets are Jethro, the father-in-law of Moses, and Elijah. Unlike other forms of Islam, they embrace reincarnation, allow women to become religious leaders, and prohibit men from having multiple wives. The Druze religion is secretive, the scriptures and laws remaining unknown to many Druze themselves. Only a few sages have full knowledge; many of them have political influence.

Most Druze accept their faith in trust. Because Druze are said to be connected to God at all times, there are no set holy days, regular liturgies, or obligations for pilgrimage. Their God, al-Hakim, is a predecessor of the Islam prophet Muhammad, to whom the Druze also pray. Speaking the truth is a command.

Even though Bothaina is a non-religious member of her community, she follows the traditions she inherited from her parents and now passes to her children. She is proud of being faithful to her words and follows advice from the elders and community leaders. Nothing, she said, is done without their approval.

Bothaina explained how believing in reincarnation helped her mourn the death of her father, whose soul, she said, was immediately transferred to a newborn boy. As is tradition, her father does not have a gravestone and Bothaina does not know the exact location of his burial.

There are no gravestones in the cemetery and no value to the body, she said, only for the soul that arises anew.

SUPPORT FOR ISRAEL

I asked Bothaina about the relationship between Druze and Arab Israelis, and she said that the Druze supported the state of Israel in the late British Mandate period through its independence. Israelis recognize their service in the IDF (Arabs are exempt from serving), and there is no military supervision or restrictions. Druze are represented in the Knesset and serve in highly visible positions, such as the presidential advisor on minority affairs. In 1962 Israeli authorities recognized Druze as a separate nationality category on their identification cards.

Ultimately, our conversation turned back to Daliyat al-Karmel and its community. Bothaina pointed to the House of Oliphant—a memorial to the bravery of fallen Druze soldiers and their loyalty to Israel—and explained that it belonged to Sir Laurence Oliphant, a British member of parliament, a writer, and a Zionist.

She emphasized how proud she is of her son serving in the paramilitary Border Police and the IDF. He will protect Israel regardless of the enemy, she said. I asked Bothaina if she has family among the Druze in Lebanon and Syria. She said they have no contact. "I know that it is possible that some of the Israeli Druze would have to fight against members of their families," she said. "But if there's war, we don't stop and ask him if he is Druze or if he is Muslim. We serve as the soldiers. If we need to kill him, so we kill him first. It is not a question. Our brotherhood is with the Jewish people. We are loyal to the people we live with. I know that our life in Israel is better than the life the Druze have anywhere else."

I asked about the hostility Israeli Arabs and Palestinians have for the Druze, whom they see as traitors, and why the Druze try to maintain friendships with everyone, regardless of religion. Bothaina said she occasionally she gets death threats from Arabs who disapprove of her loyalty to Israel and her work to honor victims of the Holocaust. She responds with an email containing a heart emoji.

Bothaina believes there are advantages to her son joining the army and her daughter a two-year national service/community service program. Her daughter can attend university in the same town that she serves, and her son, when he completes his service, will have access to a healthy job market for IDF soldiers, especially positions with police forces.

Finally, I asked Bothaina if the Druze feel discriminated against in Israel, and she said not in terms of social or economic measures. There was an incident in 2019, however, that she said offended the Druze community. Former Prime Minister Benjamin Netanyahu referred to the state of Israel as "the nation-state of Jewish people and them alone." She said this meant that all other minorities had equal rights by law, but the nation-state belonged to the Jewish people, which prompted then-President Reuven Rivlin to say, "Israel has complete equality of rights for all its citizens."

I told Bothaina that her art and her volunteer work are examples of how she is integral to the success of Israel and worldwide understanding of the Holocaust.

———◦•◦———

Bothaina discussed her artistic journey and unique exploration of the Holocaust during an online program in June 2022 hosted by the Jewish Community Center in Palo Alto, California.

PART V

THE INNOVATORS

ORNA BERRY,
former Chief Scientist and Director of Israel's
Industrial R&D Administration, Vice President of
Innovation and Growth at EMC

RONY ROSS,
Chair and founder of Panorama Software

KIRA RADINSKY,
CEO of Diagnostic Robotics, Visiting
Professor/Scientist, Technion

SIVAN YAARI,
Founder and CEO of Innovation: Africa

SHARON BARAK,
Founder and CTO of Solutum

ORNA BERRY

COMPUTER SCIENTIST, TECH ENTREPRENEUR, FORMER GOVERNMENT SCIENTIST

"In a society where men are leading and women are Number Two, I say, 'Until I find a Number One whom I could be confident to blindly follow, I will do what I think is best."

ORNA BERRY, FIRST AT ALMOST everything she does, has been blessed with a unique and extraordinary strength of character and body. The first and only woman appointed Chief Scientist and Head of the Industrial Research and Development Administration of Israel's Ministry of Industry, Trade, and Labor, her path to excellence in industry and government affairs reveals her honesty, intelligence, and sense of justice. Despite life-threatening illness, she continues to advocate for women, equal opportunity employment of minorities, and compassionate healthcare for all.

The portrait we see today of Orna has been shaped by her parents. Her father, from whom Orna said she inherited her sense of absolute honesty, was born in 1926 in Romania, and is an Israeli hero. Yoash Chatto Tsiddon made aliyah to Palestine in 1941, attended the maritime high school, served in the pre-state Palmach fighting force, served in the navy preparing convoys of World War II refugees and bringing illegal Jewish immigrants to Israel, commanded a Jewish deportees camp in Cyprus, fought in the War of Independence, and during the Arab-Israeli war in 1948 was a commander and participant in convoys to Jerusalem. He became one of the first combat pilots in the Israeli air force, a test pilot, flight trainer, squadron commander, deputy air force base commander, and finally the air force Head of Weapons and Planning. He was an industry executive (Bliss, Cyclone Aviation), later joined the Tzomet party, was elected to the Knesset from 1988 to 1992, and was one of the members who changed the election system for prime minister. (That change was reversed after two government terms.)

Orna described her father as an intellectual visionary who introduced the air force to operations research. He was a courageous pilot who, in Operation Tarnegol at the eve of the Sinai Campaign in 1956, downed an airplane carrying most of the headquarters of the Egyptian army on its way back from Syria.

He was also conventional: he expected Orna to compromise her ambitions while he encouraged his sons to become engineers. Of the three children, Orna was the one who became the engineer. Daniel Tsiddon became a professor of economics and a leader in the financial sector. Ram became a distinguished lawyer and businessman.

Orna's mother, Raisa Shrira, was a nurse who served in the Palmach and in the deportees camp in Cyprus, where she met her future husband during the British mandate. She later served in Jerusalem during the War of Independence. Subsequently, she worked at the Sheba Medical Center in Tel HaShomer and in the Orthodox community in Bnei Brak. As a child, Orna said she resented her mother taking on the Number Two role when her father was around, while taking the Number One position during his lengthy absences of service abroad. She felt that there was room for both her parents to be Number One.

Born in Jerusalem in 1949 and brought up in Tel Aviv, Orna joined the Israel Defense Forces air force. During the War of Attrition, she was an officer in flying school at Hatzerim Airbase and took responsibility for frequent changes in ground classes of the cadets, while their trainers, operational pilots, were called to the front.

"I did what I was supposed to be doing, and I filled a vacancy," she said of her first entrepreneurial idea. Orna was discharged as a lieutenant and earned a BA in statistics and mathematics from the University of Haifa, an MA in statistics and operations research from Tel Aviv University, and a PhD in computer science from the University of Southern California. During her PhD studies, she received a fellowship with the RAND Corporation.

She and her family returned to Israel in 1987. The return was never in question, but the date was set after unknown individuals stopped her son and told him to "go back to Tel Aviv." This was a clear reminder, she said, of the need for a Jewish state and a determination to return to Israel and contribute to its successful development. Back in the country, Orna took part in the evolving high-tech industry.

From a family perspective, the landing in Israel was not simple. Her husband became frustrated by the change and they drifted apart. Her daughter had a poor experience with an unwelcoming teacher, thus Orna had to assist her psychologically, eventually moving her to another school to undo the damage. Her son, who had been reluctant to move to Israel, enjoyed sports activities with his new peers and the welcoming school and classmates.

Initially, Orna worked for IBM Research Lab in 1987, then assumed an R&D position in data communication with an Israeli tech company, Fibronics, in Haifa. She left, along with four others, when she realized that the company's management did not listen to her, despite her being the chief scientist. She cofounded Ornet Data Communication Technologies in the Galilee. There, she encouraged the employment of Arab engineers who graduated from the Technion, and got them involved in tech, a space to which they previously had reduced access.

MAKING HER MARK IN BUSINESS

From an early age, Orna did not differentiate among people. She convinced her business partner of the importance of hiring the right candidate, regardless of race and gender. "The most important qualification is knowledge and productivity," she said. Hiring an Arab who graduated with top honors was merely a meritocracy. To secure the hiring of a talented worker who was initially denied work due to racial considerations, Orna and her youngest daughter traveled to his home in Nazareth to invite him to join Ornet, despite the previous discrimination. He accepted the position, becoming the first Arab employee in the company and opening the door for others. This individual later relocated to the United States, then returned to Nazareth as an entrepreneur and mentor to his community.

While fundraising for Ornet, Orna was a consultant at Intel and a project manager at Elbit Systems. Ornet Data Communication Technologies built ethernet switches and was acquired by Siemens in late 1995, the first Israeli startup acquired by a European conglomerate.

Orna always treats people as her equals and expects to be treated the same. She placed significant importance on having earned her PhD, and she was determined to employ learned and professional people on her team. "Individuals who are professional and productive create a team of high performance," she told me. In the technology field, for example, investing in the future is critical because information constantly changes. "Deep knowledge of artificial intelligence (AI), data science, and quantum science require an academic background," she said. "It cannot be learned on the job."

Orna joined the government in late 1996 and was nominated Chief Scientist and Director of the Industrial R&D Administration, the first and only woman to hold this position to date. She fostered relationships between Israel and the United States, and encouraged the participation of the Israeli government in R&D programs in Europe, Canada, the UK, South Korea, and Singapore. In 2007 she served on committees to examine management of the Israeli defense budget. From 2018 to 2021 she led national science and technology initiatives in quantum science and AI.

THE LIFE OF A CHIEF SCIENTIST

Orna's team collaborated with many government departments that had to work together to keep the country resilient. She mediated requests for funding tech companies from the education, health, and technology tiers, among others, and developed a big-picture budget to achieve maximum benefit and build for the future.

She carefully analyzed each request and ensured that public money wouldn't be used to feed someone's ego. The job was interesting, she said, because she had to understand a person's motivations for funding and the worthiness of their proposals. This blending of different views brought balance, trust, and collaboration to her teams, and led to successful relationships between the tiers of government.

I asked Orna about her strategies for surviving in the male-dominated world of science. "I identified when people would start talking to me as a woman," she said. "I shut up for a while, and then I came up with something unique to add to the discussion, so that they understood that I have a viewpoint, and that I know what I am saying. I don't try to please anybody. I am not coming with an adverse position. I am coming with my own position. In a society where men are leading and women are Number Two, I say, 'Until I find a Number One whom I could be confident to blindly follow, I will do what I think is best."

Nearly twenty years after leaving the Office of the Chief Scientist, the Academy of Sciences, the Ministry of Finance, and the Government of Israel Research Authorities asked Orna to build cross-authority national R&D programs, to promote quantum science and technology and AI and data science. Orna told me about the time when her strategic approach to the national budget was adopted over the "military approach" presented by a male colleague. His plan failed, she said, because he was too domineering, did not respect or include or empower others, was not focused but very spread out, and showed insufficient transparency for others to embrace.

To remain unfettered and unbeholden, Orna refused to be paid for her government work. She wanted to focus on doing what she thought was right for the development of a sound infrastructure, which to her went beyond the physical means for building an advanced computer system. She needed to determine other variables—including the number of highly skilled professors to employ, the number of research groups, the types of research conducted, and the tools that would keep the public sector ahead in automation, data science, and AI. "When the practice does not exist," she said, "it results in an illiterate scientific society leading a local life rather than a global one. This leads to the poor purchasing power of Israeli society."

Orna returned to the private sector in the summer of 2000 and joined Gemini Israel Ventures as a venture partner, remaining there until 2010. That year she joined EMC Corporation, as vice president and general manager of the company's center of excellence in Israel. She was subsequently promoted to corporate VP of innovation.

Orna's motto was "Performance and Productivity," and she insisted that race and gender should never be a determinant of success in the workplace. In partnership with Ben-Gurion University (BGU), she helped establish a technology park in Be'er Sheva that became a catalyst for the growth of the technology sector in the periphery. At Orna's urging, in July 2013 EMC was the first company to move into the technology park, and Orna later received the Yakirat Ha'Negev award from BGU and Yakirat Ha'ir from the city of Be'er Sheva.

After EMC merged with Dell, Orna stayed with the team temporarily before returning to public service. In 2021, at the age of seventy-two—following a complex cancer diagnosis and treatments, and after submitting two national R&D programs encompassing academia, defense, and industry (innovation authority)—Orna joined the office of the CTO at Google Cloud. Her new challenges included overcoming regulatory barriers related to restrictions on cross-border and cross-business data sharing.

"When you have people who do not understand technology, like lawyers, they need novel, transparent, trusted, and responsible sharing mechanisms," she said. "And from my perspective, digitization must provide this type of trust to its users. The area of ethics has been growing tremendously. Lawyers may limit the use of technology due to gaps in transparency and trust. But in my mind, I look at technology as the service of society. Be it defense, education, or health. I'm very interested in the solution and the impact the solution has on society."

PERSONAL CHALLENGES

Orna and I turned our discussion to the warm and loving relationship she has with her three children. "They are my children, and I feel responsible for them. But they're very smart and from a very young age, they took a lot of responsibility," she said. "When my predecessor as chief scientist wanted me to fill his shoes, I told him to talk to my kids. And he came to talk to my then-eighteen-year-old daughter, and she told him, 'If mom sent you to us, it means she's interested. And in this family, everyone does what they're good at.'"

Orna's children took responsibility at a young age, a necessary partnership that allowed the family to move forward from a failed marriage. Her greatest partner to date is her eldest child, her son. At seventeen, he oversaw the construction of her house, and he is still in charge of the most critical family assets. Her central daughter cared for the younger one during the Iraq war, when Orna was called to work, her son was drafted, the youngest was a baby, the babysitter ran away, and schools were shut.

Throughout her life, Orna has found time to dedicate herself to others. She served on the board of directors of Kav Mashve, an association that promotes Arab academic employment, and is a member of the board of directors for Ben-Gurion University Technologies. In 2021 she received the Hugo Ramniceanu Prize in Economics from Tel Aviv University, and the Peres Center for Peace and Innovation Award.

The *Marker* financial magazine ranked her fifty-first on the 2019 list of one hundred most influential people in Israel. And in 2014 Orna was inducted into the Women in Technology International Hall of Fame. She has received numerous honorary academic degrees, including PhDs from McGill University in Canada and Bar-Ilan University in Israel.

FIGHTING FOR HERSELF AND OTHERS

In 2016 surgery revealed Orna had multiple cancer carcinosarcoma in the uterus and serous carcinoma in the ovaries, while a PET CT and biopsy revealed papillary carcinoma of the thyroid. There was no systemic treatment. She consulted with seven sources who gave her three to five months to live. With the death sentence on her mind, she decided to stay in Israel, close to her family, for what she thought was the rest of her short time. Her children supported her decision.

She had aggressive chemotherapy, twenty-eight consecutive full stomach and pelvic radiation sessions, and insisted on receiving Avastin, a drug that prolonged the therapy's beneficial effects. She went for acupuncture and changed her diet. Treatment of her thyroid cancer had to wait because of potential drug interactions and the priority set with her doctors.

On top of the stress of fighting for her life, Orna had to pay, initially, for the Avastin when her insurance refused. Her successful crusade proved through research that Avastin was essential for her survival, because the drug decreased the number of cancer cell indicators. Her HMO agreed to cover the cost, only to abruptly declare her healthy five years later—less than a year following the neck surgery and the removal of the three tumors in the thyroid, without consulting with her doctors.

"They don't connect the dots, and they have all the reports," she told me. "I wrote to them an explanatory letter and they didn't answer me. So, I asked my doctor to connect for them the three facts: the fact that the other drugs that I'm receiving are alleviating symptoms from the treatment on my digestive system and danger of clots; the fact that the same year I had another cancer surgery; and the fact that it drove me to make an analysis and demonstrate what was important and efficient in my case." The doctor's letter convinced the insurer to cover the drugs.

Orna lectured and approached the media to help inform the Israeli public about self-advocacy, and how to most effectively pursue the right to live. "As in any other relationship, my cancer and I have our ups and downs," Orna said during one of her TED Talks. "The downs, when the threat of death becomes more evident, the ups, when the hope for life shines brighter. The hope for life is granted to me thanks to my family and friends, thanks to the determination to live, and thanks to the medication I am receiving, which is not covered by public health insurance. The medication was granted to me thanks to the war I waged for it."

I thought Orna would be a good person to explain how Israel became the leading country during the COVID pandemic. She said that for years the Ministry of Health has collected health data to inform budgeting for hospitals and HMOs. Then the army gathered information about the number of incidences of sickness and the spread of disease, and other experts helped determine logistics, including the numbers of hospital beds, available equipment, and medical teams. The data was analyzed by staff at the Weizmann Institute, Hebrew University, and Clalit HMO.

The key was that data was being collected for years, started by Ziv Ofek, now the cofounder and CEO of MD Clone, and Professor Yitzhak Peterburg, then the director general of the Soroka Medical Center and later of Clalit HMO.

Finally, I asked Orna what advice she would give young women. "Focus on what it is that you really want to get to," she said. "Think about what will make you feel good and what your mission is. Then develop and force yourself into becoming less sensitive to destructive forces along the way.

"Just make sure that every morning you get up, you know where you are going and take the steps in the twenty-four hours that follow," she said. "You will then be taking steps towards your goal."

RONY ROSS

FOUNDER AND EXECUTIVE CHAIRMAN,
PANORAMA SOFTWARE

"It's extremely important to build up the credibility of women in their own capabilities and in taking charge of their financial lives and their responsibility as a financial provider. They can't ignore it anymore."

RONY ROSS, CHAIRMAN AND FOUNDER of Panorama Software, has the distinction of being the first Israeli entrepreneur to "exit" Israel—a term that refers to selling technology or a business to a company outside of the country.

In Rony's case, the buyer was Microsoft Corporation. Her offering was a business intelligence (BI) product, including a unique multidimensional database, that would become the tech giant's foray into the burgeoning BI field. The price tag in 1996 was $20 million US dollars. The offer came after a single, three-hour demo.

"Afterwards, I went outside and said, 'shit, shit, shit, I should have asked for more,'" she told me. "But at the time it looked like such a huge sum. It was the highest figure ever."

Rony hasn't wasted much time fretting. She is a role model to the many other entrepreneurs and businesspeople in Israel who followed her lead. Her persistence is legendary. She once stalked a noted journalist on a conference stage to get his feedback about her product. She is a visionary. She realized the need for self-service analytics, took a risk, and invested her own money in the development of her product. She employed Russian immigrants when few other businesses were interested in that skilled labor, and helped grow Israel's stature in the tech space.

Rony walked into our meeting and lit up the room with her smile and cheerful personality. Her blue eyes peeked out from playful neon-green glasses and met mine. I was amazed by her fierce intelligence and her acceptance of risk as she described her path to selling her technology to Microsoft. But first, she shared with me her family history.

Born in 1949 to Israeli parents, Rony was meant to be a gift to her grandmother after her uncle, one of the first Israeli war pilots, was killed during the War of Independence. She grew up with a father who was a self-made, highly revered lawyer, and she and her two siblings followed an academic path that led to successful careers.

I was most intrigued by the determination and courage of her ancestors—traits that Rony would embrace—to make the state of Israel a reality. With great pride, she told me the thrilling story about her maternal grandfather, who went to Palestine as a teenager from Latvia before the First World War. Along with other young Jews, the Ottomans expelled him to Alexandria, Egypt, at the beginning of the English-Turkish war. There, along with famous freedom fighters Joseph Trumpeldor and Ze'ev Jabotinsky, he joined the first organized Jewish military group in two thousand years. The 120 young men in the Jewish Battalion of the Mules joined the English in the Gallipoli campaign in 1915 in the Dardanelles.

The Entente powers—Britain, France, and Russia—lost the battle, but the young Zionists recruited additional members across Europe to form the thirty-eighth, thirty-ninth, and fortieth regiments of the King's Army, and helped the English liberate Israel from the Ottoman Empire. They proudly wore shoulder patches embroidered with the Star of David.

Rony followed the usual path of an Israeli sabra. "I am a second-generation Israeli, having both parents born in Israel, and the only child in my class to have had both grandparents on both sides alive while I was growing up," she said. She went to the Carmel School in Tel Aviv, joined the Israel Defense Forces, and graduated from Tel Aviv University with a bachelor's in mathematics and an MBA from the Recanati Business School. She earned a master's degree in computer science from the Weizmann Institute of Science. During her studies, she married and gave birth to two children: Guy and Gali.

Rony started Panorama in 1993. By 1996 it had become the leading developer and source for online analytical processes (OLAP) software and BI in the Israeli market, gaining over 75 percent market share in two years. I couldn't resist asking about the detailed steps she took that led to this amazing success.

Rony's first venture was a development center for a US company that specialized in computer-aided design and manufacturing. In the 1990s, a large wave of Russian immigration to Israel brought brilliant technologists she recruited to work for her. When the US company decided to close the development center, she set up a consultancy business, with the same staff, to build products for Microsoft Windows, the new platform at the time. She had a customer who wanted to migrate their enterprise resource planning software (ERP) from Unix to Windows. Rony created a prototype of a reporting module to highlight the strength of Windows' user-friendly interface (UI) compared to Unix's green screen and complex coding.

Though the initial project was custom-made, the work led to the development of a universal system for managing data analytics from any industry. "Any user could exchange what they saw in the X column versus what they saw in the Y column, and slice it and dice it, as well," Rony said.

In 1994 there was no other product that offered the broad-based analytical solutions that Rony envisioned for the Windows platform and its unique graphical user interface. In order to validate the product-market fit, she approached fifteen potential customers about the need for such a product. She discovered that it was part of a field known as executive information systems, and that the need for fast response time would require the development of a special multidimensional database—a sizable development task. Rony all but gave up on the product idea when the phone rang. On the line was the last customer that she met with, a guy who headed the first direct insurance company in Israel.

Insurance companies collect data to choose new customers. Rony's system could increase a company's profit by helping select the best customers faster, in real time, by identifying people with the least risk. Her client was excited by the new software but still considered it a free trial, with payment withheld until a year after the product was successfully installed. Rony was left to compensate her employees out of pocket.

"I had to pay salaries. I had to make expenses. I had to buy new computers. I had to invest in this. I had to invest in that," she told me. "I had sleepless nights from the fear that it would not work out, that I will go broke, that I will have to admit to my family that I used up all our savings for something as stupid as that, that I will have to start looking for a job.

"I remember having pain in my knuckles from climbing on walls, trying to make it happen," she said. "But somehow, the people that worked for me were very, very optimistic." Thankfully, in a few months, they were able to build a working product to install at the insurance company.

The success attracted customers from different sectors, including the Israeli Prison Service, Bank Leumi, Cellcom, and food manufacturer Elite. Her product's unique selling point was that it could analyze data regardless of industry, that it enabled self-service analytics thanks to the attractive, easy-to-use, Windows-based UI, and that the multidimensional database that they developed was superior to others in the market. At the time, other products had multidimensional databases that pre-calculated all potential queries during the night. Panorama, however, avoided the long pre-calculation process by learning from the way people actually used the system, and stored only the frequently used queries to deliver results in a fraction of the time. As more people used the system over time, more and more queries were added, but the size of the database was still a fraction of a fully pre-calculated one.

"It worked!" she told me. "I loved it, and it was very exciting."

Rony approached several venture capitalists to help take her product abroad—only to be rejected, she said, for being a woman who didn't fit the mold of what they envisioned of a successful hi-tech entrepreneur… basically an ex-8200 technology guy, or an ex-IDF fighter pilot. "Of course, they didn't say that," she said. "But I looked at myself, I reflected and said, 'I don't care. I'm going to get there, no matter what.'"

She was determined to find a partner in the United States that would team up with her to take her product to market as part of another solution. It could be a company that built financial packages, ERP systems, database providers, whatever. It was just a question of having them believe in her and in Panorama.

Rony knew it was important to refuse public money from the chief scientist of Israel R&D, because it would limit her ability to sell software outside the country. She also had to establish herself as profitable and reliable, to show that she had customers who were worthwhile.

She told me about how she built a list of more than sixty clients in Israel in a year and a half. "I went like crazy. I sold to insurance companies. Then I went to sell it to retail. Then I went to pharmaceutical, and then I went to government organizations. I went all over the place. I zig-zagged from one industry to another."

VIGILANCE

By selling to a diverse customer base, Rony learned to modify her software to meet the needs of various industries. "For a while, every customer got a slightly different version of the software," she said, "but through this, I did manage to get a lot of functionality into the product."

She attended a conference of the Executive Information Systems in London, where journalist and analyst Nigel Pendse was a speaker. After many failed attempts to get a meeting with him, Rony physically blocked his way after a Q&A session on the conference stage and demanded that he talk with her. "I said, 'Nigel, you are not going anywhere without speaking to me first.'" When he told her to go back to her little country and do her great work there, she didn't budge. "I said, 'Listen, Nigel, you have to tell me whether my product is worth anything. Should I go and spend money trying to get somewhere, or not?'"

Rony launched into her first elevator pitch: "We built the multidimensional database based on how the users are using the data. We don't pre-calculate everything, we just do what is necessary, or what is likely, or what will take the longest."

Nigel was impressed by the idea of a learning mechanism and joined Rony and her colleague in their hotel for a demo. Lacking a Business Center, the demo took place on a computer in the hotel's gloomy accounting office. Pendse was amazed. "He said he didn't really expect anything when he came in, and that it's a beautiful product with a lot of functionality," Rony said. "He said we have a great process for our database in the way we pre-calculate that the response time is good." Then he asked if she wanted his help finding a value-added reseller in the United States.

"I remember sitting with my partner in the lobby afterwards, after Nigel left," she told me, "and in my mind, we were holding each other's hands, so as not to fly in the air. I felt it was the summit of my professional career."

Back in Israel and energized by the positive feedback, Rony attended a conference hosted by Gartner, a world-renowned technology research consultancy. Among the guests was Microsoft's head of marketing in

Israel. He directed Rony to the relevant person in Redmond, Washington, who was researching the BI market. Having established contact, Rony proceeded to supply information. When she was asked about the product's competitive advantages, Rony requested that Microsoft first sign non-disclosure agreements. When they refused, Rony decided to take a risk: she and her team wrote a white paper describing the concept of their multidimensional database and added the title "Non-Confidential" to the document.

In the meantime, Pendse arranged a few meetings, including one in Vancouver, only two and half hours from Redmond. Rony wrote to her Microsoft contact that she would be "in the neighborhood" and why not set up a meeting?

The contact replied that if she weren't coming specifically to meet with Microsoft, a meeting could be arranged. And then in an additional email asked: Are you the small company from a small country that Nigel Pendse is talking about?

On July 15 Rony and her colleague arrived in Redmond. Ten Microsoft people attended this first meeting, which lasted more than three hours. They were curious about the product, the UI, the technology, the multidimensional database, the functionality, and the plans for the next release. Then they asked the Panorama team to wait for twenty minutes, which extended to almost an hour. Then they were asked to stay for another meeting in the afternoon. They agreed and went to lunch, ordered food, and then, out of the blue, a twenty-six-year-old guy in a T-shirt and jeans asked Rony if she ever considered selling her company to Microsoft.

Rony was totally unprepared for such a proposal. She realized, however, that it might be the most important career achievement she would ever make, and said it was an excellent idea. At a second meeting, with a VP, she was asked if there were any legal reasons preventing a sale, who made company decisions at Panorama, and how much money she wanted. Rony quoted a wild range, and the VP surprised her with the response: we are in the ballpark.

They reached a tentative agreement, and in August 1996 Microsoft representatives visited her modest office in Tel Aviv, what the Americans called a "garage operation." Her brother and sister, both lawyers, helped in the negotiations. The process went smoothly, and the deal closed in October 1996.

This was the first pure software company that was sold to an entity outside of Israel, a deal known as an "exit." "One day," Rony told me, "I was walking down the street and I heard somebody say, 'This is Rony Ross. She made an exit.' And that's how I knew what the word meant." It was also the first technology acquisition Microsoft made outside of the United States.

Microsoft didn't have a plan for how to support Panorama's existing customers, so the company purchased just the R&D, intellectual property, and source codes. The R&D team moved to Redmond as Microsoft employees and stayed together for ten years, developing the Microsoft Business Intelligence and SQL Server. "This was a major component of their offering for enterprises and analytics," she said. "The analytics that they built around it was with my team." She said her R&D manager, now a Distinguished Microsoft Engineer, still leads the BI and SQL Server development with Microsoft, and that the acquisition is considered to be one of the most successful Microsoft has ever made.

WOMEN-FOCUSED PROGRESS

Rony stayed in Israel and continued to support her customers. "And when Microsoft comes up with a new product, I will be the one to install it for them," she said. "So, this way we figured out how it would work." She hired a new development team, which for five years developed products to augment Microsoft's offerings. She then expanded Panorama to a VC-funded global company. From 1997 to 2021, they developed and marketed BI solutions, operating in Canada, Europe, and the United States.

Rony engaged as a board member for several public and governmental companies. She is a member of the International Board of the Weizmann Institute, a member of the Executive Board of Afeka College, and—among other volunteer jobs with not-for-profits—is the chair of her neighborhood's country club.

In recent years, Rony has mentored a variety of entrepreneurs, mostly women, through the 8200 Impact program, the SheShe Mentoring program, the Reichman University Entrepreneurship Faculty, Afeka College Grads, and others. She mentors on strategic and product/market fit issues, and is often asked how to juggle an entrepreneurial career and motherhood. Rony's advice: explain to the child that their mother is doing everything she can to provide for the child's future.

She is also a member and investment committee member of NEOME, a Tel Aviv-based investment club for women that takes a collaborative approach to selecting companies, doing due diligence, and furthering financial education. She shares her personal success stories and encourages women to become financially independent.

"One of the things that is key for women is to be able to take risks, to take control of their financial lives and the financial side of funding their families," Rony told me. "They've gotten used to not taking the monetary responsibility for the future. But they can't ignore it anymore."

People understand that more than half of women will either not marry, get divorced, or have a husband who can't support the family. "You will be the major provider of your family for a very major period of time, if not for your lifetime," she said. "You will be the one that decides where your family will live, what schools your children will go to, what vehicle you will drive, what kind of after-school activities you can afford for your children, and where on the financial social ladder you are going to be. It's up to you, not to anybody else. You can't rely on your partner, and you can't even rely on your family money. So, it's extremely important to build up the credibility of women in their own capabilities and in taking charge of their financial lives and their responsibility as a financial provider."

HOPE FOR ISRAEL

As we came to the end of our discussion, I was curious about how Rony perceived the increasing division among Israeli citizens.

"I want you know that I am really very, very, very Zionist!" she said, and that she felt lucky to witness the country's biggest growth in its early years, whether in economics, R&D, as a startup nation, in gastronomy, music, or tech startups. "It gets into your bones and into your DNA," she said. "It's a powerful experience. Helping build a nation from a small insignificant place to becoming a light for the world is empowering." She is thrilled to see children of emigrees return to Israel and dedicate themselves as Lone Soldiers, and she is excited every day, but especially during Independence Day.

When I asked Rony if she was worried about the future of Israel, she told me that she understands threats like climate change, population growth, and Israel's internal and significant problems, but chooses to worry about more immediate concerns. Regarding the Israeli-Palestinian issue, she said more people are landing on the right side and the left is shrinking, "basically because most people realize that no matter what we do, peace is not going to happen in our lifetime."

"It's scary," she said. "People always say, 'just give back the occupied territories' without thinking of the consequences. And then what? Are we done? Are we going to get peace for returning the occupied areas?"

The agreement with the Emirates is a hopeful beginning, she said, and the more partnerships created with Arab states, the more we can change the opinion of the general Palestinian public. Israel has also made great progress in Arab relations: more Arabs have important roles in the economy as doctors and software engineers, and they are moving forward.

Finally, I dared to ask about what I thought was the most difficult situation in Israel, the ultra-Orthodox community. "It's so difficult for me to understand," she told me. "These are brilliant people, and I wish they would put their mind to something more practical than learning the Torah. They don't work, they live in poverty, and they choose to live this strange life which suits them and makes them happy. It is beyond my understanding."

Parting from Rony was difficult. She inspired hope that economic, political, and national solutions are possible in Israel, especially with a positive attitude and a commitment to lead the way for women.

KIRA RADINSKY

COMPUTER SCIENTIST, INVENTOR, ENTREPRENEUR

"Instead of me being a scientist, how could I build a machine that is going to automate me as a scientist?"

FIVE-YEAR-OLD KIRA RADINSKY LOOKED INTO the video camera when an adult asked what she wanted to be when she grew up. The little girl didn't hesitate.

"I said I want to be a scientist," Kira told me during our conversation. "For me, it was not about changing humanity. I was just excited about pushing the boundaries of knowledge, of humanity forward."

As the CEO of Diagnostic Robotics (DR), Kira has pioneered the use of AI in healthcare to lower costs, maximize clinical value from medical encounters, and predict the spread of the COVID-19 pandemic. She has also used her skills as a computer scientist and software engineer to enhance national security in Israel, leverage AI to produce drug-delivery molecules, and help e-commerce retailers benefit from historic consumer behavior.

The ability to predict outcomes, in fact, appears to be inherited. The timing of her emigration to Israel from Ukraine at the age of four was the result of her mother's near-perfect ability to predict the safest time to travel. It was 1990, and the former USSR opened its borders and allowed millions of USSR Jews to make aliyah to Israel. Among the emigres were Kira, her beloved grandmother, mother, and a twenty-one-year-old aunt.

They fled their town in Ukraine, where the oppressive anti-Semitic regime limited Jews' participation in higher education or professional careers. Fallout from the explosion in Chernobyl in 1986 poisoned the environment and further disrupted social and economic norms. The all-female "squad," as Kira affectionately named her family, looked to the holy land for a healthier, hopeful future.

The task of predicting when to leave fell to Kira's mother, an engineer whose mathematically wired brain weighed the risks of the pending Gulf War with the potential closure of the Russian door. Her timing was off, but not by much. The family arrived in Israel two weeks before the war broke out instead of the more favorable time of what she hoped would be a couple weeks after the war ended. As Kira now understands, predicting world events is a lot easier—though still imperfect—with the right algorithms and massive computing power.

They took a taxi from the airport to Haifa and knocked on the door of what was supposed to be a relative's home. Happily, the strangers who actually lived there offered a warm reception at 4:00 a.m. and a place to stay.

Kira told me that her arrival in Haifa came during a wave of immigration that disrupted work at the Ministry of Internal Affairs. "Everybody came with nothing, because you could not take anything with you from USSR," she said, and the government workers were overwhelmed trying to take care of people and process passports and ID cards. "They went on a strike. We did not get the ID, so without one we could not get a mask," Kira said. "However, kind soldiers were willing to give it to us, as typical to the lack of formality of Israelis."

The war erupted and Iraqi forces fired forty-two Scud missiles at Israel over the course of a month and six days in 1991. There was terrific panic as missiles headed toward Haifa and the Tel Aviv coast, with only minutes for Israelis to find shelter and don gas masks. I imagined how traumatic it must have been for little Kira to wear the menacing, shiny black mask with huge eyes and protruding snout. But how could she understand that some bad people in the world wanted to hurt them?

Kira came from a family of engineers and computer scientists, and education was of utmost importance. In Israel, her mother took a teaching job so Kira's aunt could pursue a higher education. "My aunt continued to study and obtain a master's degree, while everybody was doing whatever was possible and working three jobs so my aunt could get her education."

Kira grew up knowing that nothing would prevent her from achieving her passion. "I think every scientist is doing something which is unimaginable at first," she continued. "We all do something small and eventually build those huge leaps forward. I wanted to be a part of that story."

ALGORITHMS AND AI

At fourteen, Kira joined a science camp that only accepted youth ages sixteen and over. She was lucky to work in cancer research with notable professors. But during her work, she actually fell in love with building data analysis systems, such as software that could replace the manual counting of cells and accomplish tasks in a much shorter time. "I started automating a lot of work," she said of her deep dive into data analysis. "It is about how we are doing all those discoveries in one month, instead of years."

Kira set out to build a system to automate science through AI and data analysis. She smiled as she shared her hope: "Instead of me being a scientist, how could I build a machine that is going to automate me as a scientist?"

The IDF's Intelligence Force trained Kira as a software engineer, and she has been honored several times for her contributions Israel's security. In 2006, when she was twenty, she received with her department the Israel Defense Prize for Significant Contribution to the Defense of the State of Israel. At twenty-eight, Kira, representing the field of science, was one of fourteen honorees chosen to light a torch for Independence Day. At thirty-two, she received the Israel Defense Prize for a project that had a dramatic effect on Israel's security, including the prevention of hundreds of terror attacks.

"The project embodied the development of an innovative approach aimed at achieving intelligence superiority, and realizing the potential embodied in the digital age, impressive organizational integration, and unique technological achievement in the field of big data," she said.

After her IDF service, Kira received a PhD in computer science from the Technion. At fifteen she had attended the gifted student's program and received her first degree.

She built an AI system to predict world events, such as civil unrest and disease outbreaks, and in 2009 went to work with Microsoft Research in the United States. There, she built a system that scanned the *New York Times* archive and social media for information to create the algorithms to predict riots and epidemics, as well as the price of electronics and commercial goods.

"I had an opportunity to work with different aid organizations," she said. "We were able to predict the first cholera outbreak in Cuba in over 130 years, then the Sudan riots in 2013. And it was pretty exciting just to see that. Not only the predictions are happening, but there are also things you can do to stop them."

In 2012, Kira cofounded SalesPredict, an AI analytics company that was acquired by eBay in 2016. She became eBay's IL chief scientist and director of data science, "building the next generation predictive data mining, deep learning, and natural language processing solutions to transform e-commerce.

"In SalesPredict, we were trying to predict economic trends and sales conversions," she said, "using all the news data and information from companies to identify how to make better economic relationships. We work with Fortune 500 companies and quickly growing startups to increase their revenue, and also significantly make the ecosystem much more efficient."

In 2019, Kira cofounded Diagnostic Robotics (DR) to design AI systems for healthcare and enhance human capabilities. As I listened, I was secretly grateful that no machine—yet—could automate me as a physician. Kira promised that AI is not replacing doctors, but assisting them. "People do not want to be diagnosed by systems," she said. "People want to be diagnosed by people who have empathy."

DR's purpose is to make healthcare more accessible and affordable by providing the right treatment at the right time in the most appropriate setting. For example, Kira said that Rhode Island state officials used DR to help manage its response to the COVID-19 pandemic. People who responded to a web-based questionnaire could choose when to seek testing and when to seek care. The platform also provided local information and resources at a time when the wait in hospital ERs was excruciatingly long and the number of physicians was decreasing.

"The digital triage platform is a decision support system that helps manage the load flow by selecting the [patients] that need care," Kira said.

When Israel's minister of health approached DR to predict who would get COVID and how it would spread, Kira and her team designed and implemented a system to send clinical triage questionnaires to everyone in Israel. Based on the data, DR's analysis predicted how COVID would spread and targeted COVID testing for the population that most needed it. As a result, if enough symptomatic patients were identified, Israel could quarantine areas in a single day to prevent a second wave.

So-called triage from home safeguarded patients from the risk of an unnecessary trip to a doctor, and lessened a physician's exposure to highly contagious patients. DR "saw" that loss of taste and smell, as well as fatigue, were reliable predictors of COVID and helped determine who should stay home and who needed emergency care.

In other use cases, Kira said, algorithms are built using historical data sets and, with approval, information from patient medical records to detect patterns of deteriorating health. Because depressed patients, for example, are less likely to take their medications and therefore wind up in emergency rooms, a health plan or provider using DR can notify a patient to take their medications or seek help before a critical—and costly—situation.

Kira is also a visiting professor and scientist at Technion, where she investigates the time-saving effort of repurposing drugs while new drugs are in development. For example, proton inhibitors that are used to reduce gastric acid to prevent ulcers, can also improve the treatment of hypertension. Her systems also identify adverse drug effects—for example, that beta-blockers used for hypertension can increase the risk for Parkinson's disease.

YOU CAN'T PREDICT EVERYTHING

When Kira and I spoke, Israel was approaching the November 2022 elections with considerable tension between right and left, religious and secular, Arab and Israeli. Lurking in the background was the threat of Iran's nuclear capability, Russian's assault of Ukraine and its impact on the world economy, and a growing loss of life.

I asked Kira to pinpoint the biggest existential threat to Israel, and she said, "There is us versus them, and there are too many of them and too many of us. But I am most worried about education." Kira said education in general is not good or broad enough to produce the next generation of leaders, especially with a decline in the number of skilled immigrants coming to Israel. "This is our biggest next challenge."

I asked if AI could predict whether peace with Palestinians can be achieved in the near future. Kira said computers process tremendous amounts of data from numerous events, outcomes are monitored, new data is added, and an algorithm can predict an outcome based on previous examples. The Israeli-Palestinian conflict, however, is significantly influenced by the "fear/trust" index.

The index declines, she said, if Israelis worry about their safety or if Palestinians refuse to accept the neighboring Jewish state or support terrorist attacks. Monitoring the index in real time improves predictions about the conflict. For example, the Israeli "trust half" of the index increased—a good thing—when Egypt President Anwar Sadat went to Israel and said he was seriously interested in peace, and when Jordan King Hussein visited Israel following the murder of several girls at the Jordan border. Hussein expressed his sorrow when he met with the girls' parents, and explained that Jordanians don't believe in violence.

"The best way to know that there is going to be peace between the Israeli and Arab populations is actually to do a survey in Israel," Kira said. "Pretty much in all the previous times when the Israeli population had trust, it was the biggest sign of peace coming. But presently, there is very little trust, and so very little hope for peace."

Kira lives in Zichron Yaakov with two children and her loving, brilliant scientist husband, whom she has known since she was eight. I thought it was an interesting coincidence that Kira chose to live in the same place as Sarah Aronsohn (1819–1917), a heroine of the state of Israel. Aronsohn was part of a spy ring that passed information to British agents to help free Palestine from the Ottoman Regime. Aronsohn was caught and tortured and shot herself in the mouth so she couldn't reveal important information. In her last letter, she expressed her hope that her activities would help realize a national home for Jews in "Eretz Israel."

I was born and grew up in Haifa, not far from Zichron Yaakov—a cobblestoned, picturesque town in the southern Carmel Mountain Range overlooking the Mediterranean Sea. The legacy of Zichron Yaakov and Aronsohn's bravery is now joined in my heart by my admiration for Kira Radinsky, a gifted and brilliant woman who is part of a new generation of leaders.

SIVAN YAARI

SOCIAL ENTREPRENEUR,
FOUNDER & CEO OF INNOVATION: AFRICA

"What truly keeps people in poverty and without good health and education, is their lack of access to energy."

I ARRIVED AT RAMAT GAN'S Ayalon Mall early, around 7:30 a.m., in anticipation of meeting Sivan Yaari, the young Israeli woman who is known for saving African villages from drought, darkness, and disease. I passed brand-name fashion stores. I went into a large supermarket where products were precisely arranged and the fruit stand brimmed with unfamiliar items, hybrids of local invention, I was told. The meat department overflowed with options, and an ocean of fish enjoyed their final swim. Children would have crowded into the impressive candy corner, if it were not so early in the day.

Where was I? There was nothing reminiscent of the Israel I left many years ago, not even one falafel store! Nowhere to find hot pitas; just flaky, buttery croissants. I followed the aroma of brewing coffee to the small cafe to await Sivan.

She arrived dressed in blue jeans and a sweatshirt, a beautiful face surrounded by thick brown hair and adorned with a big smile. We sipped cappuccino, and she immediately complimented my choice of a fashionable Italian suit, which at first made me feel at home in the opulent mall. But humility overwhelmed me as I listened to Sivan describe how, with solar panels and water pumps, she is changing life in Africa for millions of people.

"What I'm trying to do today is to help with the major challenge that exists, which is the lack of energy," Sivan said. "Without access to electricity, there is no light or energy in schools or medical centers, which means people do not have access to quality education or medical care. Crucially, without access to energy, there is no access to clean water! Without water, there is no life."

We talked about Innovation: Africa, the nonprofit Sivan created fifteen years ago, when she earned her master's in energy at Columbia University in New York. So far, Innovation: Africa has brought Israeli solar and hydro technology to more than nine hundred villages, impacting over 4.2 million people across ten African countries.

"By the end of this year [2023], we're going to surpass one thousand villages," Sivan said. "It sounds like a lot, but it's not. We've only helped four million people. When we understand the challenges that currently exist in Africa, it's quite small compared to the amount of people in need. We're talking about four hundred million people who lack access to safe water, and over six hundred million people do not have access to electricity."

Sivan said she made many mistakes along the way—including forgetting that villagers couldn't afford to replace the lightbulbs they installed—but each misstep brought reasonable solutions, new businesses, and now, an app that allows the hydro and solar systems to be monitored live, from anywhere in the world.

FROM BLUE JEANS TO ELECTRICITY

Sivan's father was born in Algeria, moved to Paris, and then in the late 1960s to Israel, where he volunteered in the army. Her mother moved with her family from Tunisia to Israel, and as a teenager joined the army, the only one of her twelve siblings to enlist.

Her parents met at El Al, where her father was working, and her mother, a soldier, was sent to retrieve old airplane seats for her base. "My father was a real French gentleman," Sivan said. They fell in love and got married but were never successful in business. "We didn't have much growing up, and over the years, also. But they are very happy people. My father only sees the good in everything. He's always happy, and he loves dancing. He's an artist. I learned that money does not make one happy; I learned real values from my parents.

"In some way, you can say that I am African, because both of my parents were born in North Africa," she said. "So, I kind of find my way back to Africa."

Sivan was born in 1978 in Israel. She has a sister who lives in France, and a brother in Israel. When she was twelve, the family moved to France. Her mother sold pizza in the market and Sivan helped. At eighteen, she volunteered in the Israel Defense Forces, and at twenty she saw an advert for a job with Jordache jeans. Sivan interviewed with one of the owners, who told her she was "lovely," but her English wasn't very good. Her French, however, would be a good fit for the factory he owned in Madagascar. She could help with quality control.

And then Sivan had to ask him: "Madagascar, where is that?"

After arriving on the island in the Indian Ocean, off the coast of East Africa, Sivan visited villages and saw the challenges caused by the lack of energy. "But I didn't know what to do," she told me. "Truly, I was uneducated." She continued to work for Jordache and traveled to the other factories in Africa making jeans. "The more I traveled," she said, "the more I realized that the poverty is not about one or two villages, or even one or two countries; it's about an entire continent."

Over time, however, Sivan realized that water—the lack of it, and its cleanliness—was the core issue. Dehydrated and sick children did not go to school. Many hours each day were spent searching for, collecting, and transporting water. "And yet there was plenty of clean water just below their feet, in the aquifers," Sivan said, nearly shouting with excitement. "All we need is to pump the water."

WATER PUMPS NEED ENERGY

Sivan applied to Columbia, with the goal of solving the energy and water challenges she encountered in Africa. At one point in her studies, a professor advised her to invest in two solar panels, which she purchased with a grant from Columbia. "I installed the solar panels in that village," she said. "And there was light! Everyone was so happy."

A friend in New York told Sivan to create a nonprofit to accept donations for her project. Still a student, she found a pro bono lawyer and opened Innovation: Africa, which she originally called Jewish Heart for Africa. The name was meant to indicate that the technology came from Israel, but some people wrongly inferred that the nonprofit sought to convert Africans to Judaism.

I was impressed by the positive changes Sivan and her team created with seemingly little investment, yet she refused to take much credit.

"What we do is quite simple and makes an immediate and significant change in the lives of thousands of villagers," she said. "Each time we visit the villages, we see further impact. Community members are healthier, waterborne diseases are eradicated, children are going to school, and economic development begins to take shape."

"Women no longer have to go and collect water," she continued. "Suddenly, from living in a mud home, a woman is building her new brick home, because now there is water and she can manufacture bricks. People come from nearby towns to buy bricks from her, and with the money she receives, she is able to support her children. With the water, she is able to cook and clean safely—everything is different. Talk about female empowerment!"

Most inspiring, Sivan said, is the creation of new businesses that have slowly lifted people out of the worst conditions. "The most important business is agriculture," she said, and drip irrigation systems have been installed to grow more with less water. "You go back, you see so many vegetables and food. As a result of electricity and water, the village is becoming rich, and the community have improved food security for the first time in their lives."

As an Israeli, Sivan said she is quite proud of the fact that Innovation: Africa transfers knowledge about technology from Israel to empower others. "Usually when we get to the villages, it's the first time and place that the villagers hear about Israel," she said. "They heard about Jerusalem from their Bible prayers, and they relate their improved life changes to the God of Jerusalem, that God answered their prayers. It is okay with me, as long as we save lives."

FROM THE BEGINNING

The process of procuring water begins with drilling in the aquifer, and then building a ten-meter-tall tower, she explained. Next, solar panels are installed on the tower to capture energy to power the solar pump. The pump brings water up to the tank and, with gravity, water flows to taps that are installed in the village. "Once you open the water, that's it," she said. "And as long as there is sun, there will be water."

Sivan said her nonprofit started small and today has 140 full-time employees. Most are Africans, most are engineers—hydro, electrical, civil—and geologists, and many were trained in Israel. "You need to have the right people in place to make it right," she said, and villagers are involved from the beginning. In addition, ten villagers are typically hired for three months to work with the contractor. They are paid, trained, and get a diploma, so they know everything to do by the time Sivan's team leaves.

As of March 2023, Innovation: Africa had 40 contractors working on projects across 130 new villages, where Innovation: Africa's local employees are ensuring everything is completed according to the organization's standards and guidelines.

Meanwhile, a team of engineers in Israel has developed a system to install an Israeli-designed remote monitoring system, for which Innovation: Africa has received a few awards, including the United Nations Innovation Award. The app, accessible on a phone or via computer, provides alerts to engineers and can be adapted for use by donors or people who sponsor a village.

"Let's say you give [sponsor] as a gift for your child's birthday, a gift that will provide water to a village of five thousand people in Malawi, or other villages on a list," Sivan said. "Innovation: Africa will then invite you to travel with us to the village, because you are the one who's going to open the taps for the first time and see the impact of your donation firsthand!

"When you return home, you can open your app, and you can track, live, how many liters of water they are drinking each day." A webpage provides live access to maps and images, including a satellite view of the village, where you can see the tower, the taps, and the homes. "You can always be in touch," Sivan added. "You can also do a WhatsApp video call with the chief, with the people. It is a beautiful experience. And it's a way also to bond. I can imagine family members or a group of women adopting villages and traveling together to Africa."

KEEPING LIFE IN PERSPECTIVE

Sivan said she and her siblings didn't have much growing up. "But I had shoes. I was clean. When I go to Africa, only then did I realize what does it mean not to have much. Only then I realized that actually I was quite lucky. I had a bed, I had a cover, I had water. What was I complaining about?"

She showed me pictures of herself outside of Jordache in Madagascar, and with children who took her to their villages. On one visit, she wanted to help some women who didn't feel well. At the medical center in Madagascar, people were waiting inside and outside. "I asked for a doctor, but I was told that there are no doctors here, because doctors do not want to move and live in a village if there is no electricity. So I asked the nurse why she was not helping them. And she told me, 'I can't do much to help.'"

Sivan paused and looked at me. She said that I, as a doctor, would understand the challenges of trying to treat people without light.

"Imagine, in the evenings, doctors, nurses are using candles and kerosene lamps. Without electricity, because there is no refrigerator, one cannot store medicines. So the challenge is energy; what truly keeps people in poverty, and without good health and without good education, is the lack of energy." Now, thanks to Sivan, the hospital has a small refrigerator to store vaccines, and people come for their inoculations.

When she visited a nearby school, Sivan realized that the pupils sitting in the first row were the richest in the village. They could bring money to buy kerosene. "If you have money, you can sit near the light," she said. "If not, you sit in the back. And if you want to be a successful—and many of them would like to be doctors and lawyers—they would need light in order to study at home. I was thinking and wishing I could help."

LOOKING FOR ANSWERS

Sivan reminded me that she has made mistakes over the years and has failed many times. She told me about the lightbulbs, or how she forgot to consider who would replace them over time. "What was I thinking? That the nurse would take money from her own salary to buy light bulbs? That the students are going to get money to buy light bulbs? I had to find the solution."

She returned to the village and met a man who collected cell phones. The man paid the owner of a car to allow him to charge the phones every few days. Instead, Sivan asked him to charge the phones at one of the schools and pay the teacher to use solar energy. "So, the teacher will have money to do what?" she said. "To buy the light bulbs! That happened many years ago. And it worked." After a few months, Sivan said, another business opened at the school using solar energy for a barber shop.

She showed me pictures from Zambia, Tanzania, and Uganda, where people still spend the day collecting water, and told me about discovering her first critical mistake. "At a school in Uganda where we installed solar power, I thought that the teacher would thank me," she said. "But instead, he announced that they didn't use the solar energy. I asked why, and he told me to look around. There are no students. He said they are too weak to walk. He said there was famine. He said there was no water."

Sivan said the conversation reminded her of the first village in Madagascar where she saw children out of school. "I should have asked why, and I didn't," she said. "I wasn't curious enough. If I would have asked, I would have understood that the main challenge, the reason why children are not going to school, or the reason people are sick, is because of the water. And that was my first mistake. Because I only realized the challenge of the water later."

In addition to electricity, Innovation: Africa also provides schools with laptops and desks. Teams install solar energy in the homes of the teachers to attract better teachers to the village. They install solar power at medical centers to run medical equipment and refrigerators. They supply beds, mattresses, and provide electricity to homes of the nurses and future doctors who agree to move to the villages.

Innovation: Africa relies on individual donors and support from foundations and corporations. "We work closely with the local government, but we don't get funding from them," she said.

I asked Sivan the cost of Innovation: Africa's work, and she said it costs $20,000 to bring electricity to a school or medical center, and $65,000 to construct a solar water pumping system, which includes the drilling, construction, the solar panels and pump, tap stands, and a remote monitoring system.

The life-changing work used to be even cheaper, Sivan said, but last year, costs for construction materials and just about everything else jumped by about 30 percent. She said Innovation: Africa keeps no money. One hundred percent of a donation goes directly to the villages; the nonprofit's overhead is already covered. A donor who adopts a village gets all the invoices and pays the full cost of getting to the point where the tap is open. Because the cost is about twenty-five dollars per person, she said, "even someone who gives us twenty-five dollars makes a difference."

Sivan has been traveling from Israel to Africa since 2008, even when she had three young children at home. I asked how she managed. "I was only able to be successful because I married a wonderful man, a good man," she said. "He kept telling me, 'Sivan don't worry, our children are okay; go help those who are not.'"

When she realized she was too often away from home and wanted more time with her children, she brought them with her to Africa. "So, from the age of eight years old, they were traveling with me to the villages, spending time with me, back and forth," she said. "And so that's the way I'm able to combine all of it—my husband's support, and the fact that my children are traveling with me."

If she did stay home, millions would likely not have access to clean water or energy today.

———◦•◦———

Since our interview, Sivan was bestowed the title of one of the "50 Most Influential Jews" by The Jerusalem Post for her expertise in using Israeli technology to improve lives in Africa.

SHARON BARAK

FOUNDER AND CTO, SOLUTUM

———◦•◦———

"It's okay not to succeed; you need to know how to grow and learn from failure as well. And even with success, you need to know how to cope, not be afraid, and continue moving forward."

SHARON BARAK WORKED AS A senior engineer in the plastics industry until she could no longer justify her complicity in the Earth's decay. Ever since, she has devoted herself and her startup to creating eco-friendly alternatives to the millions of tons of polymers choking the planet.

The epiphany came a few years ago. Sharon and her life partner, Mike, were sitting outside watching countless plastic bags swirl through the air and tangle in trees in their Tel Aviv neighborhood. "I cannot bear this any longer," she shouted. "Someone needs to find a solution."

Mike said, "You are a brilliant chemical engineer. You should solve this."

And so, she did.

Her company, Solutum—the name is derived from the Latin word for dissolvable—creates products that could one day eliminate the traditional plastics that kill animals, accumulate in the oceans, and contribute to greenhouse gases that exacerbate climate change. Industries long dependent on plastics, including food, fashion, and agriculture, have indicated an interest.

While Solutum's product is currently more expensive, it is indistinguishable from conventional plastic and significantly cheaper than the other alternatives on the market, Sharon said. It biodegrades entirely when it reaches the end of its life cycle and is completely nontoxic. "Yesterday, I had a meeting with an investor," she said, "and I demonstrated how it dissolves. He said, 'Wow, I'll drink this!' His wife got so alarmed that she tried to stop him. I reassured her and showed her how I drink the water."

As I talked to this brilliant scientist, I learned that she thrives on failure and has already accomplished what few others have been able to do in a lifetime. Despite gender bias and health challenges, Sharon has become a leading entrepreneur in a field that she believes will benefit her children and generations to come.

When Sharon was about a year old, she and her Israeli-born parents lived in Paris for two years, followed by two years in Germany, where her brother was born. After her parents divorced, her mother—her role model, and a true lioness—raised the children in Israel and made sacrifices to ensure they never lacked anything. She worked several jobs in the cosmetics industry, but there were financial problems at home. Sharon received assistance for school and grew up with second-hand clothes. (She told me that she and her children wear second-hand items even now, because the practice is good for the environment.) Then her mother met Benny, an aerospace engineer, who became Sharon's stepfather and her role model for excellence.

Sharon describes herself as capable, competitive, and ambitious. "Perhaps because I grew up with Benny, who was perceived as a very smart man, and my brother, who could easily match that intelligence, I decided that I am smart."

A third-generation Holocaust survivor, Sharon told me how a long-ago school project to create a family tree gave her the opportunity to spend hours with each of her surviving grandparents and hear about their bravery. "They didn't think of these stories as acts of heroism; to them, it was simply their life stories," she said. "But to me they are heroes."

Sharon's late grandmother Yocheved helped smuggled immigrants through the sea at night, when she was a young girl on lookout duty. Her grandfather Yosef served in the British army. "They were apart from each other, fought for the same cause, and sent each other the most romantic love letters I have ever read," she said.

Her late grandmother Zahava was a Holocaust survivor who lost her loved ones, escaped, and rebuilt everything from scratch in Israel. Her late grandfather Dov escaped before the Holocaust and, "with a strong and generous heart," worked with Arabs, despite some of the common challenges.

"What a generation," she told me. "And what a privilege it was for me to hear their stories. May their memories be blessed."

INDEPENDENCE THROUGH SCIENCE

In school, Sharon studied "physics for the mind, and cinema for the soul. I decided that I am going to be scientific like my stepfather, because I wanted so much to be like him." She aspired to become an engineer and study "something scientific." A single mother's daughter, she knew the importance of independence and standing on her own merit.

While serving in the Israeli Defense Forces Air Force as an operations officer, Sharon visited a laboratory in the north. Scientists there had developed an application, based on the mechanism of a jellyfish's sting, to deliver substances like insulin to the body. She knew then that she wanted to pursue her own humanitarian project; but it would be years before the spark to create Solutum would cross her mind.

Sharon worked as an assistant to the security officer for El Al and lived in Paris. She traveled briefly to South America, then studied chemical engineering at Ben-Gurion University, where she met her partner, Mike, in the debate club.

CHEMICAL REACTIONS

After graduation, she worked as a development engineer in a missile production factory with her boss, L.K., a doctor of physical chemistry. Sharon was heavily involved in the development of materials and systems that seemed like science fiction. She managed projects, studied the chemical aspects of missile firing systems, identified malfunctions, and resolved them. The scientific and practical industrial experience still serves her today, as does her relationship with Dr. L.K., who is an occasional consultant and constant inspiration.

"He taught me how to research and develop, made me read hundreds of articles; he taught me the process of new developments, which helped me when I started developing the Solutum technology," she said. "Today, from time to time, I still read new science articles. He taught me how to extract relevant knowledge, and how it aids in development."

In 2011, while still working, Sharon enrolled in the MBA program at Tel Aviv University. Dr. L.K recognized her passion for management and allowed her to engage in customer negotiations, learn how to identify customer needs, shape development, and deliver projects. After five years at the factory, she had enough. "There was this saying that if you stay in the industry for more than five years, you'll remain there until retirement, and that frightened me," she said. "I felt like it was a golden cage I had to break free from."

Sharon left her prestigious, rewarding job, with a boss she loved and job security, for a position as a technology manager, working with laboratories and clients, at Delek-San—a startup that recycled organic industrial waste fluids.

"I was exposed to and fell in love with the idea of a double bottom line: a company with a business plan that also has a positive impact on the environment," she said. "There, my environmental awareness developed. Until then, I thought that environmental protection was a privilege."

At Delek-San, Sharon also learned about the integration of sustainability and business. "It's not a philanthropic venture," she said. "We're talking about business and impact, and when you operate in this way, you profit. I understand that I can't attract an investor who only looks at the bottom line, and on the other hand, even the most altruistic person won't join a business if they don't see a profit in the end."

In fact, Sharon is not willing to earn less to be environmentally friendly. "This constraint encourages creativity and innovation," she said. "On the other hand, I won't incorporate one of those cheaper polymers into the mixture. It's impossible, because the product's design, norms, and standards require compliance with strict environmental regulations. If it doesn't meet them, it simply won't exist."

When Delek-San asked Sharon to relocate to a newly opened factory, she declined and took a job as a laboratory and development manager at Tosaf Group, where she learned about the world of plastics, good and bad. Plastics are lightweight, easy to manufacture, and require low production temperatures compared to glass, metal, or paper. The problem, Sharon said, lies in how we use plastic today. "We produce enormous quantities, approximately four hundred million tons per year, and discard most of it after a single use," she said. "It accumulates in our world and creates one of the most severe ecological problems of our time."

MAKING A DREAM A REALITY

Within a year, Sharon took what she knew about polymers and set out on her own. She joined Am Sagol, an initiative founded by Oren Hayman that strengthens Israeli excellence and conscientiousness. Sharon enrolled in one of his workshops and met Victor Weis, the CEO of the Heschel Center for Environmental Learning and Leadership (now the Heschel Center for Sustainability). Weis told her about the center's Peer Program, in which participants meet once a week over nine months for a day of learning about sustainability and personal responsibility for projects.

"One could say that's where the startup began to take shape," she said. "We were asked about our dreams, and Victor answered that he wanted to create a global environmental restoration program. I was amazed at thinking on such a grand scale, and it greatly influenced me. I decided to dream big and make it happen worldwide."

In her new venture, Sharon partnered with Maya Lachman. They had met when they were both mentors and MBA students. Sharon started to look for investors by word of mouth at networking events, and even by chatting with a taxi mate one night. "We started talking, and he turned out to be Yosef, of the popular restaurant Yosef, who help introduce me to investors," she said.

A small Innovation Authority grant covered the rent for a lab, but Sharon also conducted many experiments at home. In the end, she was able to create a compound for which the degradation time could be controlled, and that would decompose into environmentally friendly components.

Very quickly, Sharon said, she understood the potential. She and Lachman entered a startup competition and spent three weeks compiling the required information, defining the product's characteristics, and developing a business model. They didn't win, but it was a critical stage in their journey. "Since then, I have failed and succeeded many times," she said. "It's okay not to succeed; you need to know how to grow and learn from failure as well. And even with success, you need to know how to cope, not be afraid, and continue moving forward."

In September 2018 Lachman and Sharon entered a competition hosted by MassChallenge, the Boston-based accelerator, and the second largest accelerator in the world. Out of five hundred candidates, Solutum advanced to the semifinals with fifty others. Sharon's startup won the first-place prize of $39,000. Combined with the $100,000 that she won three months earlier at the Tel Aviv University's Coller Prize, and other funding, Sharon began to draw a modest salary and kept the start-up running.

Solutum has since won competitions around the world, and Sharon presents at conferences and solicits investors. "Even today, in the toughest market in recent years," she said, "we continue to raise funds and grow."

Because Solutum's products have varying sensitivities to air and water, they have captured the attention of large food companies that use plastic packaging, and agricultural businesses that require plastic for irrigation and greenhouses. For example, AB InBev, a Tel Aviv-based beverage company owned by Anheuser-Busch, needed a substitute for the nylon film used to wrap large quantities of beverages. Convinced of Solutum's potential, AB InBev funded a proof-of-concept project that led to the first biodegradable stretch wrap on the market.

WHERE ARE ALL THE WOMEN?

A few months ago, at the finals of a competition hosted by LG in Seoul, Sharon was the only woman competitor, and presented to a panel of all-male judges that included LG executives and experts from academia.

"At Ben-Gurion University, we were 50 percent girls in the classroom, and that was it," she said. "Throughout most of my career, I was surrounded by men, in the factory and on the production line. In the most feminine place I worked, there were only three of us: the laboratory technician, the office manager, and myself. I thought we had made more progress."

During the dinner held in honor of the finalists—Solutum won the Gold Prize—Sharon said she couldn't keep silent. She told the judges and other attendees that she hoped to see more women compete next year, and suggested that LG appoint its marketing manager, the highest-ranking woman, to be a judge. "There's nothing like a bit of Israeli chutzpah," she told me. She also volunteers to speak wherever she is invited, to explore how women can chip away at the glass ceiling until it no longer exists.

Recently, Sharon has been meeting with the management team and board of directors of one of the Fortune 500's largest oil companies in India, where Solutum is working on a project. Even here, sometimes she is the only woman in the room. "I receive a lot of respect in my meetings with them, and I don't feel that they treat me differently due to the gender difference," she said. "I don't think it's a disadvantage that I'm always the only woman in the room in high-level meetings. I just don't understand why."

Sharon said that recently someone asked where she sees herself in five years. "A few years ago, I wouldn't have had a concrete answer. Today, being with the love of my life who supports me, which makes us a power couple, and having our amazing children, my mission is to make the world cleaner, for all of us."

LOOKING BACK

Every personal and professional setback and career choice led to Solutum, Sharon said—then quoted Apple's Steve Jobs: "You can't connect the dots looking forward; you can only connect them looking backward."

Looking back, Sharon remembers that day when she and Mike watched the plastic bags swirl through the air, and she began to envision Solutum. She contemplated embarking on a new and fulfilling professional venture, and she and Mike were preparing to live together. She thought she had it all. But just as she finished packing and returned her keys to the landlord, Mike stunned her with his decision to end their relationship. Her world crumbled.

"I was left without a job, without an apartment, without a partner, and with a crazy idea for a startup," she told me. "I felt as though I had nothing. I wondered what I should do, where should I begin anew."

Her uncles generously offered her a rent-free apartment, and she received an attractive job offer as a lead technologist at an international company. "I realized that I needed an anchor, something to hold onto while working on my startup," she said, so she took the position at the urging of her friends and family. But something didn't feel right.

Almost immediately, she had chest pains and difficulty breathing. After five days, she resigned. She left for a two-week trip to Sri Lanka, where she talked to anyone who could understand English—even those who couldn't—about her plans to revolutionize plastics.

"When someone believes they have nothing, they embark on an introspective journey within themselves," she told me about her new mindset. "The phrase, 'from nothing, everything grows,' echoed incessantly within me. Suddenly, a realization dawned on me. I understood my ability to mold my present and future."

Sharon went home and immersed herself in research and planning. Though she had some savings, her friends and parents thought she was being eccentric and irresponsible. They failed to understand how someone so diligent, who had worked since she was twelve, would choose a precarious path without a source of income.

"Faith became my means of sustenance," Sharon told me, adding that her family and community are now fully supportive of her work.

She relished her new life in Tel Aviv, frequenting a popular pub and attending lectures about startups. Casual observers might have assumed she was wasting her time, but Sharon was steadfast in her pursuit to build the Solutum of today.

Meanwhile, Mike embarked on his own journey, and they only had sporadic contact—until a dental checkup led to a biopsy and a cancer diagnosis for Sharon. Mike happened to message her right after she got the results. "I replied that I couldn't talk right now because I had received devastating news," she said. "Somehow that conversation reignited our connection."

Sharon didn't smoke, but was diagnosed with mouth cancer. She was angry at the world, threw herself into challenging activities like running, surfing, and rock climbing, and ate a healthy diet. She had a procedure within two months of the diagnosis to remove the growth. The likelihood of the growth recurring after surgery was minimal. Two days after the procedure, still in the hospital, she participated in another competition. "When you're building a startup, there's no time to rest," Sharon said. "Even in the hospital, I didn't disconnect from emails and work. And that wasn't the last time."

At the time, Mike was a consultant about building supportive communities for companies and startups. During Sharon's recovery, he invited her to his shared makerspace at ShinSheva, hoping she would be impressed and join him there.

They got back together exactly one year after they separated.

"And then, during our first date after we got back together, he said to me, 'Just because you have a startup doesn't mean you can't have children.' I looked at him and asked, 'Who will take care of them?' and he replied, 'I will. I want to have children with you.'"

A WORKING LIFE

"I was shocked," she said. "We are not married, and it was not even a priority for me, because I'm fully committed to the startup." But Sharon discovered she was pregnant shortly after that conversation.

"When we got back together, Mike and I decided to have three basic building blocks for our relationship: growth, and appreciation… and we couldn't find the third element. When our son Lavie was born, we understood what it was: tranquility. He is so calm and accepting, while Mike and I are not." Two years later, Ari arrived, the second of two "lion cubs" who teach Sharon a lesson every day.

So, I asked, how do you build a company and raise money with a newborn? Luckily, she said, her mentor, Yaron, who was one of the first to know about her pregnancy, told her that anyone who wouldn't invest in her because of pregnancy is not someone she would want as an investor.

On top of the worries about finding investors, Sharon had a difficult birth. Contractions began while she was on the phone with her board of directors. The baby didn't have enough amniotic fluid and was in distress. Sharon had an emergency cesarean delivery, and Lavie, whose name means "life" in French, was admitted to the hospital for thirty-three days. Sharon and Mike stayed with him, sleeping by his side.

"I had Zoom meetings and physical meetings from the hospital," she said. "Shortly after we were discharged and returned home as a family for the first time, I closed the company's first fundraising round."

All at once, she had moved from a place of almost nothing, to so much. "I didn't really take a maternity leave," she said. "I simply took Lavie with me to work every day. We sat in a shared workspace, and everyone there was involved in his upbringing. As they say, it takes a village…"

She was pregnant with her second son during the COVID-19 pandemic. On the day of Ari's birth, Sharon went for a checkup with the expectation that she would get back to work. Ari had other plans. He was in a breech position, with an estimated weight over four kilograms (nearly nine pounds). Considering her previous childbirth experience, Sharon was scheduled for an immediate cesarean.

"I told the hospital staff that I had a board meeting at 3:00 p.m. and asked if we could schedule the procedure afterward," she said. "After a few stunned looks, they agreed. I found a quiet room and attended the meeting via Zoom, until the surgeon came to take me. I literally worked until the last moment."

Ari accompanied her to work every day, just like Lavie had, and the Solutum team of about fifteen people helped raise him. This time, though, she invested in a crib for the office. "He brought so much joy," she said. "And so, for five months, as long as I was breastfeeding, he was with me, and I didn't stop working. From my perspective, it was a great combination."

Sharon also had help from her family, but because her own father wasn't around much during her childhood, she didn't know what kind of grandfather he would be. One day, she asked her father to watch his grandson at a café while she met in an office upstairs with a patent lawyer. "I left him with basic instructions for taking care of Lavie, who was a few weeks old, and I went to the meeting," she said. "I prayed for everything to go well. I came back and found Lavie in reversed diaper and slightly disheveled clothes, but surrounded by the loving embrace of my father, who hadn't moved because Lavie was sleeping on him. From that moment on, my father became an inseparable part of Lavie's upbringing, and they have an amazing bond to this day."

Despite their busy schedules, at home she and Mike are partners. When Sharon's mother complimented her for finding someone who "helps raise the kids," Sharon corrected her. "Mike, who I love very much, is not 'helping' me with the kids. He's my partner, and we help each other. Mike was and is an important part of my life. He is a very supportive spouse, and I believe that's the way it should be."

Mike, who has a career of his own in the tech ecosystem, was always very supportive, and helps with connections to new investors and ideas, mostly around the brand and business development aspect. "Yet," she said, "we have a clear separation, and Solutum is my baby."

Sharon doesn't separate work from life. "The startup is me. When employed, for example, I couldn't go to the doctor without requesting time off. Here, I am my own boss, working long hours without breaks; but I don't feel it as work, and I don't feel guilty if I take time for myself."

Sharon also dedicates considerable time to public and youth education for ecological and sustainable thinking. "We have a lot of work to do. Compared to the Western world, we are lagging in everything related to environmental quality, greenhouse gas emissions, climate issues, and recycling.

"And after my personal journey," she concluded, "which is still ongoing—in which I built a company while also focusing on building a family—I hope that my story and the stories of other amazing women, including here in the book, will inspire and influence, and that women will understand that there is nothing that can stop us."

PART VI

THE PHILANTHROPISTS & ENTREPRENEURS

EDNA FAST,
Founder and Director
of the LunArt Fund

ZIVA PATIR,
Independent Director of Stratasys Ltd.,
President of the Israeli chapter of the
International Women's Forum

JUDITH RICHTER,
Cofounder and Active Chairperson of Medinol,
Founder of the NIR School of the Heart

HANA RADO,
Founder and President of Group Nineteen,
Founder and President of Supersonas,
Vice Chairwoman at McCann Tel Aviv

EDNA FAST

FOUNDER AND DIRECTOR, LUNART FUND, SOCIAL ACTIVIST

"No one else in Israel was addressing this need, since art was, and still is, considered a luxury. Therefore, art education was a highly neglected topic, especially where Arab minorities were concerned."

EDNA FAST IS A SELF-DESCRIBED Israeli social entrepreneur, with rewarding careers in parliamentary research, law, and real estate. Yet it is her lifelong belief in the power of art education and philanthropy to heal cultural inequities that fuels her need to help the less fortunate.

In 2008 Edna sold her New York City real estate and legal consulting firm and dedicated the proceeds to form a small, highly focused philanthropic fund. Named after her first-born granddaughter, Luna Art Fund provided free college prep courses for artistically talented Arab Israeli high school graduates who sought admission to academic art and culture programs.

"From the practical point of view, no one else in Israel was addressing this need, since art was, and still is, considered a luxury," she said. "Therefore, art education was a highly neglected topic, especially where Arab minorities were concerned.

"On a more personal level, as 'minor league' art collectors and parents of a successful artist, we felt emotionally connected to artists, art educators, and eventually also art consumers."

The path to LunArt can be traced to October 2000, when massive demonstrations in Israel's Arab localities and clashes with police left thirteen unarmed Arab demonstrators dead. The killings led to the appointment of the Or Commission, led by Israeli Supreme Court Judge Theodor Or. The commission published a report stating that the anger behind the demonstrations was fueled by a long history of discrimination against the Israeli Arab minority. Furthermore, the report stated that the Israeli government needed to adopt a more equitable policy of resource allocation to address the needs of Israeli Arabs.

"This event had significant repercussions among liberal, progressive Jewish organizations in the US," Edna said. "It also moved me to join a newly established coalition of North American Jewish organizations, to raise awareness and spread information about Israel's Arab citizens among the diverse Jewish communities and mainstream organizations in the US."

In 2005, when Edna and her husband spent a sabbatical back in Israel, she held a series of interviews with Arab Israeli social activists and opinion leaders at the request of Rabbi Brian Lurie, the founder and general director of the Inter-Agency Task Force on Israeli Arab Issues (iataskforce.org).

"It was during these interviews that my wish to become an active participant, and not just a better-informed observer, became apparent to me," Edna said. "I would start a private family fund that would work on narrowing the gap in art education between the Israeli Arab minority and the Israeli Jewish majority."

In the Arab communities in Israel, families often fail to recognize talent or nurture children interested in pursuing art. Most school-age Arab children have never been taken to museums or galleries by their parents, nor are they offered informal art courses in or after school. The lack of exposure to art or art education leaves potentially artistic students without the necessary portfolio or basic skills to interview with college admissions committees.

With LunArt, Edna funded a series of seven pre-college preparatory courses to help Israeli Arab high school graduates build their portfolios. A substantial percentage of enrolled students were admitted to college-level art, design, architecture, photography, and film programs. Those students who decided not to apply to college, or were rejected, are also success stories, Edna said, because they were mentored to become "culture ambassadors" in their extended families and communities, with basic knowledge of art terminology and visual culture that they carry forward.

The courses were held in recognized art schools and colleges across the country, and LunArt Fund paid for rent, materials, and teacher wages. Students from different cultural backgrounds were admitted, including Muslims, Christians, Bedouins, Druze, and secular Arabs from the Galilee and Golan Heights, from mixed cities like Jaffa, Wadi Ara, Lod, the Negev, and East Jerusalem. Although Hebrew language was an essential part of the curriculum, courses were given in Arabic, taught by Arab artists and Jewish lecturers from prestigious art colleges, such as Oranim in the north and Kaye College in the Negev, as well as art schools such as Minshar in Tel Aviv and the School of Visual Theater in Jerusalem.

COVID forced the pre-college prep courses supported by LunArt to close in 2020 after twelve years of operation, but studies continued on Zoom. The challenges of teaching art without studios prompted Edna to change course and focus on studies in art administration that are better adapted to virtual teaching.

After searching for a suitable college for LunArt Fund programs to restart online, Edna found that Sapir College in the western Negev was the only educationally recognized academic institution in Israel that offered bachelor's and master's degrees in culture, administration, production, and creativity. Edna also discovered that none of the eighty-three Arab municipalities in the socioeconomic periphery of Israel, except Nazareth, had an art administration department.

Once Israel has a stable coalition, she plans to lobby the government to secure additional funding for Culture Institutions in the Arab Sector.

As of 2020, LunArt has provided Bedouin men and women with several scholarships that cover 80 percent of their tuition for a master's degree in art administration. "It was all for the better that we switched during the COVID pandemic to graduate scholarships, and we made lemonade out of the lemon," Edna said. "By now, having seen three of our graduates achieve the coveted MA degree and start an amazing cultural endeavor on their own, I am quite sure that, thanks to the pandemic, we found the right route for the next phase of the LunArt Fund."

This year, the Luna Art Fund continues to support three Bedouin graduates of the MA degree program in art administration, helping them develop an online interactive map highlighting Bedouin culture, art, and heritage. "We feel responsible for them," Edna said, "and will continue to find means for more talented Bedouin men and women to thrive. The main challenge to creating a better society is pushing Bedouins to consume art and expose their children to art, as well, while we learn to appreciate their heritage."

PATRIOTISM AND PROPAGANDA

Edna was born in 1949, a year after the state of Israel was declared. "My childhood as a pupil both in kindergarten and in elementary school was influenced by a mix of Zionist patriotism and propaganda," she told me. "My home, however, was quite cosmopolitan, and I was raised with a good measure of criticism and questioning of the one-dimensional views of Jewish Orthodoxy, as well as secular nationalism."

Both parents were refugees who arrived in Palestine in their early teens, just before their communities in Europe were annihilated and their ancestral homes demolished during the Second World War. Her German-born mother, Sonia, emigrated with Edna's Lithuanian-born grandparents from Berlin. Her father, Alan, emigrated as a teenager with his UK-born grandmother and great-grandmother, having been raised in Bucharest, Romania.

"The only language they had in common when my parents met—at a very bourgeois, upper-middle-class social club in Tel Aviv—was English," Edna said. "Consequently, the only languages I heard at home during my early childhood were English, with a perfect British accent, from my father, and Hebrew, with a heavy German accent, from my mother.

"I was raised in a very cultured home with my mother playing on her grand piano, and my father constantly listening to records of classical music on their gramophone, for hours on end. My father was a voracious reader of European classical literature in English, and an avid collector of books, art albums, and classical music records."

That her father was a high school English teacher and—when he earned his PhD at the University of Edinburgh—was appointed head of the English Language Department at Tel Aviv University, greatly influenced her childhood. "I followed in my father's footsteps by frequently visiting the local privately owned library, exchanging European novels translated to Hebrew on a weekly basis, and ended up picking English as one of my two majors at the Hebrew University of Jerusalem."

Edna and her younger siblings—brother Doron, and sister Rissa—were obligated to take music lessons and visit the local lending library. Grades at school that were less than A were met with reprimands, and scholarly tasks were the name of the game.

"On the one hand, I consider myself lucky to have grown up in such a special home," she told me. "But our childhood was infused with a series of assignments to be fulfilled: summarizing chapters from encyclopedias, practicing on the piano (or the violin, in my brother's case), and having to correspond with a dozen pen pals from the UK, in order to brush up on my English. Discipline and studying were obligatory, and just ordinary fun and games or lazing around were rare…not an easygoing childhood, indeed, albeit a very privileged and sophisticated one."

Because Edna skipped a grade in elementary school, she graduated high school when she was a year younger than her draft-age, eighteen-year-old classmates. She was already on an academic track at Hebrew University of Jerusalem when a horse-riding accident sent her to the hospital with a concussion and a skull fracture.

"During my convalescence, I was discharged from service in the IDF, the official reason being the surplus of females in military service at that time," she said. That fateful accident led to the completion of her studies in political science and English, and she graduated cum laude at age twenty. She became a teaching assistant and earned her master's degree, cum laude, in political science at the Hebrew University of Jerusalem.

Her choice of graduate study was motivated by her dream to become a cadet at the Israeli Foreign Ministry, aspiring to become one of Israel's first female diplomats abroad. Little did she know that her marriage after university graduation to a physician licensed only in Israel would derail her plans. "During my first interview for admission to the Foreign Service Cadet Program, I had a rude awakening when I was informed that my chances for admission are slim, due to my marital status. I was given to understand that having an unemployed husband was unacceptable, according to the chauvinistic standards of the early 1970s."

Fortunately, the head of her master's program, Professor Shlomo Avineri, recommended her for what would be her first job with the Knesset. She was hired by the speaker to write a master's dissertation on parliamentary reforms in the US Congress, British Parliament, and German Bundestag. "The result of this research was not just a nicely bound book on the shelf of the newly created Parliamentary Information Service at the Knesset library," Edna recounted, "but it would also open the door to a new career track in law."

LOVE AT SECOND SIGHT

Edna met her husband, Avital, at a Friday night dance party at his house during her last high school year. He was the best friend of her then high school boyfriend. "The day we met, I was already attracted to his vibrant, hyper-energetic, and positive, outgoing personality," she recalled. It didn't hurt that he was a member of the Hebrew University Student Folk Dancing Group, and a standout in the disco dance party scene that was so popular in Tel Aviv in the 1970s. At Edna's initiative, they started dating during her first year at Hebrew University; he was a second-year student at the Hadassah Hospital Medical School.

"It was love at second sight, and we dated for three years, until I proposed to him!" Avital's childhood dream was to become a physician, a profession that suited him perfectly because of his authentic care for his patients, and the constant interest and involvement in medical research that made him, later in his medical career, stand out among his peers and gain a professorship.

In 1973, the couple took off for New York with their one-year-old son, Omer. Edna had been offered a graduate school scholarship in political science at the City University of New York, and Avital a three-year residency in physical medicine and rehabilitation at Albert Einstein College of Medicine and Montefiore Hospital. Edna left the post-graduate track, and when Avital completed his residency program, they returned to Israel.

Between 1976 and 1984, the family lived in a house they built together in Jerusalem, and the boys attended a public school near their home. Avital served as a spinal cord specialist in the army's medical corps, and Edna applied for a job as a parliamentary assistant to the Civil Rights Movement Party led by the late MK Shulamit Aloni, with whom she co-authored a publication titled *On Fraudulence and Kashrut in Israel*. Aloni, a feisty, opinionated lawyer, became Edna's mentor, convincing her to switch career course and go to law school. After earning her JD from Hebrew University of Jerusalem and completing the required two-year internship, Edna became a tenured legal assistant at the Israeli Parliament (the Knesset).

In 1984 it was back to New York. Avital was offered a tempting position as a chief of a rehabilitation department at a major hospital, and the couple decided that they should settle in the United States and apply for green cards. "It is an understatement to say that this was the most emotionally wrenching and difficult life-changing decision I ever made," Edna said. She resigned from her prestigious and highly coveted position as a tenured legal assistant to the chief legal counsel of the Knesset.

In New York, she turned to a new career path in business, and became engaged in social activism and philanthropy for a more democratic and progressive society in Israel. She joined the New Israel Fund Legal Justice Committee, and later became an active member of the Inter-Agency Task Force on Israeli Arab Issues, which motivated her to start her own philanthropic endeavor, the Luna Art Fund (www.lunartfund.org).

In 2011, however, the then chief of Tel Aviv Medical Center convinced Avital to return to Israel, to re-open and run the physical medicine and rehabilitation department he left twenty-four years earlier. He also launched a project at the medical center for a day-hospital rehab facility.

The Fasts adjusted again to life in Tel Aviv, and the frequent transcontinental flights they took to visit their offspring in Europe and the United States. Edna and Avital became avid art collectors, with a special interest in Palestinian and Arab Israeli visual art, and devoted themselves to the LunArt Fund and other Arab-Jewish culture and art-oriented NGOs.

In 2014 Edna joined with Dafna Meitar-Nechmad, a prominent philanthropist and a leading member of the Israeli branch of the American Jewish Funders Network (JFN). Together with Dafna and her parents' Meitar Family Foundation, they cofounded the Institute for Law and Philanthropy at the Tel Aviv University Law School. Thanks to the Meitar family's strong ties with the school's graduate program, several prominent Israeli philanthropists, including Phillipe Weil and Marcia Riklis, provided the initial funding pledges, and Irit Rappaport joined with a long-term, substantial pledge. The institute became an academically recognized and well-funded institute after five years.

"We are celebrating our eighth year and going strong, with major Jewish Israeli philanthropies joining our board," Edna said. "We turned a dream into a viable and prolific new player in the world of Israeli law, philanthropy research and data gathering, and much needed legal reform by removing bureaucratic, legislative, and fiscal obstacles to social initiatives."

The institute's mission is: "To help integrate philanthropy into Israel's socio-economic policy and thus support the country's philanthropic sector in its quest to foster a more prosperous and equitable society." The program includes conferences in philanthropic law, mapping philanthropy in and out of Israel, and gathering data on philanthropic giving, to remove challenges of giving in Israel.

Edna is an active member of a coalition of several member organizations of the Israeli JFN, all of which support arts and culture in Israel's periphery, and which are dedicated to exploring how to promote and fund the infrastructure of art and culture in Israel, with special attention lately given to the Bedouin population in Israel's southern periphery.

Even now, after her various careers, the joy of giving fills Edna as she helps talented people from Israel's underprivileged sector hone their unstoppable energy to pursue art and promote culture in their diverse communities. A woman with high intelligence and generosity, she took it upon herself to narrow the gaps in Israeli society through art and philanthropy. She's always ready to devote her considerable energy and financial backing to worthy causes that catch her eye, aspiration, and imagination.

"There is a strong and deep relationship between art education and *tikkun olam* (repairing the world, in Hebrew)," Edna said. "To recognize and understand the 'other' requires courage that an art education and art leadership allows to express and develop."

ZIVA PATIR

BUSINESSWOMAN,
FORMER VICE PRESIDENT OF ISO

———◦———

"We as women should feel it's our duty, as we are 50 percent of the population, to make this world a better place. We make better decisions, without escalating it to war. We do better without quarreling. We embrace everybody."

IF ISRAEL IS THE "LIGHT unto nations" (Isaiah 42:6), then Ziva Patir is certainly among those who keep that light burning. Her work has been dedicated to creating large-scale change, including the initiation of international standards that make corporations more responsible and environmentally friendly. Her many successes came despite the challenges of being a woman in mostly male-dominated fields.

Ziva was born in post-war Warsaw in 1950 to Holocaust survivors Flora and Michael Ptic-Borkovsky, who created "a happy home with no room for hatred or seeking revenge, despite all the horrors of the war," she told me when we visited in 2022. This values-based upbringing provided Ziva with inner strength, grace, and the motivation to build a life helping others.

In September 1939, when Germany and the Soviet Union occupied Poland, according to the Molotov-Ribbentrop pact, Ziva's parents were denied their property under the communist regime. They were constantly on the move, yet returned in 1942 to Nazi-occupied Warsaw, where they survived with falsified documents. All relatives, except one of Ziva's uncles, perished.

"We will never understand how, after everything they had been through, after losing all their families, they could create such a happy childhood for me," Ziva said. "They made me feel that I was a princess coming from a very good family…never talking about the horrors."

After the war, her father became the chief architect of Warsaw. Her mother, a 1939 graduate of a Warsaw law school, was offered a judgeship, which she declined: she did not believe in communism. Instead, she started writing history books. When the borders opened in 1957, seven-year-old Ziva and her family moved to Israel.

Assimilation was difficult, as it was for most immigrants at the time. "They believed, and I understood it very quickly, that we came to Israel for the next generations," Ziva said. Her father found a job as an architect in a government company, and her mother started working as a bookkeeper.

Ziva very quickly got rid of her Polish accent and saw herself as a sabra. There were always plenty of books around, and Ziva's father played piano in the music-filled house. "We had friends, we were happy," she recalled fondly.

Ever since she was a child, Ziva wanted to help people. "The core idea is that I feel privileged to have a supportive family. I should share everything that I have, whether it is money, wisdom, connections, or talent. In a way, I have always felt it is my duty."

HIGH SCHOOL, UNIVERSITY, AND THE IDF

In high school, Ziva excelled in science and athletics. She became the captain of the school volleyball team, received medals, and played on the junior team of Israel. Instead of joining the IDF immediately after school—as do most Israeli high school graduates—she joined the Atuda, a program that allows students to earn a university degree immediately after high school, in exchange for longer army service later.

Though she felt supported to do whatever she desired, choosing her studies was beyond her control. She wanted to study law, like her mother, but was told to find a profession that could be practiced anywhere in the world, in case the family had to keep moving. A license to practice law, she learned, is always local. Ziva received a BS in chemistry from Tel Aviv University in 1971, followed by an MS degree from the Weizmann Institute of Science in 1977.

"Serving as an officer in the IDF definitely was the experience of my life, both from professional and social points of view," she said. Her engineering experience grew during the production of the Merkava battle tank, the backbone of the IDF's armored corps. From a social perspective, she faced another set of challenges: she was the only female professional officer among male engineers at a time when female IDF officers were assigned to mostly administrative roles. She learned to deal with challenges that came up between the sexes in the army of the 1970s, and, in her early twenties, how to manage men in their forties who worked in civil industry.

"It was fantastic. I think that whatever happened to me later was thanks to those five years in the IDF. It was a great, great experience, being able to develop professionally, but also to lead people, to manage them. The level of tasks and responsibility you get in the army in your twenties is similar to what you would hardly get in business when you are thirty. If there's something I would recommend to women who want to develop professionally and acquire leadership skills, it is to start learning in the army."

MARRIAGE AND JOINING SII

While still in service, Ziva married her handsome and smart husband, Avi, a parachuter in the IDF, and in 1976 had her son, Assaf. After his birth, she left the army and joined the Standards Institute of Israel (SII), the largest standardization, testing, and certification organization in the country. Her daughter Yael was born in 1980, and in 1984, when Ziva and Avi studied in New York, Ruth was born. Ziva was a busy mother those first years, picking up from kindergarten and spending afternoons at the park. As the children grew and demands from her career intensified, Ziva made sure the quality of time they spent together made up for the quantity.

Still under the age of thirty, she started working in the SII's standardization division, drafting standards on a range of subjects, from all kinds of products to environmental protection. Very soon she oversaw the standardization of food, chemicals, polymers, textiles, rubber, and more.

"Standardization is a very interesting field," she told me. "It creates a common language essential for trade and cooperation. At the same time, one of the ultimate goals is to ensure safety—of consumers, environment, and society in general. If you flip over your laptop, there are many, many small letters which say that it's safe, that it's environmentally friendly. Recently, standardization moved to management practices and fields such as social responsibility, which are very close to my heart."

The SII is self-financed, state-owned, and completely independent. "We had 1,100 employees, and at that time it was an absolutely male-dominated field," she continued. "People I supervised were all male engineers that were older than me. There are huge testing laboratories of various specializations: from the environment to vehicles, from engines to food, from soil to concrete, from air conditioners to the safety of kettles. So, if you asked me what my product was, I would say it was providing confidence, efficiency, efficacy, quality, liability, environmental protection, and safety."

CEO OF SII

Ziva developed a system for certification of products and management systems, bringing national developments onto the international level; and in 1996, after twenty years at SII, she became its CEO—a position that historically was supposed to be given to retired male IDF generals.

Even after reaching an esteemed level in her career, and despite her considerable experience with the company and constant self-improvement practices, she still doubted herself. "I always felt that I was not good enough," she told me. "I feel this way all my life. That is why I practice and work hard. This is the big difference between men and women. We struggle to make things work.

"And being the CEO of SII for eleven years, I had many, many struggles—working with the union, firing friends, encountering violence, being locked in my office, being threatened and defamed in the media, to name just a few. I had to do what I thought should have been done to build confidence in my customers."

Ziva let go 30 percent of her employees, and over the next few years recruited two hundred new ones in fields including high tech, telecommunication, and the environment. She was one of the initiators of the Center of Quality and Excellence in the prime minister's office. The center has been leading the country's revolution in quality, and moved to SII.

"You have certainly heard of ISO 9000 series of standards," she said. "We made these standards a key policy tool in the army: the army set a condition for all its suppliers to meet the requirements of the standard. We were involved in training and certification of quality management systems of the industry, and contributed to creating a better infrastructure for the Ministry of Defense. We were also able to replicate this approach within other industries, including government bodies and the system of education."

SOCIAL RESPONSIBILITY STANDARDS

Two remarkable stories are closely intertwined with Ziva's career: how she became the first woman to serve as an officer of an international standards developer, and how she became vice-president and chair of the Technical Board of the International Organization for Standardization (ISO). ISO is an independent, nongovernmental international organization with 167 member countries.

As she was becoming an expert in quality, environmental and safety management, and reliability, Ziva focused on addressing the "greenwashing" problem. She showed, through independent research, how many companies claim to support environmental organizations, but still cause damage to the environment themselves. Greenwashing takes many forms, she said, but generally describes a situation in which a company supports a good cause in the country where it does business, yet exploits people and resources where it manufactures.

Creating a holistic program under the umbrella of social responsibility seemed the most appropriate solution. "I combined transparency, code of ethics, safety management, environmental management, security, and anti-bribery laws, and wrote a draft in my office with a few friends there," she said, smiling. "It was kind of a startup. My wish was for it to become a global standard for the industry." She translated the standard from Hebrew into English and sent it to the ISO. "They didn't want to deal with it, so they moved it to a committee on consumer policy."

One of her colleagues suggested she become vice-president of the ISO and head of its technical board. Ziva knew it would not be an easy election: she was a woman, and she was from Israel. She didn't expect the Arab countries to support her candidacy, but she did have as a friend the director of the Palestinian Standards Institution.

"He went from one Arab country to another saying, 'Meet and support my sister.' And the guy from Kuwait, if I recall correctly, objected, saying, 'How come she's your sister? I'm not talking to her for the last ten years because of you'—to which the Palestinian director responded, 'She has helped me more than all of you together.'" She explained that the SII helped establish, certify, and train the Palestinian standardization body in Ramallah and Nablus.

During the final vote for the vice-presidency, the president said that Ziva was the only true candidate, and that the elections would be based on applause, so no one would have to leave the room in protest. The crowd *cheered*! Ziva was elected and served two, two-year terms, during which the corporate social responsibility (CSR) standards we know of today were developed and published.

"We were the pioneers," she said. "We combined environment, safety, and ethics. It created a path to justice. It is an international standard, so now a company cannot contaminate the waters in Pakistan and support athletes in the US. I created those CSR practices. It's a very fascinating and complicated issue. And it was my big baby for many years."

Ziva visited many countries giving seminars and explaining the CSR standards. For a woman to be able to travel and have a successful career, she said, the trick is to choose the right husband and to have a supporting family. Avi and Ziva were true partners in every aspect of life. He fought in the Yom Kippur War, was recruited by the army as an electrical engineer, and graduated from the IDF as a colonel in charge of electronics for the Ministry of Defense. From there, Avi became the vice-president of Bezeq, a telecommunications company. In 1996 he founded a company that created low-cost solutions for international calls. "I helped him in his 'quality journey' in all his companies, and he helped me build one of my new labs for telecom, for high tech. We were able to help each other and would consult on similar issues."

BETTER PLACE, PATIR CONSULTANTS, BOARDS, AND THE NATIONAL THEATRE

When Ziva retired from SII in 2008, a young entrepreneur asked her to join his startup, Better Place. Shai Agassi told her it would bring the world to a "better place" with cleaner electric vehicles and less dependency on oil. Agassi, she said, had a talent for striking a positive chord with every person he encountered and taking a legitimate interest in their passions, be it saving the environment or making a profit. "Shai said, 'Do what you preach,'" Ziva said.

She was attracted to the project because she cared about the impact of oil on pollution and geopolitical decisions. The presidents of large automobile companies agreed that the electric vehicle revolution would come, but they were not prepared to be first. As Better Place's vice-president of standards, policy, and sustainability, she spent five years traveling to help push the world to become free from oil dependency.

"Getting rid of our dependance on oil was a great cause," Ziva told me. "It was the right thing at the wrong time. All I have to say is that it was interesting, it was completely different from working for a quasi-government organization with hundreds of people. It was fun to go to a high-tech startup like Better Place, even though in the end, in 2013, it went bankrupt."

This was also when Ziva decided that she would never again work for someone else.

At the age of sixty-three, she created Patir Consultants, which helps regulatory agencies and businesses manage risk and build compliance frameworks. Ziva also volunteers on the boards of the Holocaust Fund and the Lahav Program at Tel-Aviv University, the leading provider of executive education in Israel. She has served and keeps serving as director of the boards of several businesses, including Stratasys, Abra Information Technologies, and others.

She firmly believes that she has learned a great deal from her three children, admiring Yael's commitment to peace, and learning from Assaf's deep thinking on everything. Taking part in their unfolding careers meant she needed to stay in the game and familiarize herself with new fields and terminology. Her youngest daughter, a practicing artist, shaped Ziva's growing love for the arts and a deepening understanding of contemporary arts and its philosophy. It has led her to not only grow her enthusiasm, but to find a new professional path, as a member of the board of the Israel Film Fund, and as the chairwoman of Habima, Israel's national theater.

Habima was facing hard times, and the mayor of Tel Aviv asked Ziva to help reinvent it. She joked that she accepted the challenge to go from "high tech to high touch." Habima, the cradle of Hebrew and Jewish theatre, was established more than a hundred years ago in Moscow. It settled in Tel Aviv in 1931 and is an important center of cultural life. In the last year, a fantastic team doubled subscribers and created a repertoire of about twenty Habima-produced plays. Ziva credited the success to new management, the board of directors, and a new vision. "I will end my career by moving or combining high tech and art, an industry that requires personal attention and service, and I love it!"

Ziva is an active grandmother to her four grandchildren, and the president of the Israeli chapter of the International Women's Forum. Following her husband's recent passing, she created a mentoring program in his name for women in science and technology.

ADVICE

I asked Ziva what advice she would give young women to help them succeed. She said: "To have leadership skills, to be brave enough to take risks, but also to study and work very hard. And always to keep in mind what is best for society. When you are exposed to tough situations, it is like being pushed into deep water. You are obliged to swim, and you rise above.

"We as women should feel it's our duty, as we are 50 percent of the population, to make this world a better place. We make better decisions, without escalating it to war. We do better without quarreling. We embrace everybody."

In some respects, she has her mother to thank for her worldview. During a trip with her children and then ninety-two-year-old Flora to Ziva's parents' birthplace, in what today is Ukraine, the family was eager to hear old stories. Flora insisted that what was left in the past must stay there.

At one point they visited Flora's family-owned brick factory, the biggest in the region, that was confiscated by the communists—then controlled by Nazis, Russia, then Ukraine, and finally privatized. It was operating as it did in the early 1990s, with the same ovens and machines. The family matriarch stood at the factory entrance and recalled how her father would ask her to check the barometer, to see if the temperature and air pressure were favorable for drying the bricks outside.

Ziva, for the first time, saw in her mother's eyes a glimpse of the child Flora had been.

That moment, followed by her mother's conviction not to fight for restitution of the family's property, impressed on Ziva the need to move forward in life and build a new future. Optimism, and the belief in a person's ability to overcome hardship and grow from pain, is the "family compass," Ziva said.

JUDITH RICHTER

COFOUNDER AND ACTIVE CHAIRPERSON, MEDINOL; ENTREPRENEUR

"Every heart beats in the same way, but the necessity to open and heal people's hearts goes beyond the medical field. Indeed, the heart is a universal symbol of emotion across culture, race, gender, religion, or geography."

JUDITH RICHTER GREW UP IN a warm, loving home environment. She was often told that she is the essence of her mother's victory, joy, and freedom of life in Israel. Those words encouraged Judith to achieve her goals by working hard, and guided her through life.

Forty years ago, when Judith was thirty-five years old, she stumbled on the incredible story of heroism and brutality behind her father's tattoo. She found in that story the source of her own power to overcome obstacles, the strength to "move mountains," and her love for humankind, as well as her tenacity and will to never give up. She realized Erno (also known as Zvi) and Anna (Rachel) Spiegel raised their daughter to continue her father's legacy of caring for the less fortunate and building bridges between cultures.

Now a successful entrepreneur, educator, and one of Israel's most distinguished women leaders, Judith was born in 1947 in Carlsbad, Czechoslovakia, following her parents' freedom from Auschwitz and their subsequent marriage. The family made aliyah to Israel when Judith was two, and they settled in Bitzaron, a neighborhood outside Tel Aviv that provided a comfortable life for the new survivors and a happy childhood for Judith.

At "Habonim" school, Judith learned about the different cultures in the pupils' countries of origin. Many of the children's parents were Holocaust survivors, and the students often shared stories about being woken up at night by their parents' nightmares. Most of the children Judith played with had parents with numbers tattooed on their arms, and no grandparents. Typical of Holocaust survivors, these parents had expectations for their children, and hope for the state of Israel. All pupils were socialized to develop Israeli identities, as they were exposed to their new country's dedication to science, innovation, the environment, and entrepreneurship. Judith emphasized that all the children around her grew up with the idea that they had to be "good children" for their parents, who had suffered in the Nazi camps.

The school was also the center of neighborhood life for immigrant families, thanks to a headmaster who understood the importance of the newcomers' socialization to life in Israel. For Judith, the Tzofim (Hebrew

Scouts movement) became an important part of her life during her adolescence and was very significant in establishing her Israeli identity.

She felt independent and confident and was often chosen by her peers to lead. "Our parents made us feel like we are a miracle. I was a good child, participating in everything—gymnastics, piano lessons, dancing, English, French private lessons—and I got the Tel Aviv municipality's 'Bialik Award' for good writing. I always volunteered to lead." She added that her family enjoyed a rich cultural exposure to theater and performances, due to her father's work as an accountant for a theater and various performing groups in Tel Aviv.

Miraculously, all nine of her mother's brothers and sisters survived the Holocaust. Seven of the Hecht family chose to live in Israel. From her father's side, the Spiegel family, all but the parents survived the Holocaust and lived in Israel. Judith home in Tel Aviv was the place they would all come for celebrations and holidays. Her mother was always the main figure of the family gatherings, where she entertained the entire tribe arriving from Tel Aviv, Haifa, and Jerusalem. As the firstborn of the Hecht family in the world, Judith attracted her relatives' attention and was the subject of warm welcomes and some tears of love, as well as competition about where and with whom she would spend her summer vacations. It was always a happy moment for her to go home, where she knew the table would be full of elegant and beautiful food.

The family from her mother's side and the Spiegel tribe still meet amidst the smell of goulash and condiments, and arguments in Hungarian end with hugs and kisses. Judith explained, "It is interesting; all of us cousins are offspring of Holocaust survivors, [and] still keep close relationship and meet happily very often…in my home. My mother kept telling me that this is the glue that helps us stick together as a close-knit family."

Judith's accountant father did well enough to upgrade and move the family to a neighborhood in Tel Aviv when Judith was fourteen. There, she enrolled in an excellent high school, Ironi Alef, a place that challenged her academically. After the move, Judith stayed loyal to the Tzofim troop from her old neighborhood. At seventeen she thrilled her parents when she was chosen to spend two and a half months representing Israeli scouts in the United States.

Judith joined the IDF Air Force, mandatory service, and soon became an officer. She was assigned to be the woman corps officer, and was in charge of one hundred women soldiers.

After her mandatory service, she debated her course of study. She explained that she was discouraged from studying medicine because of how long it would take to become a physician. As she spoke, I remembered a similar debate with my own parents: my father discouraged me from going to medical school for the same reason. Happily, I followed my mother's advice: "You are going to be twenty-seven, no matter what. You might as well have a medical degree, then."

Judith met her future husband while in the air force. Kobi was a distinguished combat pilot with a great yearning to study. They negotiated their schedules by dating on the weekends. After two years, they married, and she moved from Jerusalem to the air force base in Be'er Sheva. Two years later, they celebrated the birth of their son Yoram. For the next four years, Judith traveled back and forth twice a week—hitchhiking on a bus, then riding two and a half hours to the Hebrew University in Jerusalem—to complete her studies, eventually obtaining her master's degree in social psychology, with Nobel laureate Daniel Kahneman as her advisor.

At that time, their second son, Uri, was born.

Her training in social psychology served her well, by enhancing her natural leadership talent and developing her entrepreneur skills.

During her graduate school studies, Judith also worked at the air force, eventually achieving the rank of civilian major. Her job was to develop screening methods of the flight academy trainees. Later, she progressed and formed a special unit for training the young pilots in leadership and management skills, such as decision-making, teamworking, and motivating pilot trainees. "It was particularly challenging experience, being the only female teacher of some of the highest rank pilots." Through the work of guiding officers of high rank, she emphasized the fact that just because one is a good pilot doesn't mean he can command well. Although a pilot might fly alone for a mission, it is absolutely necessary for him/her to know how to negotiate working together as a team in the formation flying together.

At the age of thirty-two, Judith and Kobi enrolled in universities in the States. She studied at Boston University for four years, obtaining her PhD. She joked that she'd already spent more than seven years in school and would have already completed medical school if she had chosen that path. The army permitted Kobi to be absent for only three years. This led Judith to make a crucial decision to stay in Boston, caring for their two children while completing the last year of her studies.

"You know, when you take this kind of decision, there is an uncertainty of how it would end," she admitted. "But Kobi understood how important it was for me to complete my PhD in organizational psychology."

MOVING MOUNTAINS

Ilan, her third son, was born after her return to Israel.

She joined the Tel Aviv University Graduate School of Management, teaching subjects like organization behavior, company structure, team building, corporate strategy, decision-making, and career planning.

Five years of teaching were enough. "My energy is to move mountains, not hills," Judith said. She joined Teva Pharmaceutical Industries as an executive assistant to Eli Hurvitz—the company founder, CEO, and later the chairman of the board. Judith explored new ideas to advance the company, and Eli engaged her in exploring issues regarding business and strategies. "I consider Eli my important mentor. He was very generous and trusted me. I learned so much from him."

While involved with Teva, Judith stayed on lecturing at Tel Aviv University, and in 1992 her years of study, research, and work led her to publish a book, *Connecting Vessels*. The book is about boundaries and transitions between professional and private life in different careers and family stages. Proudly she mentions her visionary ideas, for that time, about the expected tendencies and wishes for corporate members to work from home. The importance of crossing the boundaries of time and location, enabling the combination of work and private life, was an essential part of her book.

In 1993, Judith and Kobi joined forces and established Medinol. His PhD from Tel Aviv Medical School and background in the medical field, coupled with Judith's pharmaceutical industry experience and enhanced business perspective at Teva, made a perfect partnership for them to build the company. At Medinol, Kobi invented stents, the tubular supports that open vessels to improve blood flow to the heart, and that help people worldwide improve their quality of life.

In parallel, a company named Optonol was founded. It developed a device to reduce pressure in the eyes of patients with glaucoma. The Richters then built a third company called Valve, which develops cardiac valves. A fourth company was also established, Microtech, which develops sensors to insert into different body organs. All four companies are under the larger company, Medinol Group. Concurrently Medcon, a telecommunication company, was formed and was sold to McKesson in 2005.

Medinol was a very great success from the start, thanks to outstanding creativity in the design and manufacturing of the stents. "Medinol is a technologically very sophisticated company," Judith said. "But we are known also for our social consideration, and we provide a very specific culture for all our employees." As CEO, she is also in charge of the organization culture, which is one area of her academic expertise. The known generosity of Medinol management is a reflection of the love and caring she grew up with, and which now radiates to employees and the larger community. "The employees remain with us for a very long time and consider Medinol a family," she said proudly.

With this success, Judith decided that it was time to give back to the community, and she created a comprehensive social and academic program to teach cardiology to high school students, and to develop their creativity and skills of innovation. She conceived the NIR School of the Heart, named in memory of a soldier—a friend of her oldest son, who sacrificed his life in an attempt to free a kidnapped American citizen. The "act of courage, unfortunately, resulted in both of their deaths," she said.

Judith's passion for educating the young comes also from lessons she learned as a daughter of Holocaust survivors. Her parents taught her that while one's family, one's friends, and one's material possessions can all be taken away, one's spirit and knowledge, bestowed by education, cannot. Therefore, she finds it important to bestow upon talented and open-minded youth the spirit of courage, curiosity, creativity, and social commitment.

The NIR School of Heart fulfills Judith's lifelong dream: to promote knowledge and creativity among young people in the fields of science and medicine, and to encourage those students to build bridges across cultures through the process of learning.

Her dream was also to encourage peace processes among adversarial groups. She created a program in which students are recruited from three origins: Israel, Jordan, and the Palestine Authority. Then, they are gathered into three groups, each composed of representatives of those different origins. The studies are all done in English. The program consists of many examinations, which are rated per group. In order to succeed, the students have to collaborate with each other within their own group. This increases their interdependency. While competing as member of their group, the students also experience and learn to respect cultural differences, overcome prejudices, and understand that they are stronger and more innovative when they rely on each other.

NIR School annually enrolls fifty high school students between the ages of sixteen and seventeen. They spend four weeks over the course of eighteen months in hostels in the Middle East, where they are taught by leading Israeli and international physicians and cardiologists about the cardiovascular system. The academic program and the curriculum were developed under the guidance of Professor Elazar Edelman from Massachusetts Institute of Technology (MIT).

For twenty-five years, the NIR School has been an educational program aimed at empowering young people with knowledge about the human heart, to help them evolve as ambassadors for health and peace. Students come together to learn about the heart, and themselves, and each other. Studying together, they explore solutions for healing the heart, consequently forming strong bonds that go beyond the academic program. They turn walls of anxiety and suspicion into lifelong voyages of friendship and hope.

Presently, there are 1,200 NIR School graduates. Out of them, 300 are in the medical field and 140 of those are physicians.

I, too, deeply believe that we all have a responsibility and an urgent duty to build bridges across different religious, ethnic, and national walls that divide so many around the globe.

In 2019, for having conceived the program, Judith was honored by the Institute of Medical Engineering and Science at MIT: "In recognition of her vision of educating ambassadors of universal health and peace, while building bridges between diverse communities." Former US President George W. Bush and President Bill Clinton attended the event in Washington, DC.

For her work with NIR School of The Heart, in 2021 she received the Global Business and Interfaith Peace Gold Medal Award and the Dare to Overcome Award from the Paralympics. In an acceptance speech, she said: "Every heart beats the same way, but the necessity to open and heal people's hearts goes beyond the medical field. Indeed, the heart is a universal symbol of emotion across culture, race, gender, religion, or geography."

Over the years, Judith has received many other awards. In Israel, she received the Ramniceanu Prize from Tel Aviv University in 2013 for "her exceptional contribution to Israel's economic, industrial, and technological development." In 2018 she was named an "Honorary Fellow of the IDC Reichman University" in Herzliya, for "the significant role she played in Israel's economy for the past twenty-five years, her expertise in business, and her vision that have led to exceptional achievement, her volunteer activity, and limitlessness of generosity, her constant pursuit of excellence, and her inspired work." She also received the title of "Yakir of the Hebrew University of Jerusalem."

Judith served on the executive committee of the Hebrew University of Jerusalem from 2009 to 2016, and presently is a member of the university's board of trustees. She has served on the boards of several industrial companies, including Bezeq and Mobileye. She is deeply engaged in social activities in the arts and humanities; funded the Richter Quartet of the Israeli Philharmonic Orchestra; and supports the Israeli Women's National Volleyball Team, shelters for abused women, Holocaust survivors in Jerusalem, and the Israeli Scouts' youth delegations to Auschwitz. She proudly added to the list her sponsorship of Arab children to join the Scouts' trips abroad.

After learning about all of Judith's accomplishments and work, I asked her where she gets the instinct to be a leader and serve the community. Judith reflected on this question for a moment and answered, "It is in my veins, my blood from both my mother and father." She explained that while her mother was a homemaker, she was very active in the school parents committee and in the Women's International Zionist Organization (WIZO). Then Judith's voice trembled. "When my mother was in Auschwitz forced labor camp, the other captives had confidence and trust in my mother to share what little bread they were given. She was their chosen leader. Later on in life I discovered my father's leadership skills, which I had inherited, as well."

FATHER'S LEGACY

As our conversation concluded, Judith told me the story about her father, and how her perspective of him and of life changed as a result of her understanding his experiences during the war.

In 1982, while working on her PhD in Boston, her husband arrived home waving an article in *Life* magazine. It was about the search for the Nazi doctor, Josef Mengele, who performed cruel experiments on twins in Auschwitz. The article displayed a picture of Judith's father and his twin sister, Magda, along with a postcard of the twin children thanking her father, Erno, for saving their lives.

Immediately, Judith contacted her father in Tel Aviv to learn more. He told her briefly that journalists from *Life* magazine accompanied a group that was looking for Dr. Mengele, and wished to question survivors in Israel. The Israeli police have a registry of every new immigrant to Israel who was identified as a survivor, and their story. The group of journalists was directed to Erno Spiegel, who underwent experiments on the orders of Dr. Mengele, which was documented. During the interview with *Life*, he recounted his story and gave them the postcard from the twins that said: "Thank you for all the good you did for us." As a result of the article, several twin survivors contacted Erno, and one made an intended appointment to meet him in six months, when he would be visiting his daughter in Boston.

Judith joined the meeting and was shocked to hear for the first time her father's full story.

It goes…

In April 1944, Erno Spiegel, his twin sister, her six-year-old son, and his mother got off the train at Auschwitz-Birkenau. They were confronted by Dr. Mengele, who was searching for twins on which to experiment. Erno responded and was asked to identify his twin, to which he pointed at his sister. From Erno's stature and comportment, Mengele assumed that he had served in the army. So Erno was put in charge of eighty of the male twin children for the nine months he spent in Auschwitz-Birkenau. Erno remembered watching his sister's hand detach from her little boy. While his sister was sent to the female twin division, the little boy and his grandparents were taken to the crematorium and extinguished.

Upon arrival to Boston and meeting Erno, the twin's memories surfaced.

As the emotional meeting continued, the stories of Erno's bravery unfolded. Judith learned about her father's role as a translator of German and Hungarian. In the camp, Erno was a father figure to the children who underwent experiments. For children that cried at night, longing for their parents, Erno provided them with love and education, and comforted them by promising that he would get them back to their homes. During the day, Erno made sure to keep the children together, preventing them from separating from the group and becoming targets for the SS soldiers.

Once, when another doctor decided to barricade the compound and exterminate the twins, Erno rushed to Mengele, who reversed the order. Judith heard how Erno risked his life to falsify the birth date of a boy who was not a twin, to keep him alive; his devotion to the teenage boys whom he taught geography and math; and the hope he inspired by his promise to help them return home.

On January 27, 1945, the camp was liberated, and the children gathered around Erno and begged him to fulfill his promise and take them home. Indeed, Erno kept his promise, and during a grueling six-week trip back to Hungary, he gathered thirty-six children between the ages of six and fourteen. On the way, the number increased to 156 as other women and other children joined.

There are many heartbreaking survivor stories, but this one revealed the truth about a modest man and loving father. His humanitarian acts illuminated unimaginable bravery, incredible mental strength, and leadership.

Not long after the meeting in Boston, Judith, her father, and her Aunt Magda attended a mock trial of Mengele at Yad Vashem, Jerusalem. The prosecutor played the role of famed Israeli jurist Gideon Hausner, and several twins provided evidence. Because Erno, the modest man he was, provided only brief answers, the prosecutor asked if anybody present knew Mr. Spiegel while at Auschwitz. One twin rose and said: "It is not Spiegel. It is Spiegel Bachi [in Hungarian] or "Uncle Spiegel." The crowd stood and applauded. The heartwarming affection brought tears to Judith's eyes. Magda whispered: "I still feel, and always will, the little hand of my six-year-old boy slipping away as I watched him and my mother walking away. I will never forget." She continued: "I know that I'm alive because of my brother, Erno, who separated me and had me put in the twin girl compartment."

At present, Judith is producing a documentary that will tell the full story of Erno Spiegel. "My father told me that everything can be taken away from me except what is in my head, so I felt that this is my legacy to give to others, something in their head so nobody could take it away from them."

———◦•◦———

Since my meeting with Judith in July 2022, a street has been named in her honor, in a new industrial park in the town of Kfar Yona. This honor was granted upon her for having been a pioneer and a role model for another woman.

Recently, the Israeli Manufacturers Association decided to award Judith a Lifetime Award for her outstanding achievement in leading the Israeli industry.

HANA RADO

SOCIAL BUSINESS ENTREPRENEUR, LIBERAL FEMINIST

"The people demanded social justice. If I will not do it, then nobody will."

ON MY WAY TO MITZPE Ramon, I traveled through the Negev desert for long hours and passed miles and miles of barren land. If not for a scattering of Bedouin camps with tents and metal shacks, or the occasional herd of camels, the scene could have come from a movie about the Wild West.

When the city appeared on the horizon, I experienced a magical moment. I stood on top of the earth looking down five hundred meters at the Ramon crater, one of the world's geologic marvels. I felt like I was at the biblical beginning, the silence disturbed only by jumping ibex and the hot wind whistling through lonely tree branches. I thought nothing could surpass this experience…until I met Hana Rado.

An accomplished executive, entrepreneur, liberal feminist, motivational speaker, and Zionist, Hana has dedicated her life to helping others. She developed a new model of outsourcing that has brought hundreds of jobs to the periphery and has helped increase the number of women in leadership roles. Whatever her mission, her warmth and simplicity create a familiarity that puts everyone at ease.

Hana was born to Holocaust survivors from Ukraine in 1959 in Karkur, a small village in the north of Israel near Pardes Hana. Her mother arrived in Israel in 1946 and her father in 1956, after serving twelve years in a Russian prison for being a member of a partisan force in World War II.

The oldest daughter of seven siblings, Hana spent a happy childhood attending an agricultural school and dividing her time between studying and working the land. Her father expected her to excel and do no less than her three brothers; she mastered driving a tractor and loved mathematics.

Hana joined the Israel Defense Forces, and after two and a half years graduated as a commander officer lieutenant. She planned to stay in the army, but had to leave to care for her ill father while her mother took care of her siblings.

She earned a BA in biology and a master's in finance from Tel Aviv University. In 1988, along with Shmuel Hirsch, she created Mister Ice, the first ice-cube factory in Israel. And in 1999, she managed the implementation of SAP's enterprise resource planning software for the Strauss

Group. Later she joined McCann and become the COO and vice president of McCann Israel, an advertising agency in the Interpublic Group of Companies. She managed five hundred people and was responsible for one billion shekalim ($250 million), until a major event changed her life.

FILLING THE VOID WITH SOCIAL ENTREPRENEURISM

In 2011 hundreds of thousands of Israelis from various socioeconomic and religious backgrounds protested the rise in the cost of living and the deterioration of public services like education and health. They erected hundreds of tents in the middle of Tel Aviv, and the protests spread to other major cities. Eventually, the government announced a series of measures to address the housing shortage, and that's when Hana took up the role of social entrepreneur. "The people demanded social justice," she told me. "If I will not do it, then nobody will."

She met Michali, a young mother of two, who commuted two and a half hours daily from Mitzpe Ramon to Tel Aviv, with little means to care for her children. Michali's plight, like that of many others who travel to the center for work, highlighted an untapped opportunity to create jobs, help save people's time and money, and develop a skilled workforce.

"There is a Zionist sentiment that without the periphery, Israel cannot exist," Hana said. In 2012, she established McCann Valley, an ad company for digital marketing, with three million shekalim (one million dollars) in seed money provided by McCann Israel. Against all odds, in the middle of the desert, she hired thirty employees who became part of McCann Tel Aviv's workforce for clients including El Al, Nestlé, and Osem (foods). McCann Valley quickly generated a profit, and the encouragement from her investors gave her confidence that she could create "something from nothing."

In 2016, Hana self-financed and established Group19, based on her model for McCann Valley. The first company under the Group 19 umbrella was Desert19 in Mitzpe Ramon, an outsourcing agency that provided quality jobs to women, many of whom were wives of IDF reservists living in the area. Within a few months, she hired twenty employees, which further increased her self-confidence.

Hana had no plans to open another center, but two women from Sefat, in northern Israel, approached her and pleaded for jobs so they could feed their families for the High Holidays. Lev19, the second company in Group19, was born in 2018, and it doubled in size in two years. It had forty employees in early 2022. Hana said the center employs predominantly Orthodox women who, despite lack of experience, learn very quickly and are grateful for the chance to provide for their families.

In 2020 Hana opened Negev19 in Ofakim and Link19 in Sderot. In 2022 Bank Hapoalim sponsored a center in Yeruham, Tech19, that employs engineers and experienced technology professionals who are mostly local residents. The center provides mechanical services and instructions for virtual and augmented reality to important technology companies in the Israeli market. In 2023 she established Agency19 in East Jerusalem, to provide digital services and administration in Arabic, with the support of the Jerusalem municipality.

Each center requires seed money of about 1.2 million shekalim ($300,000) to pay for housing, training, and employee salaries. Though she received some government help, Hana said she is personally responsible for each center and its success.

OUTSOURCING FINDS A HOME

Over the past five years, Hana's Group19 centers in the periphery have provided work for 320 local men and women and created a conduit for skilled professionals to meet the growing demand in Tel Aviv. The outsourced services include mechanical support, 3-D printing, technology for virtual and augmented reality, instructions for software, social media management, accounting, analytics, personal secretaries, marketing, and back-office support. Presently, Group19 has contracts with companies including Natural Intelligence (software), Deloitte (financial services), Gulliver Tourism (travel), Salesforce (cloud-based software), Elad (software), Nestlé (food), and Papaya Global (HR solutions).

"The purpose of our social businesses is to help companies in Israel's center to enrich their staff with excellent workers from the far periphery," Hana told me. "There are companies that approach us that would like to hire qualified people, not unlike those in the center, but those who have a sparkle in their eyes, a will to succeed, and an enormous appreciation for the work.

"The companies gain a diverse variety of people," she continued, "and our workers in the periphery wish to avoid three hours a day commuting. They would like to have a family life and look for meaningful, interesting, and rewarding work. The companies in the center understand the advantages of hiring us, and see growth in their ESG (Environmental, Social and Governance) data. We are able to answer their needs and provide stability to their company."

Group19 employees reflect the mosaic of Israeli society in age, gender, religion, and race. *People*, Hana said. "We are a tribe with no discrimination."

UNIQUE BLUEPRINTS

I asked Hana to explain the process of starting a center, and she revealed that the specific role or industry for each site is not determined until a CEO is hired. She advertises on social media for people to manage a center at a specific location in the periphery. When Hana conceived Yeruham, for example, she received CVs from fifty women and selected Inbar Cohen, an expert in technology who worked at Intel. Cohen was hired for her managerial and business talent, Hana said, not her tech experience. She gave Cohen complete freedom, providing the building and seed money to hire the staff she needed to create a center in a field in which she felt comfortable. Tech19 emerged.

The blueprint for each center is to "recognize the social problem and the need to change, looking for the right person, and then getting the seed money." She mentioned a meeting she had with Tal Ohana, the mayor of Yeruham, who wanted to develop businesses in her town. Hana, however, said she first had to find a talented CEO who could build the business based on his or her knowledge. The mayor did not get to choose the type of business that would be established.

Because all the CEOs have different talents, they are in frequent communication with their peers at other centers and fill knowledge gaps that might arise.

Hana said she is grateful for the seed money given by Bank Hapoalim; the Miraj Foundation; UJIA London; the Galilee Foundation; Galil, the office of the Negev; and others. Most of all she is grateful to the clients, who gain professionals to work for them and help change the reality of living in the periphery. She is also grateful for her husband, who taught her how to love; her children, for showing purity; and her parents, for teaching her how to fight and persevere.

Meanwhile, Hana is proud to have established Supersonas, an association for women that started in 2015 as a website and transformed into an active community and innovative platform for women to connect, discuss, and step into action. Its goal is to increase the percentage of women leaders, especially in business and government sectors, and boost the number of women in C-suite positions and board rooms.

When I asked Hana to share advice for young entrepreneurial women, she didn't hesitate. "I would tell them:

1. "Dare, dare to take a risk.
2. "Study always, don't be afraid of not knowing, and study what you don't know.
3. "Surround yourself with people that give you energy and people you can learn from.
4. "Strengthen what you are good at.
5. "Do what is right for you. Follow your emotions.
6. "Listen to others, but follow your own path.
7. "Give your managers responsibility and authority.
8. "Modesty is not a practical quality.
9. "Attach excellence to each decision."

"You have to have resilience and appreciate yourself," said Hana, who is Supersonas's president. "Take what you are doing seriously and, above, all be a good person."

ACKNOWLEDGMENTS

I AM FOREVER INDEBTED TO many people who inspired me and helped me write this book, especially the exceptional women featured in the book who opened up their lives and homes to me. Esther Margolis, a dear, loyal friend, who guided me through the world of publishing. Gideon Shavit, who introduced me to many of the unforgettable women I had the honor of interviewing. The enthusiastic David Bernstein and Aleigha Koss of Post Hill Press and its Wicked Son imprint. Lisa Kosan, my talented and indispensable editor, who believed in this book from the beginning and helped shape ideas into compelling stories. Aditi Hudli, my editorial assistant, who kept me organized and well informed. Dr. Uriel Reichman, for his encouragement and unwavering belief in the power of women. And my beautiful family, for always supporting me and my work.

ABOUT THE AUTHOR

BILHA CHESNER FISH, MD IS a board-certified radiologist with expertise in body imaging and musculoskeletal radiology. She founded Manhasset Diagnostic Imaging and then Pathways Women's Health, one the first privately owned diagnostic women's health centers in Long Island, New York.

Born in Israel, Dr. Fish served in the Naval Intelligence with the Israeli army (IDF). She went on to earn her MD from the Faculty of Medicine, University of Bologna, Italy. Soon after, she went to the United States and completed her medical training at New York Hospital—Cornell Medical Center and the Hospital for Special Surgery. It was here she became an expert in the newest technologies and accepted the position of Chief of Imaging at Beth Israel Medical Center, New York.

In 1995 Dr. Fish expanded her radiology practice and opened a women's health center that focused on preventative programs. The center invited physicians in the community to volunteer their expertise and time to teach women to be proactive about their health. The center offered group therapy for women afflicted with cancer, to provide much-needed support through their healing process.

Dr. Fish also established The Unbeaten Path, a program that provided age-specific information to adolescents on topics such as anorexia, bulimia, STDs, bullying, and recognizing mental health issues. The students received a health credit in high school for participating in this program. She also sponsored a nationally recognized community awards program for local teens and senior citizens.

Over the years, Dr. Fish complemented her scientific pursuits and experience with more creative and artistic endeavors, earning two master's degrees in art history and studio art. More recently she published a book, *Invincible Women*, a series of conversations with twenty-one inspiring and successful American immigrant women. As an immigrant herself, she decided to publish this book when there was a rising negative sentiment toward immigrants in the United States.

Dr. Fish is fluent in English, Hebrew, French, and Italian. She splits her time between New York City and Sag Harbor.

For more information, visit https://www.bilhachesnerfish.com/.